THE INIMITABLE
Adele Ferguson
Bremerton's legendary columist

A Biography & Oral History

by John C. Hughes

THE WASHINGTON STATE
HERITAGE CENTER

LEGACY PROJECT

First Edition
Copyright © 2011
Washington State Legacy Project
Office of the Secretary of State
All rights reserved.
ISBN 978-1-889320-23-6
Front cover photo: Cover portrait by Terry Poe, © 1993,
Kitsap Newspaper Group; used by permission
Book Design by Kathryn E. Campbell
Printed in the United States of America
by Gorham Printing, Centralia, Washington

Printing sponsored by Kitsap Sun
kitsapsun.com

Washington
Secretary of State
SAM REED

Adele's dedication:

To my high school English teacher, Mrs. Cunningham,
and the best editor I ever learned from, Julius Gius

John's dedication:

To *The Caruthersville Democrat* and
The Caruthersville Republican for believing in Adele

A gag photo from the '50s as Adele composes
a column about pipe smokers.

At her desk in the newsroom in 1957. *Kitsap Sun*

The Inimitable Adele Ferguson

"Th' newspaper does ivrything f'r us. It runs th' polis foorce
an' th' banks, commands th' milishy, controls th' ligislachure,
baptizes th' young, marries th' foolish, comforts th' afflicted,
afflicts th' comfortable, buries th' dead an' roasts thim aftherward."

—Legendary Chicago journalist Finley Peter Dunne,
who wrote about politics and culture in the 1890s in
the voice of an Irish saloon-keeper, "Mr. Dooley."

You can't do justice to Adele Ferguson's laugh with only one adjective. It's earthy, infectious and punctuated with delight. Although it's been 50 years since she became the first woman to invade the old boys' club that was the Capitol press corps at Olympia, her blue eyes are still mischievous. And, for the record, her name is "*A*-dell."

In her prime, the Bremerton scribe was feared and loathed, respected and courted. Her column is still carried by some 30 newspapers around the state. While her daily paper penetration has declined in recent years, she's now being cussed and discussed on-line.

During his five years as Majority Leader of the Washington State Senate in the 1980s, Ted Bottiger of Tacoma warned his freshmen members about three things: "Adele Ferguson, Adele Ferguson, Adele Ferguson." Ralph Munro, Washington's former longtime secretary of state, says, "Adele is the only legitimate tsunami to ever hit the state capitol. Elected officials would rush to the one news stand that carried *The Bremerton Sun* in the Legislative Building to see who she had drowned in her column this week. Those who weren't totally dead from the wave would often take weeks to recover their ego and energy. Adele knew how to hit and hit hard."

She never spent a day on a college campus, let alone journalism school. Yet she became one of the most influential writers in state history. She told some brazen lies to get her foot in the door of a newsroom in 1943 and never looked back. A natural born storyteller, she's a blend of Molly Ivins, Ann Coulter and Annie Oakley, the perky sharpshooter who boasted to an arrogant man, "I can do anything you can do better!"

Her worst enemies lately assert that she "truly represents the cold-hearted, racist, fascist Republican of today"—"a whack job from top to bottom." Even admirers say she can stray over the top. Notably, Adele views as outrageous the celebrated Boldt Decision that upheld Indian treaty fishing rights in Washington State. She rarely misses an opportunity to tweak the tribes. But her fans love her call-'em-as-she-sees-'em bluntness. She says she's writing for "the shipfitter who lives down the road."

She's smart, stubborn, opinionated, loyal and sentimental about some things, especially dogs and cats. If you visit her, be prepared for an exuberant welcome at the screen door by a big old slobbery Lab named Wiccy—short for Wiccan—and Daisy, a sweet Springer Spaniel. The Scarlet Pimpernel, a tabby, is less sociable. She usually hides under Adele's bed. Adele once began an interview with the flinty Dixy Lee Ray by noting the absence of one of the governor's beloved dogs, who had recently died. Suddenly, they both had tears running down their cheeks.

Adele's husband of nearly 60 years, John Philipsen, whom she called Phil, died in 2005, so she talks to her pets now. They adore her. Whenever she ventures out, people tell her *The Sun* hasn't been the same since the day she left in 1993.

* * *

Adele Werdell Ferguson was the second of 10 children born to a Norwegian immigrant and an Army sergeant with hillbilly roots and a gambling problem. She grew up during the Depression.

"I've been writing all my life. As soon as I could find a piece of paper, I think. Short stories, serials, songs. You name it, I wrote it." Her imagination

Adele, right, in Missouri during the Depression, with her sister Alice, aka "Tooddy," and brother, Grady Ferguson Jr., known to all as "Buddy." The Ferguson kids called Adele "Sister."

was the main source of entertainment in the household. The kids loved to go to the movies but admission was pricey—27 cents. "If they managed to put together 27 cents, they would give it to me. I would go to the movie and sit through it twice. Then I would come home and write what the movie was about, start to finish. I remember doing that on newspaper edges because that was all the paper I had. It would look like ticker tape. Then we'd read those movies on rainy days when nobody could go." When she missed a chapter of the Flash Gordon serials that were the staple of every Saturday matinee, "I filled in my own chapter—what I thought probably should have happened.

"The most wonderful event in my entire young life was the time when we lived in Caruthersville, Missouri, near the banks of the Mississippi. We had big floods in the spring. One time, water had gotten into the basement of a store downtown and soaked its magazines—*True Detectives, The Shadow, Hopalong Cassidy*—all these old pulp magazines. Just tons of them. First we carried them home. Then we got a wagon." They dried Hopalong around an old stove. Then all the kids sat on the floor reading—giggling or cringing over the treasure, with Adele, the oldest, as ringmaster. "God, that was wonderful! It was just like seeing a pot of gold to find all those magazines."

* * *

When Japan attacked Pearl Harbor, Adele's impetuous first marriage was all but over. With a young daughter to support, she soon found herself working as an inspector in a bomb factory at Little Rock. Then, together with her mother and all those kids, they decided to head west and join Adele's father, who was stationed in California. Her mother bought a weary Ford they nicknamed Charlie. "Neither one of us could drive. My mother had them show her how. She came home and said, 'Let's go down to the park.' I drove around the park for about an hour, learning how to drive. We packed up the next day and left for California"—two adults and eight kids crammed into Charlie. This expedition looked like a page from *The Grapes of Wrath*, but it was brightened by Adele's irrepressible laugh.

With Adele at the wheel, getting the hang of it, the first hundred miles were harrowing. She nearly sideswiped the first car they passed. One day a motorcycle cop trailed them for a mile before pulling alongside. "He saw all those kids, and he just backed away." Besides her siblings—Tooddy, Tommy, Peggy, Barbara, Nancy, Robin and Jon—there was Adele's daughter, Annette. "Our stuff is tied all over the car. On we went, sleeping in parks."

When they arrived in Los Angeles, nearly broke and low on gas, they reunited with her father. They soon surmised, however, that neither his uncertain status nor the job market were encouraging. Adele's uncles were working at the Navy Yard in Bremerton. They left the kids at a park to play while they headed to the gas rationing office. "When they found out we had *eight* kids with us they gave us enough gas to get us to Alaska."

They filled Charlie's tank, loaded up the kids and headed north. "We were about an hour out of Los Angeles when Peggy said, 'I left my shoes at the park!' And we thought, 'We don't have any shoe stamps.' You had to have stamps to buy shoes. So we had to turn around and drive all the way back

Busy Farragut Avenue in Bremerton during World War II. *Puget Sound Navy Museum*

A shift change at the Ship Yard during World War II. *Puget Sound Navy Museum*

to the park to get her shoes. We found her shoes under a tree. And sitting by them was my brother Robin. We never even missed him!" The 4-year-old wiped away his tears and declared, "I knew you'd come back for the shoes!"

* * *

When they sputtered into Kitsap County they found the epitome of a wartime boom town. Bremerton in 1943 was a gritty, around-the-clock outpost of FDR's arsenal of democracy, nestled along the shores of an evergreen paradise. To keep the Navy Ship Yard and Ammunitions Depot humming, its population had zoomed from 15,000 in 1940 to 75,000. It was now Washington's fourth largest city. The newcomers were sleeping in tents, tiny trailers, even chicken coops. Workers coming off the graveyard shift bumped others out of boarding-house bunks. "Hot bedding," they called it. More than 32,000 men and women worked at the Ship Yard at the apex of the war. Many commuted by ferry from Seattle across Puget Sound.

Adele quickly found a job, first as a messenger, then as chief clerk in the boiler shop. On the side, she started writing stories for the Ship Yard weekly, *The Salute*. When a fulltime spot opened for a women's and features editor in 1944, she was asked about her experience. Lots of it, she said, including *The Caruthersville Democrat* and *The Caruthersville Republican*, two figments of her fertile imagination. The assistant editor was showing her the ropes when he read the look on her face. "You don't even know what I'm talking about, do you?" "No," she confessed, "but you only have to tell me once." Adele Ferguson was now a bona fide newspaperwoman.

A short stint as assistant society editor at *The Santa Ana Register* in California was her next stop. Writing weddings and engagements and mandatory membership in a pinkies-in-the-air women's club was not her cup of tea. She wanted to be a real reporter and she missed her family. Now, with some genuine experience, she landed a $50-a-week job on *The Sun* right after the war. "They were very chintzy with their raises. I remember one time everybody got the rumor that we were going to get a $5-a-week raise, all of us reporters. So everybody got called in separately. The guys were told

THE NAVY YARD SALUTE

PUBLISHED BY THE PUGET SOUND NAVY YARD — BREMERTON, WASHINGTON

James R. Reems, Editor

Printed in the Puget Sound Navy Yard

Salute Office, Bldg. 50, Phone 544

VOL. IV, NO. 6 — BREMERTON, WASHINGTON — FRIDAY, NOV. 3, 1944

Man of the Week . . .

ALL-STAR COACH — Dave Spear, ex-hoop ace of the City College of New York, who, as the team's high scorer, helped hand the U. of Oregon its only defeat on a national tour in 1939 at Madison Square Garden, is now coach of the rapidly developing PSNY All-Stars. Spear predicts a good year for his squad which recently defeated the Receiving Station.

Introducing--

WOMEN'S EDITOR—Expected soon to be a familiar visitor at all shops and departments is ADELE FERGUSON, Salute's new women and feature editor. She joined the staff Wednesday and replaces JO ANN OASS, who after two years on the Yard paper, returns to the U. of W. to complete her studies. Adele comes to the Salute from the Boiler Shop where she was chief clerk. Previous journalistic experience includes high school newspaper work in the Midwest and some freelance writing.

Adele Ferguson Joins Salute Staff

As Salute went to press, the staff was just a wee bit skeptical about its latest addition, Adele Ferguson. You see, she is crazy about cats (six of them at the last count plus one stray who looked as if he might stick around a while), she raises rabbits and can't figure out why her white rabbit and her brown rabbit had black bunnies, and she has a cow that doesn't like her at all . . . this takes place, mind you, on her mother's ranch on the Canal near Seabeck, not in the office, yet.

Well, the editor gulped once, then he gulped again . . . thoughts of a PSNY Farmer's Supplement dashing madly through his mind . . . he had met some interesting women in his day; but to judge from her first hour on the staff, this one had a lot of promise.

Then Adele popped out with the fact that she's daffy about Artie Shaw and she thinks Debussy is too, too if-you-know-what-I-mean, and that she has stacks of records. Before this bit of information had sunk in, we knew that she had a daughter, Annette, two years old, who has platinum hair, unlike her mother's reddish blonde, that Adele's father is an Army master sergeant who will celebrate 30 years in the service next year, and that Adele has really been around (as a daughter of the regiment, naturally, how else could we have meant it?)

All of which finally simmered down to the general idea that we think Adele is well-rounded (personality development, and so forth), has had a

(Continued on page 4)

OPA Charges Taper Off

In view of a "declaration of policy" and signed pledge by 263 Bremerton retailers and business men to adhere strictly to OPA ceiling prices and regulations — OPA, in what is hoped to be the last of such cases involving legal procedure, filed two more suits for injunctions in the U. S. District Court, Seattle, against local merchants.

The violations alleged by OPA were before the statement of policy was signed, an OPA spokesman declares.

Edward Bremer and John Bremer, doing business as Bremer's Department Store, were charged by OPA with failure to prepare adequate base period statements, and with failure to keep required current pricing records.

Virginia Kahn, doing business as Kahn's Men's Shop, was charged with failure to keep required current pricing records.

"These statements and records are the basis of the whole price structure," George H. Layman, OPA district enforcement attorney, said. "They are necessary to compute the legal ceiling prices and to determine the amount of overcharges, if any."

Both of these stores have since joined with virtually all other retail Bremerton merchants in the united effort expressed in the declaration of policy and signed pledge, to adhere strictly to OPA ceiling prices and regulations.

The declaration of good faith was fostered by ethical merchants following an appeal by the Metal Trades Council, Navy Yard administration, and the local Chamber of Commerce to the OPA to stop the exorbitant profiteering at the expense of service men and war workers and their families. OPA took swift action.

A squad of 23 price and enforcement members of OPA, in a surprise move, screened through stores of reported violations with the result that in serious cases, a total of 37 complaints for injunctions were filed in less than three weeks.

Less flagrant violations were referred to the reorganized and enlarged panel of the Bremerton OPA board for settlement.

The declaration and pledge followed. In commenting upon the action taken by the Bremerton Chamber of

(Continued on page 4)

War Chest

Despite the fact that the 1944 War Fund Drive was concentrated in an eight-day period ending two weeks ago, contributions have continued to trickle into headquarters, and the grand total now stands at $82,212.27. This is 128.9 per cent of quota — and there were those who thought that before the books were finally closed out 130 per cent of quota might have been achieved.

Rhythm Maestro--

BAND LEADER — JOE SANDERS, known to thousands of music lovers and dancing enthusiasts as the "Ole Lefthander" will present his Nighthawks, direct from the Blackhawk Restaurant, Chicago, next Thursday night at Peri Maurer's. The Recreation Office booked Sanders and his band through the Music Corporation of America.

PSNYRA Dance November 9

Recreational press agent Bill Kropp waxes eloquent these afternoons over the booking for Thursday, November 9, at Peri Maurer's of the "Ole Lefthander" Joe Sanders and his Nighthawks direct from a record engagement at the famed Blackhawk Restaurant, one of Chicago's most popular night spots.

Heard each night over the Mutual Broadcasting network, Joe Sanders has long been recognized in the east as one of the country's top-notch band-leaders. Joe, whose particular forte is the piano, is also a composer of note and many of his compositions have been recorded.

"In addition to the distinctive stylings of the Ole Lefthander, vocal choruses are being offered for your enjoyment by the booming voice of Joe himself

(Continued on page 4)

Reduction of Co-op Surplus Gains Headway

Preliminary report of the Finance Officer, made at the last meeting of the board of the Cooperative Association, indicated that the probable net loss for September business would be $1,865. Total gross sales for the month for the cafeteria and canteen operations reached a peak for the year, mounting to $249,957.18.

The loss, brought about by price reductions on certain Co-op items, had been anticipated by the Board, and was planned to further reduce the surplus account of the association.

Further reductions in many food items was announced in last week's issue of Salute.

Personnel Management Classes Start

Beginning Monday and Wednesday evenings, November 6 and 8, respectively, a 10-unit course in "Shop Personnel Management" will be offered to Yard supervisors and personnel directors by the Training Office.

The course is to be broken down into the following subjects: brief history of industrial employee relations; functions of the shop personnel director; relationships of the shop personnel director; psychological aspects of employee relations; interpreting the workers' viewpoint; employee grievances, discovery and adjustment; the oral interview; discipline, penalties and effects; causes and methods of reducing labor turnover, and personnel policies, rules and procedure. Lloyd Prichard, X11 Chief Quarterman and shop personnel director, will conduct the classes.

Women Invited

Because of the advent of more women in industry during wartime and the consequent increase of supervision for them in PSNY, special provision will be made in the classes for women supervisors, all of whom are urged to attend.

Monday and Wednesday classes will be conducted as follows: Two separate classes, 20 hours each, split into 10 evenings of two hours each week from 7:00 to 9:00 p.m. Satisfactory completion of course merits a certificate from the University of Washington.

Registration for classes must be made with John C. Lindberg, Training Office, through personal contact or by filling out a registration slip available at all shop personnel offices and forwarding same to the Training Office.

Note: Where essential, extra gas ration slips can be obtained at time of registration.

2 Quartermen Rated Chiefs

Chief quarterman electrician promotions for Carl Bjorling and Maurice Allen top the supervisory rerate lists for the past two weeks during which time two quartermen and four leadingmen had their badges gilded. Chief Quarterman Bjorling succeeds to the position of personnel assistant for X51, left open with the resignation of Ralph Siegner.

Also promoted to the Electric Shop were George Bowles and George Erickson, both advancing from leadingman to quarterman electricians.

Leadingmen rates went to Herbert Copley, X23, who was boosted to leadingman blacksmith heavy fire, and to Ethel Grubb, Dollie Wells and Irma Shoemaker, leadingmen laborers, X72.

Carl Bjorling

The front page of *The Salute* on Nov. 3, 1944, announcing Adele's arrival as women's and features editor. *Puget Sound Navy Museum*

'This is a cost-of-living increase.' I had just written a series of stories about a Russian immigrant lady. When I went in to see Julius Gius, the editor, he said, 'Now Adele, you're going to get a $5-a-week raise. This is for Liza—for those wonderful stories you wrote about her.' And I said, 'Well gee, Julius, if I'm getting this raise for what I wrote about her, I suppose I get another five for cost-of-living?'" Gius was flabbergasted. You couldn't shine Adele. But she was money for *The Sun*. During an era when a woman in the newsroom was a rarity, she won respect with her versatility and breezy, conversational style. She wrote quickly, rarely made mistakes and was fearless. The readers loved her. She was family. Her fruitcake recipe, reprinted annually at Christmastime, is legendary. (What's the secret to producing one that doesn't taste like a Presto-log? "No citron," Adele reveals.)

A large chunk of the front page one day in October of 1961 featured Adele's tale of "How She Became First Gal to Tread Needle"—the Space Needle, that is, with Ewen C. Dingwall, manager of the Century 21 World's Fair, as her tour guide. Adele wrote:

"You will be the first woman up in the space needle, said Century 21 officials. A couple of reporters from Seattle newspapers have snuck up but they were only men—no woman has gone up before and this will be a great day."

At the needle site, a public relations man hurried up. "You've got trouble," he said. "There's another woman here who says she's going up. She's waiting in the construction shack."

Mr. Dingwall's brow furrowed. He disappeared into the shack for a few minutes. "Her name is Mrs. Lamb," he said on return, "and she's an antique dealer who's going on a trip east and wants to tell her friends she's been up in the needle."

"She can go up for all I care...but not with me."

Mr. Dingwall went back into the shack and returned.

"She's a friend of Howard Wright, the man who's building the space needle, and she says he said she could go up."

"She can go up as soon as I come back down."

Mr. Dingwall conferred in the shack again.

"Well, there is this little problem. Century 21 doesn't OWN the space needle…Mr. Wright does. How about her being the first Seattle woman and you being the first Bremerton woman to go up?"

"If she goes up with me, she will be the first Seattle woman launched into space from the space needle," I said.

Adele threatened to write that "the needle sways in the wind" if they let anyone up before her. Guess who got to be the first gal to tread the needle? And at the top, Miss Ferguson and Mr. Dingwall each ate a salami sandwich so they could say they were also the first to dine on the needle. "It was worth all the trouble we'd had, Mr. Dingwall said, wiping spatters of yellow paint from his coat. Only he'd been so excited he couldn't taste his sandwich. Mine was the only salami sandwich I ever ate that tasted like lamb."

The newly appointed women's and features editor of the Ship Yard *Salute* in 1944.

* * *

Six decades after her debut, with newspapers folding or going on-line to save the franchise, Adele took pleasure in noting that *The Sun* was still going strong at 75. Adele produced a capsule history so vivid, so authentic you can almost hear the Linotypes clack in the composing room, smell the paste and see the beige cloud of Lucky Strike smoke floating near the newsroom ceiling:

Reporters did their writing on typewriters in those days on long sheets of newsprint cut from the huge rolls the paper itself was printed on. If you had to add, cut or rewrite a story, that required snipping and pasting. *The Sun* bought its own paste, big cans of gooey snot-like stuff that was hard to get into the paste jars without getting it all over the desk.

We covered everything from stolen license plates to lost canaries. We took pride in finding out what the Navy didn't want us to know, such as a barge sinking at a dock. When one of our spies called and told us about it, one of us put a camera under a coat and took a taxi into the yard to get a picture before we were caught. Eventually we had a truce when the Navy threatened to keep us out of there for any reason.

Every reporter had a beat. Bob Wethern did the Navy yard, Curt Fortney the courthouse and politics, Paul Ryan wrote editorials and the city. Vera Pumphry was the society editor. Dot Lackey was the proof reader. I was the feature and obituary writer. John Jarstad, brother of the grocer Glenn, who eventually became mayor, was the sports editor. John drove everybody nuts when the paper came out. First papers off the press were delivered to the city room and everybody was given a copy to check for any errors egregious enough to require stopping the presses and redoing it. Julius was death on errors.

Jarstad always read his paper standing in the middle of the city room so everybody had to go around him. City Editor George Thompson got sick of it and one day lit a match to the bottom of the paper. An unflinching Jarstad stood there reading until the flames reached the top and the paper parted into two pieces. Jarstad dropped them on the floor and sauntered back to his desk, while Thompson leaped to his feet and stamped the fire out. That didn't break Jarstad's reading habit, but he was never lit off again.

A guy named Ed was the wire editor for awhile. Ed was suspected of not being as attentive to his job as need be when other newspapers ran stories we didn't have. Ed would say we didn't get that one over the wire. That set off an occasional dig through his wastebasket to see if he had discarded it. He put a stop to that by spitting periodically into the wastebasket so nobody wanted to dig in there anymore.

Ryan kept a bottle of rum in his desk and on occasion would buy a couple of cokes for him and me, lace them liberally, and we sat in the office drinking rum and coke under Julius's nose. Ryan eventually had a nervous breakdown, which was apparent when he was seen trying to get a drink of water out of the pencil sharpener.

Julius used to say that there were no hard and fast rules at *The Sun* except one: No hard and fast rules. He frowned on BSing in the city room between reporters and visitors. That was distracting. Business manager Alex Ottevaere used to wander over and chat with Wethern, his fishing partner, until Julius would come charging out of his office and order him to go back where he came from and "let the creative people do their jobs."

They had a no-smoking rule at *The Sun*, for the women. The men could smoke, but Julius and Alex thought it wasn't ladylike for the women who fought hard for that right. I didn't smoke so I didn't get involved. They also did not permit women to wear pantsuits, long after that became fashionable. Dresses it had to be for all women. I didn't join this fight either, feeling in my job dresses were preferable. The big day came when women were allowed to show up in pants. It had to be pantsuits, no jeans or slacks. Unfortunately, it rained that day. With

In *The Bremerton Sun* newsroom in the early 1950s.

nearly all the women in wool pantsuits wet from their coming and going, the whole place smelled like a barn.

When the priest at the Catholic church in Port Orchard was arrested for drunken driving, Julius wrote the story himself so no reporter had to face up to the outraged Catholics who felt their fellow Catholic, Julius, should have held it out. When his wife, Gail, was involved in a minor fender-bender that normally wouldn't rate a story, Julius wrote it anyway so nobody could accuse him of covering up for her. My favorite story about Julius, though, was when Ed Bremer dropped in, either just before or after the war was over. Ed complained to Julius that Bremerton was going to go to hell in a handbasket.

"Why?" asked Julius.

"The war's over," said Ed.

Julius said, "You sonofabitch," and stalked back to his office, leaving the most powerful man in town, who owned most of it, standing in the middle of the city room, red as a beet, while reporters hunched over their typewriters, pretending they hadn't heard a word.

* * *

Interviewing an accident survivor in the 1950s.

Adele and Bremerton were a perfect fit. She can cuss like a sailor, loves a good joke and has worked hard all her life. Adele absolutely maintains that "a woman's weight, age and salary are her own business," but she has no inhibitions about sharing her naiveté about sex as a young bride. Men are such fools, she says, offering an array of stories about how she humiliated all the guys who pinched her thighs and propositioned her when she was a young reporter. And what a knockout she was, prowling the docks for *The Salute*, covering Bremerton City Hall and the cop shop for *The Sun* in the 1950s.

A photo to go with her "Farmer's Daughter" column in the 1950s.

Bob Torseth, who'd been at *The Sun* even longer than Adele, told a classic story about her salty sense of humor: One day, she strolled into the newsroom hard on the heels of a shy young intern. Making certain they were within earshot of the staff, she licentiously wrapped an arm around him and declared, "Thanks, honey. That was fun!"

The lioness in winter is still a handsome woman, with those bright eyes and a perky hairdo featuring a tinge of red. She puts her hands on her hips in a confident way.

* * *

When Adele broke the gender barrier in the Capitol Press Corps in 1961, only one of the guys would talk to her, and he wanted her to fork over copies of everything she wrote. You can guess where Adele told him to stick it.

The *Seattle Post-Intelligencer's* reporter had her kicked out of his seat in the press gallery when she sat there unwittingly one day. She told the senior correspondent, the AP's Leroy Hittle, "You know something, Leroy, if this *ever* happens again and I'm down there sitting and they have the

Sergeant-at-Arms come and throw me out, there's going to be blood and guts *all over* this chamber. And it isn't going to be mine!"

Over the next few months, the guys came to realize they had a formidable competitor who gave as good as she got. "I was no pushover," she says. "I earned their respect."

As for legislators and lobbyists, a few became friends. But she carefully compartmentalized her relationships. "I didn't socialize with them. *Any* of them. I don't socialize with legislators. I don't make cozy friends and don't go to dinner to their houses and stuff....You can have a drink with them, but if you get too friendly then they can't understand it when you start cutting them up for something they need cutting up for. Somebody's got to cut them up."

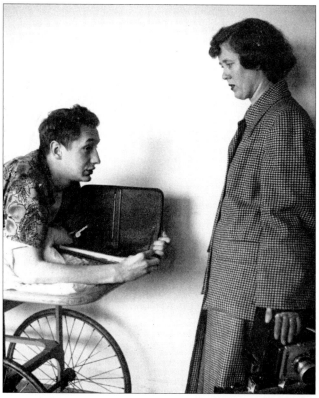

Speed Graphic press camera at the ready, Adele interviews an
injured serviceman in the 1950s.

The Kitsap County National Guard unit invited Adele to take a ride in a tank during their annual maneuvers. She was up for any adventure.

Adele receives an award from the Marine Corps League after one of her investigations led to the acquittal of a falsely accused Marine in the 1950s.

At home with husband, John "Phil" Philipsen, daughters Annette and Karen
and some of their menagerie during the early 1950s.

Adele bristles at duplicity, injustice and bureaucratic nincompoopery. She also hates sexism but she expects women to have gumption. She listens to Rush Limbaugh and admires *The Wall Street Journal*. She's fiscally conservative and socially libertarian. There's not a PC bone in her body.

Dan Evans, a liberal Republican, is her pick as Washington's greatest governor. Al Rosellini, a centrist Democrat "and the best friend the ferries ever had," is the runnerup. She admired "Scoop" and "Maggie"—U.S. senators Henry M. Jackson and Warren G. Magnuson, and holds in high regard former U.S. senator Slade Gorton, whom she first met when he was a rising young Republican legislator in the early 1960s. She's pro-choice, but was fond of the late Ellen Craswell, an evangelical Christian who was trounced by Gary Locke in the 1996 race for governor. Adele says she warned Craswell that "all that Jesus talk" would never go down with the body politic.

* * *

The late State Sen. Bob Bailey, a lanky former newspaperman from South Bend in Pacific County, was a legislator Adele admired. He was the district representative for the redoubtable Democratic Congresswoman Julia Butler Hansen of Cathlamet. Reminded that Bailey once quipped, "Julia never wore a mini-skirt because she didn't want her balls to show," Adele is convulsed in laughter. She beams at the suggestion the line might fit her, too. After all, this is the woman who once brought the U.S. Navy to its knees when it refused to let her take a ride on the *USS Nautilus* when it visited Bremerton. Describing her award-winning article on the escapade, Irwin S. Blumenfeld, director of information for the University of Washington, told an awards banquet in 1958: "Adele wanted to go on a short trip on the atomic submarine, but the Navy accused her of being a woman. She confessed this was true, and wanted to know 'So what?' The Navy hemmed and hawed and finally admitted the reason she couldn't go was that the *Nautilus* had no little room labeled 'Ladies.' Adele replied with irrefutable logic that in her own home where there is mixed company, there is no little room labeled 'Ladies.' However, the Navy prevailed and the *Nautilus* sailed without her. The story she wrote of her battle with the Navy was so hilarious that the Associated Press picked it up and it was used all over the world." In the end, the Navy gave up the ship. *The Sun's* star reporter took a ride on the *Nautilus*. On the deck, they had erected an outhouse labeled "Ladies."

"She handled this rather delicate subject with superb humor and excellent taste," Blumenfeld told the crowd. "You might even say it was uncanny." Adele chortled and whispered to another *Sun* reporter, "Oh, I wish I'd said that!"

The banquet story, a classic in the genre by her colleague James E. Hanson, was headlined **Adele Ferguson Does It Again, Only More So.** Adele had scored an unprecedented sweep of writing honors, "surpassing even her own formidable record of previous years." She won first prize for distinguished reporting for her coverage of a Shelton murder trial, first for feature writing with the *Nautilus* yarn and an honorable mention for

Testing the State Patrol's new Breathalyzer machine during the 1960s.

column-writing. Her column, The Farmer's Daughter, which appeared in *The Sun* every Friday through the gardening season, had won an award from the press association every year since its debut in the early 1950s. "Considered from any angle," Hanson wrote, "it was a triumph without precedent: Only woman to win a first for 1957 writing; only writer ever to win two firsts in one year...took two of three firsts in the under 50,000 circulation class (she didn't enter the third, editorial writing.)"

The Sun referred to her as "Miss Ferguson (who in private life is Mrs. John Philipsen of Pioneer Road, Seabeck)."

Adele's reaction to the awards? "For heaven's sake, where are my shoes?" She was wearing, intermittently, a new pair and resting her tortured feet between the announcement of each new honor. After the banquet, a reporter for *The Seattle Times* told another *Sun* staffer: "Boy, it's a good thing she doesn't take pictures, too."

"Oh, but she does," he said. "She's got some dillies she's considering entering in the photo contest next year."

The Times man reportedly exclaimed "Oh, no!" and beat his forehead.

"So at the moment," Hanson concluded, "only the sports writing division appears safe from the Ferguson threat. And even that's not certain. With Adele, you never know." In point of fact, Adele had covered hockey earlier in her reporting career at Bremerton.

* * *

Adele had a love/hate relationship with Washington's first female governor. Dixy Lee Ray was a Ph.D. scientist whose views on global warming "still make the most sense," Adele says. "But Dixy lacked political savvy, to put it mildly," and quickly ran afoul of the media. Although Adele warned the guys not to ridicule her and was generally more supportive than other reporters and pundits, the governor bristled at *any* criticism and intermittently gave Adele the cold shoulder. In 1979, Adele wrote:

"Well, now I know what it's like to be on Dixy's list. I didn't even know she was ticked at me, though I probably have given her reason. I thought I wrote as much favorable stuff about her as bad. Maybe she only reads the bad."

Adele tells how the governor greeted her frostily at a "Meet Your Governor" night in Bremerton. Arriving 35 minutes late, the governor was "all smiles until she saw me, and the temperature in the hallway dropped about 20 degrees."

"Hi, Dixy, I said, what kept you?"

"I thought YOU would be at Senator Walgren's party," she said as she swept out of the hallway into the main dining area."

The governor viewed Gordon Walgren, the Senate majority leader, as a dangerous potential rival. Adele and Walgren were a mutual admiration society.

"About that time I wished I was at Walgren's $250 bash in Seattle, the atmosphere undoubtedly being much cheerier than it was here," Adele continued. "When a reporter showed up from the local radio station, Dixy fell on him with such joy you would think he had discovered nuclear energy, and answered all his questions, all the while ignoring me. I was be-ginning to enjoy myself now. Especially when a dinner guest who had been watching all this said to her, 'Why don't you give Adele a story, Governor?'

"Oh, no" said Dixy. "I don't talk to her. I suppose she'll write THAT down."

"I didn't," Adele concluded. "I figured I wouldn't have any trouble re-membering."

Vintage Adele. "The first thing you did when *The Sun* arrived was to turn to Adele's column to see if you were in it and if you were, what had she said about you," Walgren says. At a Washington News Council roast for Adele and three other veteran reporters in 1999, he quipped that The Farmer's Daughter column honed her ability to be a good political reporter because she was "working in the dirt and manure."

When Walgren was convicted of complicity in the controversial "Gamscam" influence peddling sting in 1980, Adele stood by him, saying he was the victim of dirty tricks. One veteran Olympia reporter wrote that Gov. Ray was so pleased at the indictments that she "almost danced a jig" in front of the Capitol press corps. Adele was disgusted. Walgren, now practicing law and lobbying, will never forget her loyalty.

Even those who never got kudos in her column—and never will—can't help but admire her crusty integrity. At the News Council roast, Congressman Jim McDermott quoted filmmaker Michael Moore as observing that the relationship between politicians and the press "is like a dog and a tree." As for Adele, "There never was any doubt where she was com-ing from...and she made it clear that a lib-eral psychiatrist from

Adele in the 1980s. *Kitsap Sun*

Seattle was not her cup of tea." McDermott told the crowd that when he was in the Legislature "you knew where to find her at 5:30 every day when the Legislature was in session—in Lt. Gov. Cherberg's office" for cocktail hour. Adele cocked an eyebrow and smirked. "Don't ever run statewide!"

Former Associated Press writer David Ammons, whom Adele rates as one of the best reporters ever to cover the Capitol, considers her one of his early mentors, "both in understanding the crazy Legislature and in her admonition to 'just write for the shipfitter who lives at the end of the country road.' Don't talk 'government,' she said, just real people. I never forgot that language, and spent the rest of my journalism career translating government-speak. She's great at that."

Gordon Schultz, the retired longtime United Press International Bureau manager in Olympia, says most people know Adele for her columns "but she was also a damn good reporter, as demonstrated by the news articles she wrote about her legislators and government officials." And her antennae never drooped. "She would be working on one or more crossword puzzles while we sat at the press table when the House was in session. She was a great multi-tasker and I swear she could hear every word said by anyone on the floor while working on a puzzle at the same time."

Paul O'Connor, one of Gov. John Spellman's press secretaries during 1984, his last character-building year in office, once referred to Adele as "the conscience of the uninformed." Bob Partlow, who covered the Capitol for *The Olympian* from 1983 to 2000, says, "he meant it as an insult, but over the years as I watched Adele at work I felt it was more of a compliment. She was writing for the people who didn't give a damn about the details of the political infighting at the courthouse. They wanted to know about the impact on them as taxpayers. She was their conscience—the reporter who was always able to put things in human terms. She's one of kind."

Adele was famous for her cut-to-the-chase questions at news conferences—"usually the very question the average guy would ask," Ammons says. After serial killer Ted Bundy's execution, she asked Gov. Booth Gardner if he wasn't happy Bundy was now a "grease spot."

Ammons and Partlow both have vivid memories of the news conference where Gardner was easing out his chief of corrections, Amos Reed. "He tried to put a pretty face on it," Ammons says. The official word was that he had resigned, Partlow affirms, "and the governor was up there saying nice things. Then Amos got up to say his goodbyes." When it came time for Q&A, Adele piped up: "Didja get canned, Amos?"

"She has the most marvelous skill in getting at the guts of an issue," Dick Larsen, then of *The Seattle Times* and himself no shrinking violet, told Ammons for a 1991 story on Adele's 30 years at the capital. "When the shock of her question wears off, very often we get real, usable information. So many of us in the press use sly and intellectual language. She's so blunt. She's no-nonsense. It's beautiful. She makes it hell on those who slip below the level of her expectation. She's a tough political street guy."

* * *

Adele has had her share of scoops, but doesn't believe in gotcha journalism. She recalls the time when Senate Majority Leader Sid Snyder of Long Beach told a *Seattle P-I* reporter that Sen. Linda Smith, a Republican

Adele and Frank "Buster" Brouillet, the State Superintendent of Public Instruction, leave a ceremony in the legislative chambers at Olympia in the 1980s. *Adele Ferguson scrapbook*

Adele with Lt. Gov. Joel Pritchard on the Senate floor, 1991. *Photo by Louie Balukoff*

ideologue from Vancouver, was a "miserable bitch." He immediately thought better of it—or at least at the wisdom of saying it—and asked the reporter not to print it. "Of course she *did*," Adele says scathingly. Many journalists would argue that Snyder, a savvy politician, knew the rules of engagement and shouldn't expect to be able to retract something that deliciously revealing. Adele isn't buying that. "I never did anything like that to anyone," she says. "We all speak out of turn. I'd stop and ask someone, 'Do you really want to say that?' I'd never hang anyone out to dry like that."

Gov. Spellman tried to woo her. "We went fishing out on the Sound, with Bremerton Mayor Glenn Jarstad as the mediator, a couple of times," he recalls. "It was an attempt to reach more favorable relations. Not that it ever worked!"

Spellman says Adele did a good job of walking the tightrope between being a reporter and a columnist. "She was very accurate, and people were equally afraid of her....She had nicknames or characterizations for everyone. I think I was 'The rube in the pumpkin patch'...Adele always had a zinger, but she was fair. Mean, yes, but fair."

* * *

After 47 years with the Bremerton daily, Adele left *The Sun* on Feb. 25, 1993, taking pains to avoid any fuss. The paper couched it as a retirement. Adele says she resigned because she'd had it up to here with a new editor and arrogant whippersnappers who didn't know the difference between material and materiel. "They'd change stuff without even consulting me and make me look ridiculous."

Noting that "the office is vacant, but the aura lingers on," staff writer Julie McCormick told *The Sun's* readers that Adele left behind "a classic Ferguson touch." It was a brown paper "Disposable bull**** bag, its message to the future as blunt as the sender."

Adele can spot bullshit at 100 paces, even with asterisks. Her old friend and sometime adversary, the legendary political operative C. Montgomery "Gummie" Johnson, said she was "an elephant among mice," willing to write things no other political reporter would touch. *The Sun* quoted Dan Evans as saying that catching hell from Adele was like being "stabbed from in front." Actually, it was Al Rosellini who said it, and when Adele pointed that out to Evans, he shot back, "Well, I wish I'd said it!" Johnson observed, "You hadn't arrived until you'd been skewered by Adele." Partlow says Adele always called Olympia "a place where zippers never rust."

"She wouldn't let anyone get away with anything," Partlow says. "And she was just 'Adele.' It was one word, like 'Pele.' You didn't have to say her last name. She was just a reporter's reporter. She could drink with the boys, cuss with the boys and in every way hold her own with the boys. She came on the scene at a time when there weren't many women in the press corps. It's a tough job being a capitol correspondent....She had to fight and claw into the male establishment and cut through the crap. I did a lot of investigative work over the years and she was like a role model and mentor to me. Her work put spine in my conscience. Not that I needed a lot, but it was always a reminder of what a reporter's job really is. And she was hilarious, too. She wrote this great story about being at the Governor's Mansion for a dinner and being served these tiny Cornish game hens. Adele went into great detail about how pathetically little they were, with their tiny folded wings. How I wish I had a copy of that story. She just had this incredibly wicked wit. I'm sure she would rather cut out her tongue than call herself a feminist, but she was a role model for other women to follow. On the whole, she's just an incredible person."

* * *

An Adele autobiography doubtless would be a regional best seller. She knows where the skeletons are in the closets at the Capitol, and has a long memory for those who've crossed her. You don't dis Adele and not pay the price, sooner or later. Usually it's sooner. Over the years, however, she saw a lot of extracurricular activity between consenting adults and rarely felt it rose to the level of newsworthiness. "If it impacted the public, that's another story." After a veteran Olympia operative got an advance look at the transcript of her oral history, he paused in a capitol corridor and declared, "Well, it could have been worse!"

She loves war stories, but she's too busy writing columns about the present to spend much time on the past. Bette Davis once observed that "getting old is not for sissies," so there are aches, pains and inconveniences. "Damn it! I have to go to the bathroom again!" she grouses. But she still likes her McNaughton's on the rocks. At least one a day; maybe two, and sometimes three if it's the weekend.

From her cozy house at Hansville at the tip of the Kitsap Peninsula she has a million-dollar view overlooking Admiralty Inlet, with Whidbey Island across the channel and Mount Baker in the distance. This is Skunk Harbor, and when you suggest that her worst enemies would say the name is a perfect fit, she tosses back her head and laughs that laugh.

Writing her columns on a clunky computer in a cluttered cubbyhole, Adele is surrounded by old bottles, vintage political buttons and knick-knacks. She also collects postcards and pens. Tables are piled high with books. She does crossword puzzles—the tougher the better—and jigsaw puzzles. She has a remarkable memory. She reads several papers a day, including *The Seattle Times*, *The Kitsap Sun* and *The Wall Street Journal*, which she anoints as "very good." There are piles of clippings. All of her some 7,000 columns are neatly scrapbooked.

Recurring themes are big government, bleeding-heart liberals, fractured English and long lost dogs. Reviewing the race for state superintendent of public instruction in 2008, she noted that Terry Bergeson, the

Adele at home with her dogs, Wiccy and Daisy.
Photo by John Hughes for The Legacy Project

incumbent, was not one of her favorites, "but at least she can talk. Randy Dorn, the Service Employees union head who seeks her job, can say reading and writing but anything else ending in 'ing' stumps him. He says bein' and sayin' and goin' and extendin'. The state superintendent should at least be able to speak the English language." She was also ticked off by a new twist in the debate over "cruel and unusual" punishment:

> Because of the bleeding hearts in the legal and judicial professions, death penalty cases require vast sums of money and are years in resolving. It is to the financial advantage of public defenders we pay to represent most of those on Death Row to string it out as long as they can. Counties have nearly gone broke under the financial strain of such cases. There also is great concern expressed over the pain some rotten killer may suffer in meeting his end.
>
> …That fat slob who killed two women bank tellers near Olympia got off because his lawyer was afraid his head would come off. This, while he was deliberately stuffing himself with candy bars so he would become so gross that could be raised as a possibility. As I recall, he died in prison a while back. I believe it was his case that generated the change in this state's executions to offer a choice between lethal injections or hanging.
>
> But lethal injections have come under scrutiny as two Kentucky prisoners have taken to the U.S. Supreme Court the question of whether they are pain free, which they feel entitled to expect. Nearly all the states except a dozen back east that don't have the death penalty and Nebraska, which allows electrocution, use lethal injections now. The argument heard by the justices…was whether the three separate drugs process used by most of the states should be reduced to one drug similar to what's used to put animals to death. Justice John Paul Stevens, in particular, was worried about one of the usual three, a paralytic drug used to mask muscle spasms that might upset witnesses and cause an "undignified death." He thinks that's the cause of the pain.
>
> Well, that should be no problem, although why we worry about an undignified death for these sleazebags is beyond me. Let 'em twitch.

In 2010, her 66th year in Washington State journalism, Adele saw the year's hottest race like this:

It aggravates me no end to read news stories about Dino Rossi's decision to take on U.S. Sen. Patty Murray that say he lost four times against Christine Gregoire for governor. Let's have a little truth in advertising here.

He only legitimately lost once.

The voters elected him governor by 261 votes on Nov. 2, 2004. He was still the winner by 42 votes after a machine recount of all 39 counties. Even after that, a tearful state Democratic chair Paul Berendt and a defiant Gregoire refused to accept defeat. A sobbing Berendt asked a judge to include in a hand recount paid for by the Democratic Party 710 King County ballots that were rejected by the voting machines Nov. 2. He had worked all his life to make sure everybody's vote was counted, said Berendt. "Every vote should be counted," said Gregoire. "The race continues. A 42-vote margin, my friends, that is a tied race."

The judge denied Republican state chair Chris Vance's move to exclude the ballots and ordered poll workers to inspect each one to judge voter intent and mark it so....A lot of voters, including Democrats as well as Republican, declared Rossi had been cheated as Gregoire was declared the winner....I will never accept that Gregoire's election wasn't manipulated although I don't know whether she had a hand in it or not.

Rossi did lose in a second run at her in 2008, despite her pre-election vow not to increase taxes—which she did anyway. I think the heart was gone out of him.

So, can he take Patty Murray's U.S. Senate seat away from her after three terms? Well, in these days of recession and the blowing of vast sums of money by a Congress, most of whose members have been there too long, who better to represent us than a guy who as chair of the state Senate Ways and Means Committee, faced up to a huge deficit and put together a biennial budget with no tax increases in it?

If you believe pork barreling is what we elect politicians to do then Patty Murray is for you. ...But if you are as worried as I am at the

appalling financial state the United States is in due to spending far, far
more than is coming in, it's time to send in a new player. Especially a
good player. …

I don't dislike Patty Murray. But she's had 18 years and if she has
ever said or done anything to stem the out-of-control Democratic Party
which just can't say no, I haven't seen it. We need Dino Rossi and we
need him bad.

The voters re-elected Patty. Adele sighed, complained to Wiccy and
went back to her keyboard. The cat ran for cover. At least new material is
never in short supply.

* * *

An avid fisherman, Adele is still bitter over the landmark 1974 decision
by federal Judge George Boldt, who allocated 50 percent of the catch to
treaty tribes fishing in their "usual and accustomed" places. "There were
parts about Adele I didn't like," Partlow observes. "I thought some of her
views were racist—certainly about Indians. But I don't think it ever got in
the way of her reporting. She savaged everyone equally."

Like Slade Gorton, Adele insists that her beef with the Indians has
nothing to do with race: "I'm not anti-Indian. I just do not believe that
anybody, even if they were Norwegian, should have the fish that belong
to the people of the State of Washington. And I'm mad at the judge who
gave it to them."

In recent years, other ethnic groups and civil rights advocates have been
outraged by her columns. Exhibit A would be her 2006 offering, "Why do
blacks continue to support Democrats?"

One of these days before I die, I hope to see a shift in the attitudes of
so many of my black brothers and sisters in this great country we share,
from perpetual victimhood, to pride in their achievements on the road
from slave to American citizen.

Remember Ronald Reagan's story about the kid who had to shovel a huge pile of manure? He went about it with such joy he was asked why and said, "With all that manure, there's got to be a pony in there somewhere."

The pony hidden in slavery is the fact that it was the ticket to America for black people. I have long urged blacks to consider their presence here as the work of God, who wanted to bring them to this raw, new country and used slavery to achieve it. A harsh life, to be sure, but many immigrants suffered hardships and indignations as indentured servants. Their descendants rose above it. You don't hear them bemoaning their forebears' life the way some blacks can't rise above the fact theirs were slaves. Besides freedom, a job and a roof over their heads, they all sought respect. But even after all these years, too many have yet to realize that to get respect, you have to give it.

Verily, this is The Gospel According to Adele—child of the Depression; self-made woman in a man's world. It's "Stop sniveling and deal with it!" In his second Inaugural Address, Lincoln surmised that "The Almighty has His own purposes," adding that American slavery was something God allowed but "now wills to remove" through "this mighty scourge of war." Adele is definitely no Abe. With malice toward some, she just wades right in when the muse strikes her and opens fire, better angels be damned.

Predictably, the pony manure hit the fan when the slavery column appeared and—if you'll forgive the mixed metaphor—spread like wildfire on the Internet. Outraged readers lobbied papers to pull "the racist rant" or apologize for running it. *The Kitsap Peninsula Business Journal* reportedly received 1,500 e-mail protests. *Seattle Post-Intelligencer* columnist Joel Connelly, one of Adele's least favorite people—and the feeling is mutual— reprised the uproar in an April Fools' Day roundup of that year's most memorable stumbles. "She was once the archconservative of the Olympia press corps," Connelly wrote, "a formidable crone whose columns…criticized Native American tribes and even tossed darts at the driving habits of Asian Americans. Still, few would have expected that Adele Ferguson would hold forth on race relations as she did…"

No apologies from Adele on that one or any of the other hand grenades she has lobbed since 1965 when her column began syndication in Northwest newspapers. Some, however, suggest that Adele has strayed farther right and become ham-handed because she no longer has the benefit of strong editing and wise counsel from the likes of her late editor, Gene Gisley. They say he knew how to temper her more extreme instincts. Adele gives high marks to Gisley but denies being a loose cannon without him.

Lillian Walker, one of the thousands of blacks who arrived in Bremerton from all over America during World War II, strongly disputes the notion that Adele is a racist. Mrs. Walker helped found a chapter of the NAACP in Kitsap County and led civil rights demonstrations at segregated soda fountains and lunch counters. "We felt that we were moving forward," she says of the post-war years. It was grating, however, that *The Sun* "would not print a Negro picture on the front of the paper unless he had committed some terrible crime, like raping a woman or killing someone." That changed when Gisley and Adele gained influence in the newsroom. "If we went down to the paper, we could either talk to Mr. Gisley or Adele, and we knew that we were going to get what we wanted," Mrs. Walker said in 2010 at the age of 97 when her oral history was published. All they wanted, she emphasized, was "to be treated like everyone else in Bremerton." Adele was color blind. "She wrote for everyone."

"The black people in Bremerton were first-rate folks," Adele says, "and Lillian Walker was amazing."

* * *

Adele does have some regrets over the column she wrote in 2002 about how to bring an end "to the suicide bomber terrorism inflicted on Israel by the Palestinian Arabs."

"So what is my solution for ending this carnage?" she wrote. "It stems from the words of the late, great Prime Minister Golda Meir: 'This won't be settled until they love their children more than they hate Jews.' The next time a bunch of Arab youths are throwing rocks at the Israeli tanks, mow them down. Kill them. Keep doing it until the Arabs decide whether they really hate the Jews more than they love their children. I don't think the Israelis would have to dispose of many Arab children before the white flag would go up. The world would hate them for it, a world that has been surprisingly tolerant of the Arabs slaughter of Jewish children, but I'd bet the suicide bombings would stop."

The "Voices of Palestine" Web page went ballistic over the "hate-filled" column and *The Eastside Journal* published an apology for running it. Her sin, Adele says, was in being too blunt—too Adele. "I should have listened to my husband." In fact, that's how she began the column: "Don't write that," she quoted him as advising. But Golda Meir fundamentally had it right, Adele insists, adding that she guesses they both just flunked Political Correctness 101.

Julie McCormick would seem to deserve an "A" for the ending to her story about Adele's unhappy sayonara to *The Sun*: "And now she's gone. Who's going to take on the brown bag now?"

Adele in her office at her home in Hansville overlooking Puget Sound.
By John Hughes for The Legacy Project

When asked about the "Disposable bull****" bag, Adele looked startled. She had never bothered to read the 1993 story about her departure
from the newspaper. "I never left behind a brown paper bag!" she insists.
"Someone else must have left it on my desk."

That makes the symbolism just that much better. The staff understood
her legacy: Comfort the afflicted and afflict the comfortable. There will
always be a never-ending supply of bull****. But there's only one Adele
Ferguson.

And she's still writing a column.

The capitol correspondent for *The Bremerton Sun* takes a break outside
the legislative chambers in the 1970s. *Adele Ferguson scrapbook*

Oral History

Research by John Hughes, Lori Larson and Don Brazier
Transcription by Lori Larson
Interviews by John C. Hughes

ADELE FERGUSON INTERVIEWS
October 23, 2008

John C. Hughes: We're at the home of Adele Ferguson at Hansville, Washington, overlooking Puget Sound. In 1961, Adele became the first female legislative reporter at the state Capitol in Olympia. She retired from *The Bremerton Sun* in 1993, but has maintained her column, which is syndicated in some 30 Northwest newspapers.

Adele, you have been quoted as saying that you should never ask a woman her weight, her salary or her age. But, for the record, this is an oral history, and I'm duty bound to ask you to state your full name, including your maiden name, and your date of birth. It's for posterity.

Ferguson: It's going to go in that book.

Hughes: It's going to go in an oral history, on the website, then in a book.

Ferguson: Well, my full name is Adele W. Ferguson.

Hughes: Not "Uh-DELL" but "A-dell"?

Ferguson: Yes. You know why I do that?

Hughes: Why?

Ferguson: Because when you answer the phone and say "A-dell" they understand "A-dell." But if you only say "Uh-dell" it kind of runs together. I was named after my father's only sister, who was an invalid of some kind. I never knew for sure what was wrong with her. They never called me anything but "Sister," just as my brother, Grady Jr., was "Buddy" and my sister Alice was "Tooddy." They quit doing that with their last seven kids.

35

I should tell you something interesting about my mother and my father's family. I never met either one of my grandmothers. Well, I did when I was little baby—one of them. The one that came over from Norway with her kids in World War I. The other one is from the hillbilly section of Tennessee. And my grandfather had brothers, several brothers, and one of them was found dead by the railroad tracks one day, all bloodied up. Now the question was, "Did he get beat up and killed or was he run over by the train accidentally?" You know how they found out?

Hughes: No.

Ferguson: You take the body home and you get a new quilt, and wrap the body in the quilt, and then you wash the quilt. And if the blood comes out of the quilt then he wasn't murdered. If the blood had remained in the quilt he would have been considered a murder victim. Now that's old hillbilly stuff.

Hughes: That's Hillbilly CSI.

Ferguson: Oh yeah.

Hughes: I think we got interrupted on your full name. What's the "W" for?

Ferguson: My middle name—Werdell—is my mother's maiden name. She was a teenager, I think, when she came over from Norway in World War I. What happened was this: A great number of Scandinavian men were inclined to come to the United States ahead of the family, settle, find another woman, have another bunch of kids and say, "I'll see ya!" So the poor grass widows…they're left alone back in Norway or Sweden. It happened to a lot of them. Eventually when they get the money, first they send the kids over one by one. They pop the kids over as soon as they got the dough. And the kids come over and stay with the father. My grandmother came over with her two girls—my mother and my aunt. I think she had five boys and two girls. Her boys were all excellent floor layers. They were wonderful figures in my life.

Hughes: Grandma's sons we're talking about?

Ferguson: Grandma's. My Norwegian grandmother. She settled in Minnesota. Interestingly, as a young woman, she had a mastectomy and that was *very rare* in those days.

Hughes: Yeah, to survive it no less. Talk about disfiguring.

Ferguson: And I don't know how it happened, but—what's the name of the big medical clinic there?

Hughes: The Mayo?

Ferguson: The Mayo somehow learned about that and asked her to please come to the clinic, would she talk to some of their doctors in a meeting about what happened—all about her operation? And she did. As a matter of fact I've got a book on the Mayo Clinic but I haven't run through it yet to see if I can find that written up in there. I think it might be.

Hughes: So Werdell is your mother's maiden name?

Ferguson: Yes. My father's name is Ferguson.

Hughes: So you are Adele Werdell Ferguson. What was your father's first name?

Ferguson: Grady, Grady Ferguson.

Hughes: And the derivation of Ferguson?

Ferguson: Mostly Scotch. I don't know where the Grady comes from. When I was little we used to laugh at it. We didn't like it….I'm half Norwegian and half Scotch.

Hughes: That's a pretty formidable combination of gene pools.

Ferguson: Oh, I think so.

Hughes: And how about your mother? What was her first name?

Ferguson: Christine.

Hughes: Were they married as young people?

Ferguson: Well, they must have been. I don't know. Was she 18 when I was born? No that wasn't me. That was somebody else. I'm thinking of Barack Obama's mother! (Joking) She was 18 when he was born. I was their second child. They had a boy before they had me. Then they had a lot more kids.

Hughes: What was the span between you and your brother?

Ferguson: Probably a couple years. Kids at school used to say, "Gee, how do you remember all of the names of all of your brothers and sisters?"

And adults would say, "I didn't know they gave that much furlough in the Army!"

Hughes: And how many siblings in all?

Ferguson: Ten.

Hughes: You were number two of 10. Holy moly! That's a big family. So, do you want to negotiate over this? What year were you born?

Ferguson: (after lengthy pause) I was born near the time of the Great Depression. That's as close as I'm going to give you.

Hughes: OK. And where was that?

Ferguson: Fort Snelling, Minnesota. My father was an Army man. He was career Army.

Hughes: Were your early growing up years in Minnesota?

Ferguson: Well, no. I was just a baby in Fort Snelling. Between Minneapolis and St. Paul. I think it's the oldest fort in the United States. And then they moved to Fort Omaha.

Hughes: So you stayed there for how many years?

Ferguson: I don't remember. I went to school there. And then in Caruthersville, Missouri. My dad was transferred to a National Guard unit in Caruthersville. That's in Southern Missouri.

Hughes: What was your dad's job in the Army?

Ferguson: He was a soldier. I don't know what he did. He was in the office, and of course he fought. As a matter of fact he joined the Army when he was 16 because he had thrown a boot out the front door of the house and hit a goose and killed it. And they took him down and enlisted him into the Army. So he was 16, but of course they didn't care how old you were. He was big enough and able.

Hughes: Where was that?

Ferguson: Tennessee. But then he went to the border, fighting Pancho Villa. He fought with those troops.

Hughes: With General Pershing along the Mexican border in 1916?

Ferguson: Yeah, and then he was in World War I, too. He went overseas. And he got mustard gassed. He never talked much about his Army service. He eventually became a sergeant, and then he became a First Sergeant He got in some kind of trouble toward the end of his career and got busted. But I never knew why. Someone in the family may know why.

Hughes: What did you call your parents—"Mom," "Dad"?

Ferguson: I called my mother "Mama." Some of the other kids called her "mother." Neighbors called her "Mrs. Ferguson." I never heard anyone call her "Chris." My mother called my father "Dad." He called her "Ma."

Hughes: Tell us about what your mother did.

Ferguson: She stayed home.

Hughes: A housewife—classic housewife?

Ferguson: Yeah, she never worked.

Hughes: What was she like?

Ferguson: Oh she was fine, which was really odd since she had six daughters and four sons. Anyway, Frances, the last one born—born in this state—she was a Down syndrome baby. I'll tell you something later about her. But what was your question?

Hughes: What was your mother like?

Ferguson: My mother was the kind of woman anyone would like to have as a next-door neighbor. She was an expert by experience with her brood of 10 in childhood diseases, broken limbs and internecine warfare. I never heard her gossip. I never heard her swear. I don't recall ever seeing her lose her temper. She treated neighbor kids like her own. I remember a couple of ragamuffins coming by the house one day, selling berries, I think. And my mother gave their unkempt hair a good combing with the family comb. On discovering they had lice, she gave them the comb, which meant her own kids had to comb their hair with a fork until she or my dad got to town to buy a new one. My dad had his own comb.

My mother milked a cow for a while and the neighbor's cow, too, when the neighbor was not home to do it. She and the neighbor's wife both knew that if the wife ever learned how to milk the cow it would become her job. Neighbor kids walked to our house in the mornings to wait in our living room for the school bus. When the girls in the neighborhood got the itch for a 4-H Club, my mother wound up running it when no one else volunteered. She was such an eager reader that the bookmobile made its weekly neighborhood stop in our yard.

She made most of our clothes, and the thing I thought was so unusual was that she had six daughters, but we never cooked. She did all the cooking. She never taught me to cook. I learned to cook from a cookbook. My sister and I would do the dishes, and the two oldest boys had to sweep the floor and do some other damn thing. But then we sort of swapped off. They'd do the dishes and we'd sweep the floor.

Hughes: So these 10 kids came in pretty rapid succession in the Ferguson household?

Ferguson: Oh yeah, there was always a baby. I never played hooky from school. *Never*, because I knew if I did I'd probably end up taking care of the baby.…You know, after we moved up here to Washington, I think it was the University of Minnesota had heard about this family of 10 kids, and they called up here and wanted to know about us. We were older then and fairly successful. I've been kind of successful my whole life. They wanted to know from the principal of Central Kitsap High School—a guy named Jim Huey—how all these kids were doing. And he called one day and told me, "You know, I told them all about you." I said, "I didn't go to Central Kitsap. I went to high school before I got here." And he said, "Well I told him you did. I wanted him to be proud of all of you." I always wondered if they'd ever written about all this and if I could lay my hands on it. Because every single one of us was successful. My brother worked for this outfit that demonstrates airplanes. What do you call those little things you sit in and pretend you're in an airplane?

Hughes: A trainer. When I was in the Air Force we called them a Link Trainer.

Ferguson: Yeah, I think that's it. And I was in the newspaper business all my life. My sister Tooddy ran a nursery school, and a wonderful one. They were just in line to go to her school over in Seattle.…And then my brother Tommy was in the Navy 20 years, and then after that he worked first for a private company. And Robin was a hot-shot supervisor at Boeing. And my brother Jonnie, we think he's a spy because nobody knows what he does. And when he comes to this country he always goes to states where they have spy schools and stuff. But when you ask him about it, he just buzzes around. He's so blank sometimes I don't know how he could possibly be a spy. He was just here recently. But he won't tell you anything… But he's been on the federal payroll and he's just really weird. Jonnie the spy. He lives in Las Vegas now and has 18 cats.

Hughes: With all those kids, were your parents Catholics?

Ferguson: Want to hear a joke?

Hughes: I do!

Ferguson: The guy went to Catholic priest and he says, "My dog just died, and I just loved that dog. Could you possibly say a prayer in the church for my dog?" And the priest says, "No, I'm sorry but we just don't do things like that." The guys says, "Well, I don't know what to do." The priest said, "Well, try the Baptist Church down the road there. Maybe they'll do it." "Oh, OK," the guy said. "Do you think it would be forward of me to offer them 5,000 bucks to say a prayer for my dog?" And the priest said, "Holy Mary, you didn't tell me it was a Catholic dog!"

Hughes: So Jonnie the spy has 18 kids. That's pretty incredible.

Ferguson: *Cats!* 18 cats.

Hughes: I thought you said "kids"!

Ferguson: They take in strays. And my sister who has visited them says, "Yes, you can smell the cats." But they have scratching posts and litter boxes. And I asked him when he was here recently, I said to Jonnie, "How do you feed all these cats?" He said, "I line up so many bowls, and they eat…" It's nice that people will do that—take in that many strays. But I couldn't. I've had up to eight cats at one time and they didn't all like each other.

Hughes: Do you have cats now?

Ferguson: One. The Scarlet Pimpernel. She's somewhere around the corner here. She's a tabby.

Hughes: Were the Fergusons a religious family? Did you kids all go to church?

Ferguson: *No.* Well, we occasionally went to Sunday School, the nearest Protestant one. But we didn't go very often to church. In her old age, as a widow, my mother attended my church, Our Saviour's Lutheran, but didn't like it because they have a statue of Jesus up front and she said they were worshipping graven images. She was a Lutheran as a child. My dad wasn't anything.

Hughes: What was it like growing up in that household as a girl—the oldest girl?

Ferguson: We did everything. We made our own toys. Like if we didn't have cards, we'd make them out of thin cardboard if we could find it. My sister and I we made our own dolls, rag dolls. An oatmeal box would be their bed…And for fun we hunted up snakes, tied them to sticks and brought them home to my mother.

Hughes: This is in Nebraska?

Ferguson: This is in Missouri.

Hughes: OK, so relocate me here. Where are you when you're a young girl going to grammar school?

Ferguson: Probably in Missouri.

Hughes: And your dad's in the Army all this time. You're a classic Army brat.

Ferguson: Yep.

Hughes: Did you enjoy school? Were you a good student? Tell me all about it.

Ferguson: Oh yeah, loved school, loved English. In high school I was taking five different kinds of English classes. I'm not that good on mathematics.

Hughes: So when did it hit you that you were a writer?

Ferguson: I've been writing *all* my life.

Hughes: Tell us about your first memory of doing that, Adele.

Ferguson: As soon as I could find a piece of paper, I think.

Hughes: What did you write?

Ferguson: Short stories, serials, songs. You name it, I wrote it. I composed songs We all loved to go to the movies, but we never, hardly ever had the money. It was 27 cents to go to the movies. But if they managed to put together 27 cents, they would give it to me, and I would go to the movie and sit through the movie twice. I would come home and write what the movie was about, start to finish. I remember doing that on newspaper edges because that was all the paper I had. I stole all that my mother and father had up in the cupboard. I'd get these long strips of paper and it would look like ticker tape. Then we'd read those movies on rainy days when nobody could go.

Hughes: What were some of your favorite movies?

Ferguson: Oh well, Tarzan and all that. But the Flash Gordon serials were crazy. When I missed a Saturday, I made it up. I filled in my own chapter—what I thought probably should have happened.

Hughes: You could have had a career as a novelist. Did you ever think about doing that?

Ferguson: Well, I've been too busy.

Hughes: Actually some of the things you've covered in your life are stranger than fiction.

Ferguson: I'm trying to think of some of the people I have interviewed. I once interviewed a lady whose *hobby* was to make little bitty coffins with little bodies in them, out of clay. I wrote about it; have a picture of her and everything.

Hughes: When I was a reporter in Aberdeen, there would always be a farmer who would come in with a giant rutabaga or whatever. All sorts of characters wandering in.

Ferguson: Ours here (in Bremerton) was named Andy Rogers. And one time they brought in one that was shaped like a man's everything. And his wife was with him, and she was, "Hehehehehe," snickering and caring on. I could have slapped her! And there she was with this *thing*. We couldn't even take a picture of it probably, it was so realistic.

Hughes: But back to you as a girl in Missouri during the Depression. Tell me more.

Ferguson: I collected everything that was collectible. I collected bottle caps. I collected cigar bands. It didn't bother me to stop in the street and pick up somebody's little cigar butt and take the end off and take it home. And I collected those katydid skins that were on the trees. We tried skinning snakes. We were all going to make wallets, so we took and put them on top of a chicken house, but they all rotted. Today I collect so much stuff. The only thing I never collected was Depression glass. I just didn't care. Well, where were we?

Hughes: We were in school and we were at Flash Gordon, and making up stories.

Ferguson: I loved school. And the teacher, Mrs. Cunningham, she frequently let me be the substitute teacher in English class.

Hughes: How old were you then?

Ferguson: I don't know, probably a sophomore.

Hughes: Oh, this is in high school. Where did you attend high school?

Ferguson: Caruthersville, Missouri.

Hughes: Did you graduate from there?

Ferguson: No.

Hughes: So you started high school at Caruthersville, Missouri, and you got to be a substitute teacher.

Ferguson: Yeah, I thought that was great.

Hughes: What were you like as a girl at that age? Were you like you are now—voluble and fun?

Ferguson: Well, I don't know if I was fun.

Hughes: You loved to talk—you liked to read?

Ferguson: Yeah, and I had fun, but sometimes it would aggravate me. I guess because when we'd go out and play soccer outside, if Deborah Baker got hit in the face with a soccer ball, everybody said, "Oh Deborah! Oh gosh! Where do you hurt, Deborah?!" When I got hit in the face with the soccer ball, they laughed. It was funny. I was a funny person.

Hughes: Were you popular?

Ferguson: Not with boys, I don't think much. I was sort of a smart mouth.

Hughes: Were you athletic?

Ferguson: Sort of. Although I remember telling them that I didn't want to play basketball because—what do you get when you play too much basketball?

Hughes: Bad ankles and knees. So during that time, tell me about your favorite thing to do.

Ferguson: Read, read and write.

Hughes: What were you reading?

Ferguson: Anything. The most wonderful event in my entire young life was the time when we lived in Caruthersville, Missouri, near the banks of the Mississippi. We had big floods in the spring. The water comes up and it makes these holes. You can catch great big carp in them or catfish. One time, water had gotten into the basement of some store downtown in Caruthersville and soaked its magazines. *True Detectives, The Shadow, Hopalong Cassidy*—all these old pulp magazines. Just tons of them. I bet we took them all home. First we carried them. Then we got a wagon, and we wagoned them home. And all the kids would sit around reading. You had to dry them out a little bit first. But, God, that was wonderful. It was just like seeing a pot of gold to see *all* these magazines. And we just had a ball with those magazines.

Hughes: Did you listen to radio, too?

Ferguson: Oh yeah, every night. As a matter of fact we were *experts*, as most kids were then, because my dad would be waiting for the news to come on. But if there was something on we wanted to hear instead, we were right there by the radio so the minute the station (was about to change) we'd change it and he wouldn't hear. So we'd get to listen to the next half hour of what we wanted and he didn't realize that we had aced him out of the news.

Hughes: Born in 1943, I'm probably the last generation to grow up on radio rather than TV. I listened to "Gangbusters," and "I Love a Mystery" and "The Shadow." I remember rivetingly that my mom had the records from Orson Welles' "Mercury Theater." What were your favorite shows, Adele?

Ferguson: Those kinds of shows, and as a matter of fact we were listening the night that Orson Welles did his thing, you know, on Halloween in 1938.

Hughes: "The War of the Worlds" scared millions into thinking the Martians were invading.

Ferguson: We had listened to so much radio that we knew exactly (what was really happening), because we recognized his voice and we recognized other voices, and we knew this was a put-on thing. All these other people were going nuts thinking that the aliens were landing, and we're sitting there thinking, "Well, that's a pretty good show." We weren't the least bit fooled.

Hughes: So this is Roosevelt era. Tell me about the politics of your dad and mom.

Ferguson: I don't know. I just remember that when Roosevelt died, my father or somebody said, "Well the old son of a bitch is dead!"

Hughes: That must have meant that dad was a Republican!

Ferguson: Well, not really. He never talked politics. But my brother Buddy, my older brother, he was hot for Roosevelt. He had a teacher who brought him into the Roosevelt "New Deal," and so he was crazy about Roosevelt. The rest of us were not.

Hughes: Did you listen, nevertheless, to FDR's "fireside chats" on the radio?

Ferguson: No, we didn't. My father didn't. He read editorials and all. But the thing that really kind of impressed me about my parents is that here he was a hillbilly and she was an immigrant from Norway, yet they spoke good English. You watch "Judge Judy" some night. You'll see college students on there saying, "Well, me and her went down here" and so forth. I think, "Where did you learn English?!" and "My god, what's the matter with these people?" But my mother and father never spoke like that.

Hughes: That's very revealing. So did you learn any Norwegian growing up?

Ferguson: Oh no, no, no. Mother was one of the *few* members of her family who never had an accent. All her brothers did. We came here because her brothers were here.

Hughes: Did your folks place a real premium on education? Were they high school graduates?

Ferguson: No, but it was just assumed that everybody went to school. Everybody did the best they could, and don't lie, cheat or steal. That kind of thing. Just an ordinary, common raising, I guess. One thing I remember is that we had a *great big* American flag in a buffet just like this one. (points to her buffet) Boy, were we ever told, "Never let that thing touch the floor. Never. If you ever take it out of there, be very careful. Do not touch the floor with the flag."

Hughes: Dad being an Army guy, was the atmosphere in the household very strict?

Ferguson: Nah! And we learned to play pinochle as kids—double deck pinochle. So every Ferguson kid is a good pinochle player.

Hughes: That's a classic Depression-era thing—you entertain yourself with cards—Hearts, Bridge, Pinochle and Canasta.

Ferguson: But we only played Pinochle—Double Deck Pinochle. I was kind of unhappy with the fact that my brother was the favorite because he was the first baby. I remember one Christmas so well. He got a bicycle for Christmas. I got a *game*. And then it was cold out and he couldn't ride his bicycle, so they made me let him play with *my* game with me. I was so insulted over that!

(Adele's daughter comes in, asking if she can get us lunch.)

Hughes: You're a great cook, aren't you, Adele?

Ferguson: I'm a *good* cook, oh yeah. I cook every night just like there were two of us here. My husband died in 2005. It's funny that when you become a widow, sometimes you think he's still here. You know what I mean?

Hughes: I do. My late mom, whom you would have liked a lot, said that the best thing about people who were so alive when they were alive is that when they're gone they're not really gone. They're always here.

Ferguson: That's his chair over there with all the holes in it. It was my other cat—Raisa Gorbachev—that did that.

Hughes: When I look around this house, it's clear that you are a book worm.

Ferguson: See all those books over there on that table? I bought them at the St. Vincent de Paul. And some of them I take back after I read them, so they can sell them again. Some of them I keep. The political ones, the ones I can use for resources, history and stuff I keep. But I buy most of my books there. And I always like to say I'm not going to read so and so's book until it reaches the St. Vincent De Paul for 45 cents! But I love autobiographies. I'm reading an autobiography I've never read before by H.L. Mencken (the celebrated newsman, critic and commentator).

Hughes: I've read it too.

Ferguson: It's in several volumes, I think. I've got volume one and volume two. There's supposed to be a three but I didn't see it there.

Hughes: What do you think of Mencken?

Ferguson: Well, I thought he was great. What a writer! I love it when he says, "My father hated labor and labor leaders so much that he would pick the paper up at night and scan through it looking hopefully for a picture where some labor leader had been arrested, clubbed and hanged."

Hughes: And Mencken once said, "No one ever went broke underestimating the intelligence of the American public." Mencken's *Newspaper Days* is just terrific. He's a reporter in Baltimore at the turn of the century. Speaking of segues, when did you start reading newspapers?

Ferguson: Oh, I've *always* read newspapers.

Hughes: What newspapers did they have in the house when you were growing up?

Ferguson: Whichever was the local paper. It was usually just one. And I remember when I was a little kid that the funnies were always green. The paper was green.

Hughes: In the old files of *The Aberdeen Daily World*, there are color comics—an experiment about 1902 on green newsprint. They sometimes used yellow newsprint for the funnies, too.

Ferguson: Well, I don't date back to 1902! Also, if I had the money, which I rarely did, I'd scrapbook stuff. I saved everything that was written about John Dillinger. Ah, and other things. I still do scrapbooks; I've still got all kinds of scrapbooks floating around. I do political cartoons in scrapbooks. They're pretty interesting to look at and go back and see.

Hughes: They really are. David Horsey, the cartoonist at the *Seattle P-I* is a genius. Do you follow his stuff?

Ferguson: I've known him since he was young in Olympia. But I wish he'd stop trying to be a political writer. And I told him that to his face: For God's sake, Dave, you're a wonderful cartoonist, even if you're terribly biased. But give it up. Don't try to be a big star in both because you're not going to do it. You're not going to make it.

Hughes: When you have two Pulitzers as a cartoonist, that's got to tell you something.

So when you got newspapers when you were a youngster did you read everything in them?

Ferguson: No. I read what looked interesting—the murders, and all that. In those days a guy could get shot down on the street and they'd put a picture in the paper. Blood all over, you know! Remember that?

Hughes: People keep telling me that the media is so sensational today. But in *The Aberdeen World* or *The Sun* or whatever paper you read anywhere in early 1900s on through the 1930s, the front pages were replete with the goriest, detail by detail, stories of some poor Olof getting minced by the saws in the mills—losing limbs, blood on the deck. And murders, executions, kidnappings.

Ferguson: Oh yeah! I read all that kind of stuff. And I wasn't really all that interested in the editorial pages back then. As I grew older, when I became a political writer is when I really became interested in editorial pages. Now I take four daily newspapers, plus *The Washington Times*. I just read yesterday that it's now run by two ex-*Washington Post*-men and that they're thinking of endorsing Obama, but they're afraid it will drive people away. It will drive me away, I tell you, by God!

Hughes: So did it hit you there in high school that you wanted to be a writer? Were you on the high school newspaper?

Ferguson: Yeah, and I took journalism.

Hughes: What year did you graduate from high school?

Ferguson: I'm not going to tell you.

Hughes: OK, but what high school was it?

Ferguson: Central High in Little Rock. Before all the trouble (with desegregation)

Hughes: So you really had a close up of segregated society in the 1930s and 1940s. Tell me about that.

Ferguson: Well, there was a black high school just around the corner, so I'd have to walk up from where I stayed. I stayed in a little rooming house down there because my mother lived way out in the country. So she gave me money for this rooming house so I could go to school.

Hughes: Wait a minute, I'm lost here now. You lived so far out in the country?

Ferguson: My mother lived so far out in the country that I couldn't commute to school from there. I didn't have a car or anything.

Hughes: You said only your mother. You mean your parents?

Ferguson: My father was gone a lot. (As for segregation) the black kids would come down the street. They would be going to their school and the white kids would be going to their school And the unwritten rule was that whoever had the most in their number stepped off the sidewalk, onto the grass, and let the others pass by. If I would meet two black girls I would step off on to the grass and they would come on down. Of course, I hardly had anybody with me because I was alone.

Hughes: Were you prejudiced in any way?

Ferguson: No. As a matter of fact, when I was a kid I always appreciated the black guys because you need to have a little muscle. They weren't going to bother you (because you were a white girl), and if you needed anything you could stop by one of the black people's houses and they'd help you.

Hughes: Did you have any ideas about the races and racial relations that you quickly outgrew when you broadened your horizons?

Ferguson: No, I just never thought about it, I guess. I lived in the South, and in the South the black people lived on the alleys or in other parts of town.

Hughes: But is it wrong to think that most everyone in the South, during that era, was deeply prejudiced?

Ferguson: They weren't. As a matter of fact, most of them had black people working in their homes. When we lived in Caruthersville, we lived in town at 610 West 7th Street. Why, we had a black couple that lived in what used to be a smokehouse up in back. Her name was Eliza, of all things, and his name was Bill. He was our hired man and she was our cook. We had another lady whose name I kind of forget—maybe it was Hannah—she came in and did the ironing. My mother *always* had a baby, so some things she couldn't do.

Hughes: Were you living in military housing some of the time?

Ferguson: In Fort Omaha we lived in military housing. Long rows of buildings. Your neighbor was right through the wall.

Hughes: With mom not working, dad an enlisted man and all these kids, your family was not that well off.

Ferguson: We were all right. We didn't consider that we were poor. Well, we were pretty poor for a while there. My dad was a gambler. He often came home broke from a night of cards, so sometimes the light bill didn't get paid. I remember when our set of encyclopedias was repossessed, and I used to have to go to the door and tell the bill collector that my folks weren't home when they really were. But we never asked anyone for help. Sometimes we lived on the field corn. Field corn was raised by the farmers to feed their stock. Terrible stuff. But we would go and steal it out of the fields at night and bring it home. And we didn't have any real salt to put on it. We didn't have any money to buy it. So we used curing salt—that brown stuff you cure meat with. It was just awful. And one day we sold a brass bed to a guy who would come through buying metal and stuff. We sold one of the beds to get some money. And we gave my brother Buddy the money to go to the store and get a loaf of bread.

Hughes: What did a loaf of bread cost then?

Ferguson: Probably a dime because we always bought day-old bread. When you haven't got any money, a dime is a lot. Buddy was so weak from not eating. We weren't eating that well, not when you're just living on field corn.

Hughes: And dad is away in the Army?

Ferguson: He's gone. And my mother had a baby while we were there. That was terrible because I'd never been exposed to anybody having a baby before.

Hughes: Your mother delivered a baby when you were looking on?

Ferguson: I wasn't looking on. She went and called the doctor and the doctor didn't come. So she said to me, "Go down to the end of the road and tell Mrs. So and So to come up. I need her for the baby." So I ran all the way down the road, which had to be a good mile, and got this old lady.

Hughes: How old were you then—a young teenager?

Ferguson: Yeah, I suppose. And I told this lady that my mother was about to have a baby, and could she come and help. And she said, "I'll be right there." When she arrived I had to somehow handle these kids. I had all these kids there. And my mother is beginning to make noises of some pain, you know. So I gave the kids a tub. I said, "Now, you see that faucet way down there at the end of the cotton field? You go down there and fill that tub with water and bring it back." So they walked down, filled the tub with water, what they could carry, and brought it back. And right in front of them I poured it out and I said, "Now go back and get another tub." Now they're crying!

Hughes: This is a variation on the theme of telling the husband to go boil water.

Ferguson: *Now they're crying!* I make them fill tubs, and I dump it right in front of them until the baby is finally born. That was Jonnie. He was a nice fat boy.

Hughes: That's just classic stuff, Adele. But let's go back to this issue of race: Did you have any black friends? Play with black kids?

Ferguson: No, well you never really saw them hardly. I mean they went to different schools.

But I picked cotton with them. The fellow we rented our house from had huge cotton fields. And he didn't have kids pick cotton because they were lousy pickers, but we did anyway. The black people were always very nice to us kids. And we're out there picking cotton. We had to rent the cotton sack from the guy who owned the cotton field, and we paid a nickel or something for a cotton sack. And I was thinking, "I wonder if I can ever save enough money to buy a tar-bottomed cotton sack?" It drags down the row easier than a regular cotton sack. And the black guys were so funny because frequently there would be snakes in there. Not poisonous ones. When they'd find one, they'd throw it up at everybody! Everybody would go "Whaaaaaa!" It was funny. But they treated us kids like royalty; they didn't dare do that kind of stuff with us kids because we'd go tell our folks. And our folks would say, "OK, you can't pick out there anymore."

Hughes: These are great stories.

Ferguson: I was going to get you to when we came out West.

Hughes: I still want to get you out of high school.

Ferguson: Well, I'm out of high school.

Hughes: So you graduate from high school in Little Rock. Then what?

Ferguson: Then I got married. I've had two husbands. My mother always said my first husband just married me to not be drafted. Maybe he did. I don't know. He was a guy who was about to be drafted into the Navy. And I had known him for a while, and his parents and everything. His name was Tolbert White. Typical Southern name. So we got married. We didn't even sleep together because we didn't have the *time* to do it. We just got married and that was it. I don't think we ever went to bed together for nearly a month or two. I was petrified with fear. You know, I'd read all about stuff. They never told you much about it in books, but they sure leaned toward telling you that, for one thing, it was messy. But eventually we did it, and I didn't like it. Never did, with him anyway. So he went off in the Navy, I moved in with my mother. My mother moved in with me really, in Little Rock. So she and I went down to get jobs during the war.

Hughes: What's your recollection of Dec. 7, 1941?

Ferguson: My recollection was that my brother had stopped by to see me in the apartment I was living in. Little, lousy one-and-a-half-room apartment I was living in with my husband. And we went downtown and the newspapers were telling us that Pearl Harbor had been bombed.

Hughes: You didn't hear it on the radio?

Ferguson: Heard it on the street from the newspaper boys. So then we thought, "Oh gosh, that's really something." I wasn't that sure what it was going to mean to me. But eventually my mother and I had to go get jobs. So we went down to this place in Little Rock where they made nose bomb fuses—little things, you put the bomb in it. They had all these women there for the jobs, because there weren't any men. They were all in the service. So the guy looked out into the crowd, and said, "OK, now you, you, you, you, and you will be inspectors." (pointing at herself) And I thought, "That's really good he recognizes talent when he sees it."

Hughes: What did that pay?

Ferguson: Probably the same as the other workers. I don't remember. You'd walk behind the old women who were pulling the nose bomb fuses and testing them and so forth. I asked them, "How come I got to be an inspector?" He says, "We always take the tallest ones." I thought, oh God, here I'm so flattered to be an inspector.

Hughes: You were kind of a tall girl.

Ferguson: I am a tall girl. I'm 5-7. I was that tall then. So anyway, then my father was out stationed in California. He never went overseas in World War II. He did in World War I, but he didn't in World War II. Oh, I've got to tell you this story! We were speaking of being poor and not having any money. So I told my mother one time, I said, "You know I have to have some new shoes. I really need new shoes." And she said, "Well, I haven't got the money to buy them." And I said, "Well listen, I've got the worst shoes in the whole school. And I really have to have new shoes." And she said, "Well, I wish I could buy them for you, but I just can't. I'm sure there's somebody who's got worse shoes than you." A couple days later, I went into the girls' bathroom at school, and I was sitting on the toilet, and it was open between the stalls. I see these feet hanging down under the toilet next door to me. "God, look at those shoes." I mean the toes were all stubbed off, and the laces were just knots; the heels were worn to a nubbin. And I thought, "My god, my mother was right. There is somebody who's got worse shoes than I have." So when I got out I waited, and the door opened, and my sister Alice walked out!

Hughes: From growing up during the Depression, are you still pretty frugal?

Ferguson: *Oh yes!* And I am *furious* if I'm billed for something I already paid. I just go wild. And I pay everything on time. I pay cash for everything. I paid cash for my cars. I *own* this house, you know. Paid it off early.

Hughes: Was John, your second husband, that way too?

Ferguson: *No.* He owed 21 different people when I married him in 1946. He didn't have any money at all, and I had money in the *bank.* You know what I did? I wrote a letter to all the people he owed money to. And I said, "He's married now, and I will see to it that you are paid. To begin with I can't give you very much, but as I pay you off I'll increase the amount until you are all paid off." *Nobody complained.* Nobody even answered; they just let it go at that figure. And by God I did it, I paid everybody off. That's the way it ought to be with people.

Hughes: So you're in a nose bomb factory in Little Rock, inspecting. Were there a lot of people there?

Ferguson: I don't know. I was only in one part of it. But it was a large operation. The war was on. So they were operating continuously. Anyway the time came when we were going to go off and join my father out on the West Coast. We decided to leave Arkansas and go to California. Now the one little problem was that we had no way there. Neither one of us could drive. So my mother went down and bought a car—a Ford. We named it "Charlie" after a boyfriend I had at the time. My mother had them show her how to drive it. She came home and said, "Let's go down to the park." So she drove down to this park near our house, and she showed me how to drive. I drove around the park for about an hour. We packed up the next day and we left for California. I did *all* of the driving.

Hughes: From Arkansas to California as a beginning driver!

Ferguson: And the first car I passed on the highway, I just brushed the side of it I was that close. (using her hands to demonstrate and laughing) But I just kept going!

Hughes: Go Charlie, go!

Ferguson: I can remember one time when a policeman pulled up alongside us on his motorcycle. He looked in and saw all those kids, and he just backed away.

Hughes: How many kids were in Charlie?

Ferguson: Well, let's see. There was Tooddy, Tommy, Peggy, Barbara, Nancy, Robin and Jon. And my daughter Annette. So we had eight kids in the car, plus all our gear is in the back. The stuff is tied all over the car. And I knew *nothing* about driving a car. So we would go to a gas station… and there were long hoses lying out between the pumps. And I'd always stop the car and have Tommy get out and move the hose. And the guy standing there would just marvel.

Hughes: That's hilarious. The hoses were there, of course, to alert the attendant that you were there. Someone would run over it and it would make a "ding."

Ferguson: And we moved it every time we went to a gas station! But anyway, on we went. We slept in parks overnight. We slept near a reservoir. One night we slept at somebody's lovers' lane because people kept stepping over us all night long, you know, to go in the bushes and do their thing.

We finally got near California, but we were running out of gas. We stopped to find my father. My mother got a hold of him, and he was at camp near Los Angeles. We found out we couldn't stay there. So my mother thought, "Well, if we can't stay here, let's go up to Washington." My mother's brothers were all up there working in that Navy Yard. So we thought, "OK, let's go." But we had to have gas. We headed to the gas rationing office. First we went to a park because we didn't want to take all the kids with us. We left all the kids at the park. My mother and I then drove back to the gas ration office, and as soon as they found out we had *eight* kids with us they gave us enough gas to get us to Alaska. I mean they gave us all the stamps we could possibly use. So we went back down to the park and picked up the kids. We were about an hour out of town, Los Angeles, when Peggy said, "I left my shoes at the park!" And we thought, "We don't have any shoe stamps." And you had to have stamps to buy shoes. So we had to turn around and drive all the way back to the park to get her shoes. We found her shoes under a tree. And sitting by them was my brother Robin, who was about 4! We never even missed him. And he's crying a little, but he said, "I knew you'd come back for the shoes."

Hughes: Adele, that's priceless.

Ferguson: It's a *true* story. But every now and then we'd stop at a service station to get gas or to go to the bathroom or something. When Robin would go to the bathroom, I would start revving up the car so he'd think we were about to leave without him. He'd come running out zipping up his pants!

Hughes: So, you're en route to the Bremerton Naval Shipyard.

Ferguson: Yes. One place we went through, the car sort of broke down. So the next man who went by we asked him if he'd take a look at it. He gets in the car. He's going to try this and that. I said to my mother, "He's pinching me!" She said, "Let him pinch. He's going to fix the car." So he does fix the car. So we push on, and we sleep by the side of the road. One place we had a coupon for a new tire, but we didn't have any money for a new tire. So the guy at the tire store gave us two used tires for our coupon.

But my brother and I had to walk *way* back into town to do that. Oh God, we did a lot of walking. But we finally got up to Washington and learned where my Uncle Eddy lived.

Hughes: This is at Bremerton?

Ferguson: Yes, out by Crosby. And they were out there. How would you like to suddenly have your long lost sister and eight kids show up on your doorstep with no money, or anything? But they treated us like we were kings and queens. I mean they were so good to us. They welcomed us; they fed us; they found us a place to sleep.

Hughes: Now that's what kinfolks are all about.

Ferguson: *That's what kinfolks are for.*

Hughes: That's a wonderful story. Meantime, your first husband is overseas?

Ferguson: He's in the Navy. He's gone. And I had divorced him by then. I actually divorced him before we left. So my mother took us down to enroll us in the Bremerton Navy Yard and get a job. And we lied about our ages. I had to lie about my age in order for my sister to work because she wasn't old enough to work.

Hughes: Which sister was that, Adele?

Ferguson: Alice, nicknamed Tooddy. We spelled it T-o-o-d-d-y. We *had* to get these jobs. Years later, they had this thing in the paper saying, "Do you want to find out how your Social Security is?" So I sent a card in, and they sent a card back and it said, "We've corrected your information." And I thought, "What would they have to correct." And then I remembered I'd lied up my age by two or three years in order that Tooddy could work. So they never really checked on you in those days.

Hughes: How old did you have to be—21?

Ferguson: I think you had to be 18. And she wasn't, so I lied my age forward so she could be 18. If I said I was 20 then she could say she was 18. Otherwise, if I was 18, there was no way that she could be 18.

Hughes: Tell me about the job you got.

Ferguson: My first job was being a messenger.

Hughes: So you weren't a "Rosie the Riveter"?

Ferguson: Oh no, I was the messenger who worked in the office. Eventually I became the chief clerk of the boiler shop at the shipyard. I liked clerical work. I could write and all this kind of stuff. Whatever needed to be done. Keep timesheets and all that kind of crap. Although I got in trouble, with one of the top supervisors. Our desks were open to the door. People would come up the stairs and come in the door, and they could see under the desks. So if you didn't have your skirt down, they could see up your skirt. The girls were complaining that this particular guy made an awful lot of trips up the stairs. So I had the desks enclosed with wood. Without asking anybody. I just simply ordered it done. And they put panels in front of all the desks. From then on my efficiency report was poor. The peeper was the guy who made out my report. But anyway, I worked, and I wrote some stories.

Soon after she joined the news staff of *The Bremerton Sun* in 1946.

Hughes: For whom?

Ferguson: For the ship yard paper, *The Salute*. And I wrote one about my father and the time that he stole a pound of butter or a bottle of wine… something that he had pilfered from a train car of supplies. But they hadn't proved it, so they couldn't get him on that. Everybody was stealing stuff to eat. You know what the really funny thing is? Later on when I started collecting postcards, I found one that told all about a guy named "Fergie" who had stolen something, and I just know they were writing about my father.

Hughes: Did they give you a byline in *The Salute* for that story?

Ferguson: Oh yeah, picture and everything.

Hughes: So what year are we in now?

Ferguson: 1943. We got here in '43.

Hughes: What was Bremerton like then in the middle of the war?

Ferguson: Jammed, *jammed.*

Hughes: Tell me about it.

Ferguson: When I worked at the shipyard paper, I asked the Navy to give me peak employment in the Navy Yard during the war—and that was the figure. (She writes down the number)

Hughes: 32,343 on a day in July, 1945?

Ferguson: I remember it because of the threes and the two doubles to a four, so I sort of got it fixed in my head. But that's how many people were working on a day in July '45. (*The Bremerton Sun* and other sources say that employment at the shipyard was "nearly 34,000" at its high point.)

Hughes: That must have been one hopping town. Were there a lot of women working there?

Ferguson: Ah, sure.

Hughes: Were there buses just around the clock?

Ferguson: Oh yeah, a lot of people. I lived on Pioneer Road near Seabeck, and went to work in the morning. I lived with my mother then. Went to work in the morning with a guy who had a big truck. The back of it was enclosed, with seats along the wall. And he took about 15 people to work every morning and we all paid him. Being a girl, I would sit up front a lot.

Hughes: Who took care of your daughter?

Ferguson: My mother.

Hughes: Was there childcare there at the Navy Yard?

Ferguson: *No*, we didn't have anything like that. Not a bit. My daughter Annette did so dearly love my mother that when I got married again and took her home she really resented it.

Hughes: So did some of those stories lead to a job on *The Salute*?

Ferguson: All of a sudden in 1944 they needed somebody to hire at *The Salute*. But I didn't get the job. So that's where Charlie comes in. Charlie was the Admiral's aide—nice looking guy. Went to Groton. God, if I could have married him I'd be sitting pretty. They had another opening, and I had to be interviewed. Charlie interviewed me. He said, "Now you realize you have to have some experience working for a newspaper to go to work for *The Salute?*" "Oh yeah," I said. "Gee, I worked for *The Caruthersville Democrat and The Caruthersville Republican*." I made these newspapers up. So he said, "Well, OK, you go on down and see how it is." So I went down to *The Salute* office and met a fellow there named Don Allyn Nice Guy. He was the assistant editor and Jim Reams was the editor. So Don said, "If you're going to go to work here, let me show you what's here." So he started to show me this, and this, and this, and this. Suddenly he stopped and said, "You don't even know what I'm talking about, do you?" He's right. I don't know *anything*. And he says it again: "You don't really know what I'm talking about do you?" I said, "No, but you only have to tell me once." He said, "OK." And they hired me. Unfortunately, the boss got kind of a crush on me. And he started telling people we were going to be married. And I said *we were not*. So he stopped speaking to me.

Hughes: He's your editor and he's not speaking to you?

Ferguson: He's my editor. And he would leave me notes for what I was supposed to do for the day. Well, one day Charlie dropped in on the office.

Hughes: This is the Admiral's Assistant?

Ferguson: The AA. In uniform. And he stops by my desk and says, "What are these notes?" I said, "Well those are my orders for what I'm supposed to do today." He said, "He sits right behind you. Why can't he tell you?" I said, "I don't know. I think he just doesn't want to." So obviously things were not going well and I knew I had to get out of there. You were not supposed to be able to leave a job in that Navy Yard during the war. But they realized it wasn't going to work out. If Jim was going to be that way—and they'd had him a long time—that it was OK to let me go.

They weren't going to make me go, but if I wanted to go they were going to allow me to leave the Yard, so I did.

Hughes: How long did you work for *The Salute,* Adele?

Ferguson: A couple years maybe.

Hughes: Do you remember what you were paid?

Ferguson: No. I had tried to join the Army too but they wouldn't take me because of Annette. I had the child. I had a friend down in Santa Ana, so I thought, "Well, I'll go down and get a job down there." You could get a job anywhere during the war. So I went down there and got a job on *The Santa Ana Register.*

Hughes: When I was a kid hanging around *The Aberdeen World* in the 1950s, Barbara Elliott was the Adele Ferguson of Aberdeen. She was the first female in the newsroom, as opposed to the "soc" department, which wrote the weddings and engagements and society stuff. The guys were all off at war, so Barb got a spot in the newsroom. Is that how you got a job

Adele, a reporter for the Bremerton Navy Yard *Salute,* inspects an octopus that was discovered tangled in the propeller of a vessel being repaired in 1944. *Adele Ferguson scrapbook*

at the Santa Ana newspaper?

Ferguson: No, they hired me to work at the society desk, with the society people.

Hughes: Were there any women out in the regular newsroom?

Ferguson: No female reporters. Just men.

Hughes: You were the Assistant Society Editor for *The Santa Ana Register*?

Ferguson: Right.

Hughes: Tell me what Santa Ana was like then.

Ferguson: Oh, busy. Everything was busy during the war. Lots of people. Like in Bremerton, you'd walk down the Bremerton streets and the sidewalks were jammed most of the time. I mean constantly jammed.

Hughes: What was *The Register* like? Was that a good newspaper?

Ferguson: Yeah, it was good. They were good to me. I worked five days a week. I did write some feature kind of stuff, too, and turned it in, and they ran some of it. But that wasn't what I was paid to do.

Hughes: Did you write the classic kind of grind-em-out weddings and engagements?

Ferguson: Oh yeah. And I had to join the Junior Ebell Club.

Hughes: The what?

Ferguson: They call it the Junior Ebell Club; it's a fancy young women's club. And I had to learn how to play Bridge.

Hughes: I imagine you made do. Is your personality pretty much the same now as when you were a young woman? You love to talk. You're easy to talk to. Were you ever shy?

Ferguson: *No*, I was never shy.

Hughes: Was there certain gentility to the society pages?

Ferguson: Oh yes, oh yes.

Hughes: Tell me about that.

Ferguson: Well, it's like any society department. There's the upper class and the Altrusa Club, these kinds of things, and we'd cover what they'd do.

Hughes: Yes, and the mayor's daughter got a three-column picture when she got engaged?

Ferguson: Oh yes, what people wore and all this kind of stuff. But the editors were pretty nice and they paid pretty well, and I kind of liked it there. I don't know why I left. I guess, maybe the war was over and I decided to go home.

Hughes: Tell me about the most memorable story you did there in Santa Ana?

Ferguson: I don't know, but it was a feature I did on some damn thing.

Hughes: By then, being a fast learner, had you already got the hang of newspaper lingo, and writing leads and headlines, and all that sort of thing?

Ferguson: Well, I was getting it. Of course when you're new in the business you go to bed at night wondering how you're going to lead the story in the morning. After that you just forget it. You know that when you get there it will come to you. But I got to be real good—except I got so irked at editors. I always tried to write the leads so people would want to read the rest of it. And I always wanted a snapper on my stories, features. You couldn't always do that with news stores, but you could do that with features. But it would get me when the goddamn editor would steal the snapper and put it in the headline. That just *infuriated* me!

Hughes: That is every reporter's bane. So, along about the end of 1945 you meet John M. Philipsen.

Ferguson: I met him when I came back to Bremerton. His name is John, but I always called him Phil. His name was P-h-i-l-i-p-s-e-n…The English spell it with two "l"s and "s-o-n." But the Danes spell it with one "l" and "sen." He was staying with some people down the road a ways. Everybody stayed with somebody if they could because there was no place to live. It was very difficult to find a place to live during the war. But now the war was over. He had been in the Navy for eight years and now he's out. So we started going together.

Hughes: What kind of guy was John Morgan Philipsen?

Ferguson: Nice, good-looking guy—tall and blond. He was an electrician in the Navy Yard.

Hughes: On this Digital Archives record I have it says you were married on July 5, 1946.

Ferguson: Yeah, it was right after the Fourth of July. I was working at *The Bremerton Sun.*

Hughes: Wait a minute. How'd you get to *The Sun*?

Ferguson: Oh, I went down to *The Sun* dressed to the nines. I wore a beautiful black coat and white little straw hat. I really looked great. And I went in and saw Julius Gius, the editor, and asked him for a job. He was the founding editor of *The Sun*. He was half Finnish. Great guy. Wonderful guy. He was a *brilliant* newspaper man. I mean he was the kind of guy who would stop the presses for a misspelled word that would be embarrassing to somebody. And I learned everything from him. One time I wrote that a fire was caused by a short in the wiring. And he said, "It is a *short circuit* in the wiring." I said, "Well Julius, everybody writes short in the wiring." He said, "Yes, but you know better."

In the *Bremerton Sun* newsroom in the late 1940s. *Kitsap Sun*

Hughes: So what year did you start at *The Sun?*

Ferguson: I was working at *The Sun* when I was married.

Hughes: So it must have been 1945, right after the end of the war.

Ferguson: The war was over when I was in California.

Hughes: If you were married in 1946 it must have been late in 1945 or early in '46 when you joined *The Sun.*

Ferguson: Yeah.

Hughes: So you're all dressed up—

Ferguson: All in black, with a little white straw hat. I looked great.

Hughes: Were there any females in the newsroom at *The Bremerton Sun?*

Ferguson: No.

Hughes: And what job were you applying for?

Ferguson: Reporter. I wasn't trying to break any glass ceilings. I just wanted a job! So they hired me.

Hughes: What did he ask you about your newspaper experience?

Ferguson: "Where have you been working before?" And I told him, "I was working over at *The Santa Ana Register.*" And I lied a little bit there. I told him I was a reporter. Of course, they didn't check on me. And I told him I'd been on *The Salute* and so forth. I had a little background. I was nice looking. That helped. He always appreciated a pretty girl.

Hughes: You are a great looking woman now, and you were gorgeous then, judging from these photos.

Ferguson: Thank you. So he hired me I didn't make much, maybe $50 a week. They were very chintzy with their raises. I remember one time everybody got the rumor that we were going to get a $5 a week raise, all of us reporters. So everybody got called in separately and told that they were going to get the raise. The guys were told this is a cost-of-living increase. And I got called in. I had just written a series of stories about a Russian immigrant lady named I forget what. Let's say it was Liza. When I went in there Julius said, "Now Adele, you're going to get a $5 a week raise. This is for Liza, for those wonderful stories that you wrote about her." And I said, "Well gee, Julius, if I'm getting this raise for what I wrote about her, I suppose I get another five for cost of living?" You know what he said?

Hughes: Tell me.

Ferguson: "You sonofabitch!"

Hughes: When did *The Bremerton Sun* get started?

Ferguson: 1935. Before *The Sun* there was *The Searchlight*, which was then purchased by *The Sun.*

Hughes: Who were *The Sun* guys?

Ferguson: It was Julius Gius and Alex F. Ottevaere, who were funded by John P. Scripps in California. They bought *The Searchlight*—merged it with *The Sun.*

Hughes: So Bremerton once had two daily newspapers?

Ferguson: Yes. Julius and Alex founded *The Sun.* This was our new newspaper—*The Bremerton Sun.*

Hughes: Was it a morning paper, hence the "sun"?

Ferguson: No, an afternoon newspaper. Both of those were. By the way, the lady at *The Searchlight* rationed toilet paper to her employees. They got so many sheets per day. She made her own paste.

Hughes: And you said that the Scripps family helped found *The Sun*?

Ferguson: Yeah John P. Scripps, who was the founding guy down in California, owned some other newspapers on the West Coast. So Julius and Alex founded *The Bremerton Sun,* with the help of Scripps.*

Hughes: What was the reputation of *The Sun* when you got there? Was it a good newspaper?

Ferguson: Oh yeah.

Hughes: What made it such a good newspaper?

Ferguson: They covered everything. They even wrote when somebody

---

* *The Daily News-Searchlight,* owned and published by Mary E. Jessup and her sons, John, Wilford and James, was purchased by *The Sun* in April of 1945 and printed its last issue on April 30 "after more than 40 years of continuous service" to the community. *The Sun* had been established 10 years earlier, in 1935. It was purchased by the John P. Scripps Newspaper Group in 1940.

stole a hubcap. After I went to work there, we were known as the best small daily newspaper in the state.

Hughes: *The Sun* has always had a good reputation.

Ferguson: Not now they don't.

Hughes: They don't?

Ferguson: No, no. When I left, and not just because of me (things started to get worse). But I left angry.

Hughes: I didn't know that. I want to get back to that later. What was it like in *The Sun's* newsroom there in 1946? What was it like to be the first female reporter there?

Ferguson: Well, everybody was trying to make it with me—the guys. Back then I just laughed about it. But later on girls would come and talk to me about that kind of stuff, and say, "Well what do you do when guys are after you? Especially guys that you have to talk to you because they are your news sources?" And I'd say, "Well I learned the best way to handle it is this." And I've been propositioned by some pretty high up guys. I'd tell them, "That would just get us in nothing but trouble." That way they can't get mad. You haven't said, "No I won't go to bed with you by God for a thousand dollars" or anything like that. It just simply said, "That would just get us in nothing but trouble."

Hughes: How many reporters were there on the news staff of *The Sun* in 1946?

Ferguson: They had quite a few. I'm picturing the room. We all sat at tables in a big room.

Hughes: Where was *The Sun* located then?

Ferguson: It was on Fourth Street, just across the street from *The Searchlight*.

Hughes: Is that building still there?

Ferguson: No, I think they made it into a store. But I'm trying to think, I don't remember the desks very well. There must have been desks, though.

Hughes: Everybody had a typewriter?

Ferguson: Yeah, and I could type, of course. I had gone to business school.

Hughes: When did that occur?

Ferguson: Sometime.

Hughes: When I first started hanging around the newsroom in Aberdeen in the 1950s, there was this carcinogenic plume of cigar, pipe and cigarette smoke. Everybody smoked. And they had guys who were still wearing green eyeshades at the copy desk. Was the atmosphere at *The Sun* classic "Front Page" kind of stuff when you were a young reporter?

Ferguson: Yeah, yeah, yeah. I had a picture of all the employees of the *Sun* back around that time, but I gave it to the museum downtown. And I'm in there, with all those guys. People stayed there quite a long time. You had to have a real good reason to get fired.

Hughes: Did you feel like you really had to prove yourself, being a female there amidst a dozen guys?

Ferguson: No, I just had to be a good writer. I was a good writer.

Hughes: Tell me about one of those first big stories you remember where you really showed your stuff?

Ferguson: Well, of course the time I went on the submarine.

Hughes: You went on a submarine?

Ferguson: On the *Nautilus*. It was 1957, and the *Nautilus* was coming to town. The *first* atomic submarine. It was going to make a trip up onto the icecap or some damn thing. So they let the newspapers know that they could take a certain amount of press for a visit. So we sent a letter and applied for me to be one of those persons. And they wrote back and said, "No she can't go because she's a woman." And we said, "Well, we already know that. What's wrong?" And they said, "Well, we don't have any restrooms for women on board the submarine." So then I wrote a story about the incident. And we tried everything. We even talked to that lady Senator up in Maine or someplace.

Hughes: Margaret Chase Smith?

Ferguson: Yeah, I guess. And she hadn't been on it either. And other women were trying to get on board. All they were going to do was run us up to Everett, put us on a bus and we'd come back to Bremerton.

Hughes: Were they going to actually submerge?

Ferguson: I think so. So I wrote a story, but they absolutely refused. We tried Sen. Jackson; we tried Sen. Magnuson. Nobody could get us on board the submarine. So I wrote that we didn't have any trouble without a separate bathroom for women in my house. We just took our turn and it wasn't any problem. It was kind of fun to write.

Hughes: Well, you got an award for that one. Here's the clipping from *The Bremerton Sun,* April 12, 1958. It says, "She won first prize for distinguished reporting for coverage of a Shelton murder trial. First for feature writing with her renowned account of her controversy with the Navy over a proposed trip on the *U.S.S. Nautilus.* And an honorable mention on the Farmer's Daughter column."

Ferguson: I submitted the story in the Sigma Delta Chi journalism society awards competition. And I was notified to come to the awards banquet. What I didn't know was that Abe Glasberg, who was then the editor of the Everett *Herald*, was the overall chairman of the awards that year. He had happened to be back in Washington, D.C., when that story (about the *Nautilus*) came out. And it had been picked up by newspapers all over the United States and overseas. Abe said the Navy was just getting razzed unmercifully by every other branch of the military. And he thought it was the funniest damn thing—the reaction to this story. So he looks over the winning entries for the awards and mine isn't in there. So he looks in the rejects and there it is. He takes it out of the rejects, puts it back in the awards pile, and it wins! So the next time, the *Nautilus* came back to Bremerton, they invited me to go aboard. And this time I went. And they had a little ceremony up on the deck. I've still got the cartoons. They showed a little outhouse built on the deck of the submarine, and a sailor marching back and forth, you know, with his gun.

Hughes: At least the Navy had a sense of humor. That's a wonderful story. Was Julius Gius a good editor?

Ferguson: He was a wonderful editor.

Hughes: What made him a great editor? He had the good sense not to mess up your work?

Ferguson: Yeah, but I had to stop him sometimes. I was the church editor for a while. In fact, I was a little bit of everything. I did hockey for a while, too.

Hughes: Hockey?

Ferguson: Yeah, I wrote the hockey stories and I got $10 for doing it. The sports guy gave me the $10. I said, "What's this for?" He said, "That's what I get every week from the hockey people." But anyway, Julius he came up to me once and he said, "You've got all these church stories to write yet. You've got to get out of here. Here, give me some of those. I'll do them for you." And I said, "No." He said, "Why not?" I said, "I don't like the way you do them." Oh God, he just turned and walked out. Julius got to a point where he wanted to do something else. Now he was either going to run for Congress or he was going to go down to California and be top guy in the Scripps chain. Eventually he chose the Scripps job—being editorial director, which he was great at. When he was leaving Bremerton, I went up to him and I said, "Julius, I'd like to be the editor of this newspaper. I think I can do a real good job of it." He said, "No you can't, and you won't. Writers like you only come along once in a hundred years. If you were editor of this newspaper, you'd want to change everything everybody did to make it the way *you* would have done it. And you'd never be able to get anything done because you'd be so busy improving everything. So you don't need to be an editor. Stick to what you do best."

Hughes: Was that good advice?

Ferguson: Yeah, it was. As a matter of fact, KOMO once tried to hire me. One of the top guys at KOMO called me and said they wanted to hire me. They said, "You can either be our investigative reporter or you can be our"—what was the other thing?

Hughes: Consumer affairs maybe?

Ferguson: Editorials or something. It was a pretty good job. He said, "We will pay you well and you can keep your column. You can continue to do your column and keep the money (from it)." So I thought about it and then I called him back and told him, "No, I know I'm a writer. And if I go over there now I'm with new people. Where I work now I know what everybody does, and what they want of me, and what I can deliver for them. But if I go over there and suddenly I get in with some people who don't like me that much, or want me to do something I don't want to do, I'm disconnected." So I turned it down.

Hughes: Were you otherwise ever tempted? Or did they offer you any jobs at *The Sun*, like to be city editor?

Ferguson: No, no, no. I was a writer.

Hughes: So what was it that made you a great reporter?

Ferguson: I was curious about everything. One time when they were going to have a trial over at the courthouse, they picked somebody else to cover it. I had other things to do. This guy came over to cover it for the *Seattle P-I*. He said, "Boy, I was sure glad Adele Ferguson isn't going to cover this. She sees so much stuff that nobody else sees." I thought that's a pretty good compliment.

Hughes: Could you write quickly once you hit your stride?

Ferguson: Yeah. In fact some of the best stuff I've written, I just wrote off the top of my head.

I tried to write leads that people would be encouraged to go through and read the rest of the story.

Hughes: Try to get the "grabber"—the lead sequence.

Ferguson: Make people want to read. And I read some things in the paper today and sometimes they're so boring. And I think, "God almighty, you didn't have to do it this way."

Hughes: Was Julius Gius the greatest teacher you had early in the going?

Ferguson: Yes, yes he was.

Hughes: Was he also a classic stickler for attention to detail?

Ferguson: Oh yeah, and he was a good writer himself. He won prizes. But he was proud of his whole staff. He was so mad one year because just he and I won. I won very often for various types of stories.

Hughes: Like the murder trial?

Ferguson: Yeah. The trial went on for a whole month and I had to drive down to Shelton. That was a problem because Julius was pretty cheap. He didn't want to pay anybody mileage to be going down there. But he did.

Hughes: How many hours a week were you working?

Ferguson: Well, I didn't have to put any hours down. Most other people worked 40-hour weeks. But I was paid so much a week and I could work however many hours I wanted to work. So I always worked more than the other staff.

Hughes: How did they get away with that if you weren't a supervisor?

Ferguson: I had that kind of a deal, like being the boss' secretary. And I always worked more. I always was the first one to the office in the morning. I went to work at seven o'clock; deadline was eleven.

Hughes: So *The Sun* was an afternoon paper six or seven days a week?

Ferguson: Six days a week. Eventually it became seven.

Hughes: Did you work six days a week?

Ferguson: No, I only worked five days a week.

Hughes: Tell me more about Julius and some of the things he really inculcated in reporters, like the classic stuff about spelling names.

Ferguson: Oh he got so mad at me once when I got a name spelled wrong on the front page. And I did something once that got the city editor fired. I had worked every beat, see, and at this point I had the Navy beat, and the Navy Yard beat. I had done cops, and courthouses, city hall, and hockey, just everything.

Hughes: Was hockey a big thing in Bremerton?

Ferguson: Oh yeah. So I enjoyed going to the games.

Hughes: What were the names of the teams?

Ferguson: I don't remember. Anyway, they had one guy on there who was a really mean rotten guy, and he would always go up to me crossly with a stick. Where was I?

Hughes: About the mistake you made and getting the city editor fired.

Ferguson: Oh well, that wasn't a mistake. That was a deliberate thing

I did. Every week I had to write up a little story that said, "Boaters are advised to stay out of Dabob Bay on Mondays, Tuesdays and Fridays from 11 A.M. to 3 P.M because there will be torpedo testing." So I wrote that little story, and one day I felt real good about it. So I wrote that, "Boaters are advised to stay out of Dabob Bay because there will be Tornado testing." And then I added, "So keep the hell off the beaches then." And it got into the paper. It proved to Julius that the city editor wasn't reading the copy. He should have caught that. They fired him.

Hughes: Aberdeen and Bremerton were still classic, wide-open, whorehouse, sailor-and-logger towns in the 1950s. Who was the Bremerton mayor back then, Whitey…?

Ferguson: Domstad.

Hughes: He worked in Aberdeen for a while. I interviewed him. And I said, "Well, what do you think about Aberdeen?" And he said, "Seems just like Bremerton to me." The Shore Patrol was always on duty, I suppose, in Bremerton, but you did have houses of prostitution, lots of bars and tattoo parlors?

Ferguson: Oh yeah, right downtown, owned by the cops. You know that kind of a thing.

Hughes: What?!

Ferguson: Oh yeah, everybody knew who owned them.

Hughes: Tell me about that.

Ferguson: No!

Hughes: So when did you start writing a column? Was "The Farmer's Daughter" (in the 1950s) your first outing as columnist?

Ferguson: I forget who got me to write that. But I wrote that once a week, and it was supposed to be funny.

Hughes: But your father wasn't really a farmer?

Ferguson: *No.* That was just funny stuff. I found it easier later to do five columns a week on anything than to do one column a week and be funny. Because you'd have to sit down every Thursday afternoon and be *funny* for the next day's paper. And that's hard to do. So I really never enjoyed writing The Farmer's Daughter, although I did get some prizes for it. I didn't want to have to be funny. When I wanted to be funny I could be funny but I didn't always want to be funny. You can't do it like that.

Hughes: Someone observed once how few comedians have ever won Academy Awards and how wrong that is. I mean, it's hard to be funny.

Ferguson: Yes it is.

Hughes: Did you work with some great reporters during that time (the 1950s), some people you really admired?

Ferguson: No.

Hughes: So pretty early on, you were a star reporter for *The Sun*?

Ferguson: I was. I was. To this day people stop me in the grocery stores and on the street and say they miss me. But you know where I really made friends in this city? I loved to do obituaries. Most reporters hate obituaries. I didn't. I always called the family if I could get a hold of them. And I'd say, "This is Adele Ferguson from *The Sun*. Now I hate to bother you at a time like this but I know you want this to be the way *you* want it. You want it to be accurate. So could I just ask you a couple of questions?" And to this day people say, "You wrote my mother's obituary"…"You wrote my father's. I'll never forget. It was so nice of you" and so forth. But there's where you make friends because *every* newspaper is going to reach *every* family through the obituary columns one way or another. So you have to be nice about it. But I've seen reporters who refuse to do it. They just hated obituaries.

Hughes: Those are *dumb* reporters. There are so many great stories in obituaries.

Ferguson: I wrote one time about a guy who was on one of these fishing ships that disappeared. The family was just frantic. And I had to call and break the news to them that he was among the missing. And then about three, four days later they found him in a boat. Alive. So Casey Davison, the city editor, ran to the phone and said, "Well, I've got to call the family and tell them." Julius said, "Wait! Let Adele. She had to call and tell them he was missing. Let her call and tell them he's found."

Hughes: That must have been a wonderful call.

Ferguson: Well, the worst and best thing about it was that there was still time that I could write a story about it. I picked up the phone and I said, "Mrs. So-and-so." "Yes." And I say, "They found your son and he's alive and well." "Whaaaaaaa!!!!" She dropped the phone and was gone. Now, I've still got to write a story! I had to get in my car and drive out to her house and ask her how she felt about all that and rush back and write the story. God, I could have killed her. I always tell another story anytime I give speeches, about how I called this woman who'd just lost her husband. I said, "This is Adele Ferguson and I hate to bother you at a time like this, but I know you'd like to say some things and I want to check some facts. Now, he worked in the Navy Yard for 20 years, and he's been retired for 20 years. What has he done for the last 20 years?" And she said, "He didn't do a *damn thing!*"

Say, I didn't tell you about when I was a justice of the peace, did I?

Hughes: No. Tell me.

Ferguson: Well, when I was at *The Sun* in the 1950s or '60s, the county coroner went over and paid a dollar and filed my name for Seabeck Justice of the Peace. I was elected and I was authorized to perform marriages. So I performed about six marriages. One marriage was an elderly black couple who came into the office and wanted to see the editor. So I referred them to Julius' office. And they told him that they wanted to get married. They had never been married. They had a bunch of children, and nobody in the family knew that they had never been married, but they wanted to *get* married. And could he please keep it out of the paper, because we always printed the names of everybody who applied for a marriage license. "Oh sure," he said. "We'll keep it out for you. When are you going to get married?" And they said, "We don't know, we haven't found anybody yet." He brings them out to me and says, "Now, Adele here is a justice of the peace. She can marry you." "Oh," they said, "Really? Will you do that?" And I said, "Well sure." And Julius says, "We can do it right here." So they said, "Well, fine, where are you going to do it?" I almost said "in the darkroom," but it quickly occurred to me that that would be a poor choice of words, and I said, "We can do it down in the photography laboratory." So we went down to the photography laboratory and I performed the marriage ceremony and we had some coffee, and cookies that were kicking around there. And those people were so happy.

Hughes: So this is a classic question I always used to ask every reporter applying for a job: Tell me about the most character-building mistake you ever made? Something you really screwed up.

Ferguson: Well, very early in my career I went out on a story with a photographer. We didn't have a staff photographer at *The Sun*. We hired a guy. So we went to this house to interview this woman and she insisted when it was over on giving us each five dollars for coming to the house. We said no, and she absolutely insisted, following us clear out to the car, stuffing the money in our pockets. And we left with the five dollars. When I got back to the paper, I went straight to Julius and told him. He should have fired me. I realized what a rotten thing that was. I should have never have done that. I didn't need the five dollars; the woman was pushing it on me.

Hughes: Did you take the money back?

Ferguson: No.

Hughes: What did Julius say?

Ferguson: He just shook his head.

Hughes: Did he appreciate your conscience?

Ferguson: I don't know, but he didn't fire me. I guess I was too good a writer to let go.

Hughes: Did anyone ever come close to wanting to fire you, for stepping over the line, for being too bold?

Ferguson: Well, I think my last editor, just before I quit in 1993 would like to have fired me.

Hughes: So you had all these beats you were covering. When did you really start covering politics?

Ferguson: I started covering politics in 1961, I think. Because at that time, the political writer was Gene Gisley, who later became the editor of *The Sun*. He was also an avid Democrat. His best friend was Gordon Walgren, who was in the House (1965-68) and then in the Senate (1969-1981) from our district. Frances Haddon Morgan was running against Walgren for the State Senate. Gene wrote something for *The Sun* endorsing Gordon Walgren.

Hughes: In a column?

Ferguson: Well, he wrote it in a news story, as a reporter. And the editor then, Jack McHenry, called him in and said, "*I* decide who we endorse, not you." Now Gene realized that his time was going to be short there. He had pissed off Jack so badly. So he called and he wrote Julius Gius and they offered him a job down in San Diego. Gene left *The Sun*, went to San Diego and became their political writer.

Hughes: Despite that mistake, was Gene a good reporter?

Ferguson: Oh yeah, he was a good reporter, and a good guy. He's dead now. So then the editor called me in and said, "Well, now you're going to be the political writer." I wasn't even reading political stories. I didn't give a damn about politics. But I'm now going to be the political writer. So I'm sent down to Olympia.

Hughes: So being the political writer for *The Bremerton Sun* involved being the correspondent in Olympia? And by this time you've got a couple of kids, right?

Ferguson: Yes. Annette and Karen.

Hughes: You didn't commute to Olympia, did you? That's quite a ride.

Ferguson: Not at first, mainly because they didn't want the expense. Eventually they paid, and I'd go down on Mondays and stay in a hotel in Olympia till Friday. In the beginning I just went back and forth when there was something going on that was of some local interest.

Hughes: So this is 1961?

Ferguson: Yep.

Hughes: Jack Kennedy has just been elected president. Al Rosellini is the governor.

Ferguson: I liked Rosellini; I think he was a good guy. Best friend the ferries ever had in the Governor's Office.

Hughes: OK, so it's 1961—

Ferguson: And I'm going to be a political writer. McHenry also said, "I'd like to have you write a column every day."

Hughes: On politics?

Ferguson: Well, whatever I choose. I only agreed if I could do it on anything. I mean he wanted it on politics. But I said, "I can't guarantee that. If I can write about anything, then it will be easier to do. But five columns a week on politics might be a little difficult."

Hughes: He wants you to be a columnist writing five columns a week, in addition to being a beat reporter on politics? That's a tall order.

Ferguson: I was up to it. I mean I liked to write; it's no problem. Eventually, he said five columns a week are too many, so he cut me back to three. Which was fine with me because I was doing five. I started writing my syndicated political column in 1965. I moved up here (to Hansville) in '65, and my father died in 1965, on December the seventh.

Hughes: Had your mother died before that?

Ferguson: No, no, no, she lived on for a while after. After he was dead, she now suddenly had money, because he had spent it all at the racetrack. He was a gambler, so he was always spending the dough. One time they went picking apples over on the east side of the state, to make some money.

Hughes: For the record, your dogs are lapping at me.

Ferguson: (Smiles and nods approvingly) And they made quite a bit of money picking apples. But the night they were supposed to leave and come home, my father lost it all in a card game. So after he was dead—even though I know she cared for him—she said to me one time, "You know, I've never had it so good." She found $5 bills tucked away in the closet and stuff. He was hiding money from her so he could go gamble.

Hughes: So it's 1961. You're going to Olympia as *The Sun's* political reporter at the Capitol. Tell me about it.

Ferguson: Don't know anybody. Well, I do too. I know Red Beck—C.W. "Red" Beck. He was a state representative and then he was a state senator.

Wonderful guy.

Hughes: And he was "Red" because he was a redhead?

Ferguson: He was a redhead is what he was, a big heavyset guy.

Hughes: Are you indeed the first female Capitol reporter?

Ferguson: I am the first woman to become a *regular* correspondent at the Legislature. They didn't speak to me, the men, except for Leroy Hittle. He was the longtime head of the AP office in Olympia, and he liked me. We were never romantic, but he liked me, and he wanted to help me.

Hughes: He was a personable guy. Gov. Evans appointed him to the Liquor Board in 1967.

Ferguson: Yeah, he was, and he gave me a little desk. There was a row in there and then you sat at it. They weren't desks. They were little nook and crannies. And so Leroy gave me one next to his office and told me, "Now you know, Adele, when you write your stories you're going to have to give me a copy because everybody has to give a copy to the Associated Press." And I said, "Not me. I'm not going to do that." Leroy said, "What do you mean?" I said, "Well, what's the point of me being down here and them paying me to be here, if I have to give you a story and you beat me on it in the Associated Press?" Well, he said, "Everybody else gives me a copy." I said, "Well, that's them. That isn't me. I'm not going to give you a copy." I said, "I'm going to give it to my paper first and you can have it after it runs in my paper." Well, he agreed.

Hughes: Do you remember who was working for *The P-I* and *The Times* at that time?

Ferguson: Yes.

Hughes: Were they the guys who were stinkers to you?

Ferguson: Oh yeah, all of them except Leroy. Who was it that was with the UPI (United Press International) at that time? Was it Gordon Schultz?

Hughes: No, he came to Olympia later.*

Ferguson: Yeah, that was before Gordy Schultz. Later on, Gordy wooed

---

* Norm Kempster was a UPI reporter in 1961; Schultz arrived to become bureau chief in 1963.

me to come over to his office (relocate) and leave the AP office. He said, "I'll give you a big desk I'll give you this great big desk right here. Move in with me." So, I did.

Hughes: Tell me more.

Ferguson: I'm trying to think of the name of the guy who was with *The P-I.* I thought about him just the other day. It's a little short name.*

He was "Mr. Big"—the senior member of the press corps. He was the everything. But the thing was that he was so stressed out sometimes that if things really bugged him he had nosebleeds. And he'd be standing like this, you know, trying to keep his nose from bleeding. I remember one time we were at some meeting over in Eastern Washington. We'd all gone there—convention I guess. And I'm standing in Leroy's room. Everybody goes in everybody else's rooms. And I'm in there with him and (the P-I guy) has a *big* nosebleed. And I said, "Well, what's the matter?" And he said, "Oh I've got to write this thing about Al Rosellini, and I just don't know how to even start the story." And I said, "Well, if it was me I'd call Al up and ask him." He stopped, looked at me, went to the phone. From then on he was nice to me.

Hughes: Tell me the story about you sitting in somebody's chair and causing a ruckus.

Ferguson: Well that was him. (the P-I guy) They had a desk-like counter that went around the room in front of the House and the Senate, too, with seats for *The P-I, The Times, The Tacoma News Tribune,* AP, UPI, *The Spokane Chronicle* and *Spokane Spokesman-Review* and then "other" correspondents. I belonged in *Other.* (the P-I guy) never even showed up until afternoon because his deadline was late at night. So one morning, Leroy Hittle said, "Come on, Adele, sit down here and we'll talk" There was nothing going on. *The P-I* seat was right next to the AP seat, so I sat in *The P-I* seat and was talking to Leroy. So I'm sitting there, and it's noon, or thereabouts, and (the P-I guy) came in and saw me sitting in *his* seat.

---

* It was Stub Nelson.

And he went to the Sergeant-at-Arms and said, "Get her out of there! That's my seat." So the Sergeant-at-Arms came down and said, "Adele, could I see you for just a minute?" And I said, "Yeah." And he said, "Bring your stuff." So I picked up my stuff—purse, books—went up there. And he says, "What's his face says you're sitting in his seat and he wants you to get out of it." And I said, "Well, I'm out of it." Meantime, *The P-I* guy has disappeared; he didn't want to see me. So Hittle came up to me, and I said, "You know something, Leroy, if this *ever* happens again and I'm down there sitting, and they have the Sergeant-at-Arms come and throw me out there's going to be blood and guts *all over* this chamber. And it isn't going to be mine!" He believed me. And he told (the P-I guy), "Don't do that again. You'll have to just suffer it and wait till she leaves." But it went on for about six weeks that none of them would speak to me. They thought I was an interloper. They really thought I was one of these women who just comes down to cover what the women are wearing to the Governor's Ball. But I wasn't!

Meantime, I made friends with all the lobbyists. They couldn't have been nicer. They were all so friendly and helped me. So I really made out with the lobbyists. They invited me to dinner. The banking lobbyists said to me, "Hey, Adele, we're having this dinner down at so-and-so. I'd like to invite you to come but we're having some of these certain people and it would have to be off the record." And I said, "Oh well, I couldn't go to anything like that." So he said, "Well, I can't invite you because that's the way it has to be." So I didn't go. But I learned that it has to be that way. You have to agree that some things just have to be "off the record."

Hughes: You were looking over this tiny, high-tech tape recorder of mine. It's essential for oral history. But I really agree with a story you told earlier about not liking to use tape recorders. I always felt that as a note taker I could get 98 percent of everything on my notepad. I never had anybody really quibble and say, "Well I really said, such and such, instead of that."

Ferguson: No, I never did either. The only boast I ever made was, "If it's got quotes around it, you said it."

Hughes: And someone once said, too, that a "misquote" is seeing something you actually said in the cold hard reality of 8.5-point body type the next day. Did you ever have somebody try to do that to you, to really try to say, "Oh she took me out of context. She misquoted me"?

Ferguson: No.

Hughes: So there you are. It's Olympia, 1961. Tell me about what finally really broke the ice with the guys in the Olympia press corps?

Ferguson: I don't know.

Hughes: The fact that you had gumption?

Ferguson: I guess, I was getting good stories and they weren't. I was getting some really good stories I was talking to lobbyists. They didn't do that. I wrote some really funny stuff too.

Hughes: What was the atmosphere like then in Olympia when you were covering the Legislature? I read a great quote the other day by Ed Reilly of Spokane, who was Speaker of the House in the 1940s. He said, "For 60 days you're a king. Then the medals come off."

Ferguson: Well, it was *wild*. There were dinners and receptions every night. Of course it eventually got to where it was too expensive; the lobbyists couldn't afford to pay it. But there were parties every night, and everybody crashed the parties or went to them A lot of dancing and everything, I can remember that. I remember (State Sen.) Jim McDermott of Seattle told me he was going to dance with me at the Governor's Ball. And I said, "Well, it won't be yours buddy!" They began to respect me. But I didn't have any buddies to start with. None. Leroy Hittle was the only guy who was ever friendly to me. But they got over it eventually.

Hughes: I heard a story about an incident at the close of that first legislative session you covered in 1961.

Ferguson: It's the closing night. The place is full. Everybody's drinking. This one reporter was plastered. And so we're all sitting down front in the press row and there's a bunch of pages sitting down there.

Hughes: Young kids, teenagers?

Ferguson: Yeah. And he leans over to me and he says, "I've got eight inches." And the pages look at me to see what I'm going to say. And I said,

"Well it's too bad you haven't got 12—you could get a job as a carpenter!" It went over pretty good. And when I went by Slade Gorton at that dinner that night I said to Slade, "Did I go too far?" And he said, "No!"

Hughes: Your syndication of the column began in 1965 when Robert L. Charette, a legislator from Aberdeen, went to Ed Van Syckle, editor of *The Aberdeen World,* and said, "You ought to run Adele's column."

Ferguson: Oh, yeah.

Hughes: So *The Aberdeen World* was the first link in the chain of your syndication?

Ferguson: I think Aberdeen and the Centralia *Chronicle* came on at the same time. I'm still in the Centralia paper. They *love* me in Centralia! Bob Charette was a wonderful guy. He was somebody who could explain unemployment compensation like nobody else. I wrote quite a bit about Bob. He was a very good source and liked reporters.

Hughes: He was an amazing storyteller.

Ferguson: Oh yeah. The only thing I ever found unusual about him was once he had to be up at the Speaker's rostrum, and be the Speaker, and he was nervous as a cat. It was strange to see that in such a bright and confident guy.

Hughes: So you wrote for *The Sun* and then *The World* and then *The Centralia Chronicle.* Did a number of other papers come on pretty quickly?

Ferguson: Yeah. It was in *The Wenatchee World* for while and the Tri-Cities paper for a while.

Hughes: How many did you have at the peak?

Ferguson: Oh, 35 or 40. Where you lose columns is when they get a new editor. Or you write something that irritates somebody, or some legislator who like doesn't like you. That's how I got out of one of my papers. I think it was Wenatchee. I had some of them who made it a point to stab me in the back for something I had written.

Hughes: Did you have any particular theme that you tried to bring to the column?

Ferguson: Whatever interested me, I thought would interest them.

Hughes: How many were you doing in '65?

Ferguson: I was doing five columns a week. I think I was doing two for the *Sun* and mailing out twice to the state. Monday, Wednesday in one mailing and Friday in another.

Hughes: Did you have anybody helping you mail out these columns?

Ferguson: No. I did it all.

Hughes: Well, you had a lot of material, that's for sure. What was the atmosphere like in the Legislature then versus now?

Ferguson: Well, I think then we had a lot more people who were members because they wanted to do something, not because they wanted money. It now pays too well. The benefits are too good. They now are career legislators as opposed to citizen legislators. When I first went down there they were citizen legislators. Marshall Neill from Eastern Washington became a Supreme Court judge (in 1967), but he'd been in the Legislature for years. (1949-1967). Perry Woodall, a Republican from Toppenish who served in the House and Senate, was a wonderful, funny guy, brilliant lawyer. He loved to tell me dirty jokes, but he would never tell you what went on in the caucus room because with him caucuses were private. But I could skim what happened in those caucuses from everybody else and pour it right back. He was the main guy who was nice to me down there; gave me a ride back and forth, so my paper didn't complain about the cost.

Hughes: Tell me about the whole flavor of "citizen legislators" back then versus the legislator of today.

Ferguson: It's gone. Back in the 1960s when I began covering the Legislature, there was a lot of emphasis on the cost of the legislative session. In 1967, it was $22,000 a day. But, I wrote at the time, "When does any taxpayer ever sit down and figure what he's got in the way of talent and experience and knowledge available right at his fingertips? Within this gathering of 148 citizen legislators there were some of the finest brains west of the Mississippi." For instance, a legal opinion by attorney Francis Holman would cost $500 in his office, but he put his brain at the people's disposal. Brian Lewis was one of the leading engineering consultants. The state paid him thousands before his election to find out what he thought about the feasibility of a Fletcher Bay Bridge. As a legislator, he shared his knowledge for practically nothing. George Clarke as head of the Washington Survey & Rating Bureau knew as much about insurance as anybody in the state. Wilbur Halluer was one of the leading fruit processors in the Northwest. Irv Newhouse was one of the foremost hop growers in the world. Dr. Homer Humiston was a gold mine of information on health services and pension plans. Bill Kiskaddon was a Boeing research engineer. Bill May was a strong labor figure. John Stender was an international vice president of the Boilermakers' Union. August Mardesich and Dick Kink were lifelong commercial fishermen.

There were printers and publishers, doctors and dentists, truck drivers and loggers, longshoremen and envelope salesmen, housewives and school teachers, bankers and you name it. For $3,600 a year plus $25 a day expenses, these people offered to take time away from their regular jobs to serve the public in writing the laws they were to live under. The most expert opinions could be sought on almost any subject. As the pay increased over the years to today's $42,106 a year, plus $100 a day expenses, the legislative mix changed from people willing to serve the public to people legislating for a living. The pay was handsome enough to attract housewives, retirees and public employees. The citizen legislator is a relic of the past. The state Legislature has become a profession treated like a fulltime job.

Hughes: Who are some of the people, legislators and others, who really made an impression on you of being really bright, upstanding?

Ferguson: Of course, Sen. Augie Mardesich of Everett, Bob Goldsworthy of Spokane, Slim Rasmussen of Tacoma, Sen. Bill Gissberg of Snohomish. And Marshall Neill. Neill used to sit behind Perry Woodall. And Perry Woodall was a wild talker. If he had something that needed to be looked up, he'd turn back to Marshall, and Marshall would get the law book and find what Perry wanted so Perry could recall exactly what he wanted to quote.

Hughes: Tell me more about Mardesich, the fisherman who was a power in the Senate in the 1960s and '70s.

Ferguson: Augie was a guy who *rarely* put a bill out with his name on it if he really wanted it. He got it on somebody else's name so then he wasn't targeted because he figured they would go after it because they didn't want Augie to have it. But between him, gillnetters and purse seiners, those guys ran the committees in both houses; you couldn't get a thing through there that they didn't want. He was very powerful.

Hughes: Did you know (future Senate Majority Leader) Sid Snyder early on?

Ferguson: Oh yeah.

Hughes: He was the deputy chief clerk, then the chief clerk of the House, wasn't he?*

Ferguson: Sid Snyder is a really wonderful guy, a savvy politician and a great storyteller. He's got the memory for these details. If ever there is something I need to know, and I can't quite pick it up, Sid knows.

Hughes: When you were a Capitol correspondent during that era, was it sort of free and easy to talk with officials? You could just walk in and get to talk to the governor?

Ferguson: No, no, no, no, it was never like that.

Hughes: So Al Rosellini was the first governor you covered when you arrived in 1961?

Ferguson: Al was the first governor I covered.

Hughes: Did the governor have routine press conferences?

Ferguson: Yeah he did, and he was good. Of course, they treated him kind of mean. Let's see what is it that Jack Pyle (of *The Tacoma News Tribune*) used to say to him? "Well, governor, are you going to tell us the truth now or are you just going to sit there and dangle…" I forget what exactly, but anyway, they talked down to him.

And when Dixy Lee Ray became governor (in 1977) and had her first press conference, the guys didn't think anything of her. They were not respectful. They thought she was just an old lady professor. So they were

---

* Snyder was deputy chief clerk from 1957 to 1969 and acting chief clerk from 1965 to 1967.

sitting out in that big room where they have the press conferences, making fun of her. And I said, "You guys better watch out. I bet this place is bugged. I bet she's sitting back there in her office listening to every word you're saying." Hahahah, they'd think; that's funny. And when she walked in that room she was breathing fire. I mean *mad*. And I knew she had heard every word they had said about her. That was the last press conference for weeks. She was so mad that they were just running her down and just being so snotty. And I warned them. I said, "She's listening to this."

Hughes: We skipped around Al Rosellini too quickly. You say you admired him.

Ferguson: Oh some. Yeah, I admired him.

Hughes: What was it that you admired?

Ferguson: Well, he did good things. He brought the institutions in this state up to par. He hired good people. Even Martin Durkan (a powerful Democrat from King County), who was no Rosellini fan, would say that. One time I said something like, "Why don't you say something nice about Al? What could you say nice about Al Rosellini?" Durkan said, "Well, he hired good people." And that's important.

Hughes: Who were some of those good people that he hired?

Ferguson: Oh, Dr. Garrett Heyns, (who gained national recognition for his dedication to improving prisons) as his director of institutions. I can't think back. It's just too many people.

Hughes: He picked good staff people?

Ferguson: I'm talking about his agency people. His own staff—the ones who should have been looking out for him—they were too busy looking out for themselves. By the way, one time I dared to ask Rosellini, "Why do you have this little slurp, this click, when you talk?" He used to have a little click, and then he had a slurp. He said, "It's just habit." That's all it was, there wasn't anything wrong.

Hughes: Talk about eye for detail—or ear for detail, in this case. You ask unusual questions. During that era—1961 to 1964—you're covering the rise of "Straight Arrow"—this bright young Republican civil engineer,

Daniel Jackson Evans. Could you spot him as a comer right off?

Ferguson: Oh yeah.

Hughes: What was it about Dan Evans?

Ferguson: Oh, well, probably the best thing that would answer that is that Dan lived down in Olympia in a house with a bunch of the other members of the House. I remember Jimmy Andersen, Chuck Moriarty, Slade Gorton. Four or five of these guys rented a house. And they told me Dan was the only one who made his bed before he left in the morning. Now *that's* Dan Evans.

Hughes: Attention to detail. Discipline.

Ferguson: Slade was great too. I really liked Slade Gorton. He's a wonderful guy. Brilliant guy. They were good guys. They talked to me, and they confided in me. Rep. Joel Pritchard (a future GOP congressman and lieutenant governor) was one of that gang. Don Brazier from Yakima was another of those bright young Republicans in the Evans era. Don was a guy who really believed in public service. And he wasn't one of those ambitious guys who'd walk over the top of someone to advance his career. As a legislator, as a deputy attorney general for Slade and then as chairman of the Utilities & Transportation Commission, he lived public service. Back when the energy conservation thing really started, he also kept his office at about 60 degrees! It was that way at home, too. He made the family wear sweaters.

Hughes: With Evans, Gorton and the others, the cumulative IQ power in that house must have been really something. I never interviewed anybody I thought was brighter than Slade Gorton. Do you agree with that, in terms of brain power?

Ferguson: Yeah, I do. And there's something else about Slade, too, despite the fact that he's considered kind of standoffish. I had every phone number that he had that I needed to reach him by. I had his phone number at McChord Field where he was in the Air Force Reserves; I had his phone number at home. I could call him in the morning when I knew whether he'd gone jogging yet or not. He was good. But he never tolerated small talk. He never sat and gossiped like you and I are talking. It was all business with him. Nonetheless, if you needed to talk to him about something, he was available. Some of them aren't that available, but he sure was.

Hughes: What was it in that landmark year of 1964, hard on the heels of the Kennedy tragedy, and during LBJ landslide, what is it that propelled young Dan Evans, at 39, to upset Al Rosellini for governor?

Ferguson: I don't know, and I don't have any columns to look back in because my columns only started in '65. I have all my columns from '65 forward.

Hughes: Your impression then about Dan Evans as an up-and-comer, possibly the next governor?

Ferguson: A lot of this involved John O'Brien being ousted as Speaker of the House in 1963. He'd been speaker since 1955, and Evans, Slade Gorton and some dissident conservative Democrats wanted to get rid of him.

Hughes: Who became Speaker when they ousted O'Brien, Adele?

Ferguson: Bill Day, a Spokane chiropractor. His nickname was "Big Daddy." My biggest scoop was probably when I wrote that they were going to dump O'Brien. Nobody else did. I found that out and I put it in the paper a week before the session opened.* I quoted Rep. Bob Perry, a Democrat from North Seattle, as saying, "O'Brien is as dead as last year's garbage. He's through. He's finished. He is NOT going to get it." Later on, Perry said to me, "I wish you hadn't had me saying that." I said, "What do you mean?" He said, "Well I mean, it's really disrespectful to say 'Dump him like last year's garbage.'" "You said it!"

Hughes: Jim Dolliver, a Republican staffer who later became Dan Evans' chief of staff, said O'Brien "didn't realize what was happening until the knife was going in." You wrote that O'Brien was absolutely livid. "In a bitter outburst that could only be compared to that of Richard Nixon after his recent defeat for governor in California," O'Brien called the maneuver "dishonest and immoral." As he "continued to rail at the Republicans and

---

* Legislative historian Don Brazier, a longtime friend and admirer of Ferguson's, says she did indeed have a scoop, but she was lucky, too, because Rep. Perry was over-confident. The plan to dump O'Brien wasn't a done deal until the Sunday night right before the session started.

Democrats who'd thwarted him, voices rose and the man who once was king was obviously just another House member talking too long." That's good writing.

Ferguson: I was the *only* one that had John O'Brien getting kicked out of office after all those years. He'd been speaker since 1955. The Republicans voted for Evans for speaker, then swung their votes to Bill Day. Another scoop I had was that I also knew it when Dan Evans was going to endorse Nelson Rockefeller for president in 1968. I had that. Nobody else had that. I went in and talked to his folks. They knew it; they didn't tell me. But I could tell it by the way they were talking that that was going to happen.

Hughes: Whenever they want to roast you, they always talk about how you were feared. At a roast in 1999 someone said that if you were in politics you'd pick up the newspaper with rapt anticipation just wondering what Adele Ferguson had written about you. And you said at that time, "People who have resented me in the past are being nice to me now. People who have been snotty now go out of their way to come up to me and make amends." That was when you'd been in Olympia for 30 years. Why were you such a fearsome person? What was your reputation built on?

Ferguson: *I found out what was going on.* Ted Bottiger would always have little classes with the new members of the Senate. He said, "I always tell them there's just three things you want to look out for while you're down here in Olympia. And that's "Adele Ferguson, Adele Ferguson, and Adele Ferguson."

Hughes: Well, let's go back to 1964: So there they were—the bright young guys—Evans, Gorton, Pritchard. And interestingly when you look back on Al Rosellini's career, and the reforming that he did, was there nevertheless sort of an inference by the Evans campaign that Al was *old* politics—a new day was dawning? (Adele is nodding.) And here were these bright young progressive Republicans?

Ferguson: Yep.

Hughes: Those Evans guys were pretty much Bull Moosers—pretty liberal Republicans, weren't they?

Ferguson: Oh yeah. They're liberals. So is Ralph (Munro), so is Joel (Pritchard). They're all liberal Republicans. I mean they're about as liberal as the Democrats.

Hughes: It's kind of interesting in Washington State how much sometimes there hasn't been a lot of difference between a conservative Democrat, like Henry M. Jackson, and a "mainstream" Republican.

Ferguson: Yeah, like in the Senate, see, Hubert Donahue was a very conservative Democrat. Here's something good about Dan Evans and his staff: I remember a story about Bill Lathrop, an ex-State Patrol guy who was Dan Evans' driver. And when he became Evans' driver, Dan told him, "I don't want you to be sucking up to me." Well, he didn't use that line, but that was the gist of it. Dan had been an admiral's aide when he was in the Navy and didn't like that sort of thing. So one day when they came to town, the two of them picked me up and we went down to some event that was going on. So when they came back with the car when it was time to leave, Dan was standing there and I said to Bill, "Aren't you going to open the car door for him?" He said, "There's nothing wrong with his arms!"

Hughes: Gov. Evans preferred it that way?

Ferguson: Oh he did. That's the way he wanted it.

Hughes: Dan's press secretary at one time was my former fellow *Aberdeen World* reporter, Jay Fredericksen

Ferguson: Oh, he used to tell me a lot of fun stuff about Dan.

Hughes: Jim Dolliver and Ralph Munro were also very impressive people that I met among Evans' people in the late 1960s. Tell me more about the Evans Administration.

Ferguson: They were great.

Hughes: They were great because?

Ferguson: Well, he was a smart man; he was a loyal Republican, and he didn't fool around. Of course he did want an income tax. I remember when he went on this trip promoting the income tax. He was going to go all around the state. They asked me to go with them. They said we'll make all the arrangements for the hotel rooms and everything. I would pay them of course, but they would make it so we were all staying in the same hotel. There were just four of us, I think—Dan Evans, Bill Lathrop, his driver, and Jay Fredericksen. So we got up north of Wenatchee someplace. The four of us got out of the car, and we're walking down the street. A man comes up, he stops, and he looks at us. And then he goes over to Jay and he says, "Isn't that Adele Ferguson?" I thought that was great! He didn't say anything about Dan Evans, the governor.

Hughes: Let's skip ahead to 1972 and Dan Evans is running for an unprecedented third consecutive term. Well, it wasn't unprecedented to run for a third term, but he actually won one. Al Rosellini, in a debate, referred to Evans as "Danny Boy." Al had been ahead in the polls. Was that a real turning point in the race?

Ferguson: Yeah, because it showed a lack of respect for the governor. Al shouldn't have done that.

Hughes: Do you suppose that was just sort of a knee-jerk reaction by Al, or somebody put him up to it?

Ferguson: No, I think he just got carried away, and he was sorry later.

Hughes: Sort of pumping his chest a little bit?

Ferguson: Yeah. It was the straw that broke the camel's back. Evans was gaining.

Hughes: Did you see any difference in that third term of the Evans Administration compared to the previous two?

Ferguson: No.

Hughes: How would you characterize it?

Ferguson: Well for me it was just four more years because I knew all the people. He changed a few people. But he had such good people working for him. His press people were good people.

Hughes: Philosophically some of those reforms that Dan picked up on were started by Al Rosellini, weren't they? He made some really significant reforms in state institutions, didn't he?

Ferguson: Well, Dan is the one who organized the Department of Ecology.

Hughes: And also the Department of Social & Health Services. Was that for better or worse?

Ferguson: Worse, worse, worse, because eventually they had to start picking it apart again. I mean they jammed all these things together. It didn't work, so they had to take them apart again. I think Charlie Elicker (a Republican state senator from Kitsap County) is the one Dan relied upon in the Legislature to come up with the Department of Ecology.

Hughes: Ralph Munro says he was standing near the elevator on the Senate floor the night the bill passed, and Elicker, with a twinkle in his eye, said to you, "Can you spell 'Ecology'?" There had been a fight over what to call the agency. Do you have some pretty strong environmental feelings, Adele?

Ferguson: I do not believe that the United States economy should suffer because some people don't believe global warming is all man-made. There are an awful lot of scientists who haven't been heard from, or are not being quoted on what's causing global warming. I agree with Dixy. Global warming has been around for many, many centuries. It will come and go; it will be cold; it will be hot. Just the other morning I heard some politician who was saying, "It's a consensus now that we're causing all this." It is *not* a consensus. There is no consensus yet. It's just a whole bunch of people who want to do it that way. I think a lot of these people are looking at it from a money standpoint too, or how much it's going to cost.

By the way, when Evans went back East to announce the SST with Nixon, they invited me to go, so I went. We flew back. But we never got to talk on the plane. Dan reads novels on planes. He doesn't talk. He was reading. So the rest of us started talking. Was it Jay again?

Hughes: It might have been Neil McReynolds, Evans' director of communications.

Ferguson: I think it was Neil. So at one airport we lost Neil. He was a making a phone call back home for something and the plane took off without him.

Hughes: Kind of like leaving your little brother behind.

Ferguson: So we got to Washington, D.C., and I had a room in the Mayflower. Dan always let Lathrop make the arrangement for them because Lathrop always had the smaller expense account. So he put him in kind of a cheap hotel. The next morning we agreed to meet for breakfast. And I take a taxi over to their hotel. Now they've got a car provided for them, and we drive down to have breakfast before we go up to the White House. So we get into this little restaurant, and after we eat, Dan starts to button his coat and the button comes off.

So he said to Jay and to Bill, "Have you got a needle and thread?" And then he looked at me. And I said, "Yes, I have a needle and thread." And it turned out to be the Washington State Labor Council sewing kit! So I said, "I will sew this on only if you swear that you will never tell anybody that I did this." OK, they all swore. So I sewed the button back on.

Then we went up to the White House, and we get just inside the gate. The guard at the second gate says, "Let's see your identification." Now my identification is my driver's license. It says Philipsen on it. He says, "Who's this Philipsen?" And I said, "Well that's me. That just happens to be my married name." And he says, "Well, I have to see something that says Ferguson." I said, "I don't know if I have anything like that, because I'm identified by my married name." "Well," he said, "you can't go in." And Dan said, "Well, I'm the governor of the State of Washington, and she's with us; she's going in with us for this announcement about the SST. The guy says (motioning with his thumb back toward the gate), "No she's not. She has to go back out to the first gate." So now the time is going by. So those three, the governor and his aides, they go on up and leave me. I go back down to the first gate. And I'm down there trying to explain to this guy who Philipsen and Ferguson are when this big black limousine drives up. It's Scoop Jackson. "Adele!" he says, "How are you?" And I said, "Scoop, for God's sake, will you inform this guy who I am so I can get in?" "Fine," he said, "She's OK by me." The guy says, "OK, you can go in." I thought, well, that's something: The Republican governor could not get me in the Nixon White House. But Scoop Jackson, a Democrat, can get me in just like that. So I ran on up there. Tom Pelly was then a congressman so he got me a seat in the back of the room. There was still a seat vacant. He had a picture taken of me sitting—you can only see my back and side, except there I am and there's Nixon and Evans and everybody.

Hughes: Great story. We skipped over something: Who ran against Dan Evans in 1968? John J. O'Connell?

Ferguson: Oh yeah.

Hughes: He was our Democrat Attorney General for three terms.

Ferguson: Oh, they had the goods on him from the start.

Hughes: Yeah, about what?

Ferguson: Well, his gambling—Wasn't it is gambling that got him? I could look it all up back in my column.*

Speaking of staff, I saw Sen. Warren Magnuson's wife mad just once.

Hughes: Jermaine wasn't it?

Ferguson: Jermaine Magnuson, yeah. Lt. Gov. John Cherberg had Sen. Magnuson and some other people in his office. And I was big pal of Cherberg's. Well, we had drinks together.

Maggie was there and his wife was *really* ticked because he had dandruff all over his shoulders. It was her feeling that his staff should have seen to it that he didn't have any dandruff on his shoulders when he arrived. Oh, she was mad. Maggie was so good. Any time he came to *The Sun* when I was there he'd come into my office, over the editors, and he'd say, "Adele, we just want to stop by and see you, see how you were."

Hughes: Of course he had Norm Dicks as an aide, right there at the hem of his garment, learning those lessons.

Ferguson: Well, Norm's a good congressman, but you know what they say about Norm, which is true? When you're shaking hands with him he's always looking over your shoulder to see if somebody better is coming along!

---

* During the campaign, *The Seattle Times* revealed that the attorney general, whose reputation for integrity rivaled Evans', had a line of credit at Las Vegas casinos.

Hughes: Norm would love that one. But you regard him as a good congressman?

Ferguson: Well, he's the pork barrel — he gets the pork. That's what makes a good congressman.

Hughes: Does Norm Dicks have good staff people?

Ferguson: Yeah, he does. Norm's a good guy. By the way, I was a big buddy of John Cherberg's. His wife didn't come down on Monday nights. She came down on Tuesdays. So that left him and Orlando, his driver—

Hughes: Excuse my need for a history lesson, but was Cherberg always lieutenant governor?

Ferguson: Well, he was a football coach at the University of Washington (1953-55) and then lieutenant governor for 32 years, from 1957 to 1989. My husband and I went on a number of trade missions with Cherberg. You pay your own way. But the thing you get out of it is you get invited to these big dinners and stuff. So we went a lot of places. I talked him into going to Egypt. I always wanted to see the pyramids! I'm glad we went....But as I was saying, everyone ended up in Cherberg's office at day's end.

Hughes: What kind of guy was he?

Ferguson: He was a great guy. He was a super patriot and stuff. But he could get annoyed. He was standing on the rostrum one time and one of the speakers got up and said, "Well, I can't give my speech if the TV cameras aren't on." So Cherberg waved to the TV guy in the corner and said to turn the TV cameras on. The guy had a pipe in his hand and pointed up to show Cherberg that the lights weren't on, and it wouldn't do any good to turn the TV on because you couldn't see. Cherberg thought he was giving him the finger. He rushed down there and grabbed him and the guy had to explain that it was just his pipe.

Hughes: That's funny! So could you have a cocktail at the "Ledge" Building, the Capitol?

Ferguson: Oh sure. I had cocktails there all the time. And also the Speaker of the House always had cocktails once a week, and the Minority Leader had cocktails once a week. In the Senate, even Jeannette Hayner, who doesn't drink, had cocktails once a week when she was majority leader—and dip and potato chips, you know.

Hughes: Was that pretty much press corps and legislators? Were there lobbyists in there?

Ferguson: No lobbyists. Just press. And the whole idea was that you could ask questions that you wouldn't ask otherwise.

Hughes: So were you doing a column for *The Sun* as well as news reporting at the same time?

Ferguson: Yeah, I was.

Hughes: Was that a tightrope, hard to walk, when you're doing straight news reporting?

Ferguson: It got me up early in the morning, I'll tell you that.

Hughes: That is a really hard thing to do, to keep respect on both sides of that line—when you're covering a story about how the delegation's doing, covering the governor, and then you're writing your own opinions.

Ferguson: Well, it was supposed to be different, and I tried to keep them different.

Hughes: Did you know my friend Bob Bailey of South Bend, a lunch-bucket Democrat who served in the Senate? A great newspaper man, too, by the way.

Ferguson: Yeah, he was a great guy. I loved Bob. The caucus was always mad at Red Beck because they thought Red Beck was telling me everything that happened in the caucus. Well, he was, but so was Bob Bailey. He trusted me. I didn't ever use anything that I thought was going to hurt somebody. You know what I mean?

Hughes: Yes, I do.

Ferguson: Get them in trouble for it. I know some big secrets today that I'd never be able to write, or tell.

Hughes: You'll take those to your grave, will you, some of those secrets?
Ferguson: Yeah.
Hughes: Is there real smoking gun stuff?
Ferguson: Oh yeah.

Hughes: Well, what's the general nature of it? Is it about graft, corruption—?

Ferguson: No, it's about—(long pause)

Hughes: Sleeping around?

Ferguson: Yeah, that kind of stuff.

Hughes: That's an interesting thing, too, about the way things have changed in the press corps, isn't it? It's well documented about Jack Kennedy's dalliances, and the like. And we in the media often had a gentleman's, gentlewoman's agreement to not print that sort of thing back then. Was that the way it was in Olympia?

Ferguson: Yes. Well, I don't know that that's the way it was. Maybe they didn't know it. But some of the things I know, I don't know who else knows.

Hughes: But if Senator Smith were having an affair with Aide Jill or whatever, was that just sort of viewed by the press corps as consenting adults?

Ferguson: Well, I think it was viewed as "What good would it do you to write it? What have you gained? It isn't anything that anybody *has* to know." It isn't anybody's business if it doesn't affect their work. That's the way I felt. If these guys want to run around or get drunk or whatever, as long as it didn't affect their job as representing the people, or if they were a doorman, or whatever they were doing. I don't care what anybody does if they don't let it affect their work as the people are paying them to do.

Hughes: Tell me again about the advice you gave to anyone coming to Olympia for the first time.

Ferguson: Well anybody coming to Olympia for the first time I told them, "Everybody down there is related to somebody else who is there—I mean the doorman, the legislators and all. So whatever you say, they're just *dying* to go and tell that person that you said it So you've got to be very careful." Martin Durkan, he used to complain to me about a reporter. He said, "I don't know what good it does me. I try to tell him and explain something to him and he just gets it wrong and screws it up every time." I said, "What do you talk to him for then?! Just let him alone, don't talk to him. And pretty soon his boss will want to know why he never has *you* in his story and then you can tell him, 'Well because the son of a bitch always reports me wrong.'"

Everybody down there is related to somebody and *dying* to have something to go report. And it's a *gossip factory*, it just grows gossip. Of course you know the old story about when the State Patrol had the right to stop cars for no reason. They could just pull cars over, and say "Let's check the next 10 cars." And the reason they had to quit that is because they stopped a car that had a very prominent (lawmaker) in it, who was not with his wife. I always thought during all the Walgren ("Gamscam") stuff that some of those State Patrol men would talk because they were in the car with Dixy and some of the other people who were out to get Gordon Walgren and John Bagnariol. There's some untold stuff there, but nobody has done it.

Hughes: We might as well skip ahead because I know you have very vivid memories of that incident and some strong opinions as well. This is the so-called "Gamscam" case in 1980. It involves Gordon Walgren, majority leader of the State Senate.

Ferguson: And John Bagnariol (the co-speaker of the House).

Hughes: And then there was the lobbyist.

Ferguson: Pat Gallagher.

Hughes: Tell us all about that. What did they accuse those fellows of doing?

Ferguson: They accused them of conniving with members of the suspected mob to advance gambling in the state.*

And how they ever got Gordon (indicted), I don't know, because he refused their money, turned down their five thousand bucks. And the only thing they got him on was answering a phone call that came across state lines, but he didn't know it. I thought it was really rotten the way they

---

* A federal racketeering indictment charged that they conspired with undercover FBI agents posing as organized crime figures to allow gambling in Washington in return for a share of the profits.

got him. But I noticed that everybody who got involved in it later—the Supreme Court, the Bar Association, all these people, including Justice Jim Dolliver, who wrote the opinion for the Supreme Court, couldn't figure out how Gordon Walgren was considered to be in on this. Of course, he was targeted in the scam by the FBI because he was the majority leader in the Senate. And Dixy thought he was going to run against her instead of for attorney general.

Hughes: You're convinced that Gov. Dixy Lee Ray was getting the goods on these guys in a Nixonian way because she saw them as rivals?

Ferguson: Well, the U.S. Attorney, John Merkel, was the guy who kept it going when the FBI tried to drop Gordon out of the scam because they couldn't get anything on him. Merkel told them, "Get something." Gordon found that out when he got an order to go through the FBI files after he got out of prison. He found the memos from the FBI to Merkel.

Merkel and Gordon were both from over here (Kitsap County). And Merkel's father was the prosecuting attorney here. And then after he died, they wanted Merkel's law partner named prosecuting attorney, and Gordon got that job instead. So they were out to get Gordon. And Dixy of course thought Bagnariol was going to run against her, while Walgren was considering running for attorney general. But she thought *both* of them might run against her. And I always thought, boy, one of these days maybe one of those State Patrol men riding in Dixy's car will tell. But nobody has yet.

Hughes: That would really be something wouldn't it?

Ferguson: Oh yeah, because I imagine they heard a lot from Dixy and her sister riding in the car.

Hughes: Tell me about 1979 when Bagnariol and Republican Duane Berentson were co-Speakers of the House in the 49-49 tie. That must have been a moveable feast for you.

Ferguson: Oh they got along OK. Bagnariol had a terribly hot temper. He'd snap at you for no reason, and then he'd apologize for it because he didn't really mean to do it. He was just mad about something else. He did that to me a couple times, but he always apologized. And he was a good guy.

Hughes: Had you known Gordon Walgren well before all this?

Ferguson: Oh yeah, sure, because he was my editor's best friend. (Gene Gisley was back at *The Sun* as editor.)

Hughes: You had a strong feeling that Walgren was innocent. How would you characterize him as a legislator?

Ferguson: He was a good legislator. He stopped a lot of efforts to raise fares on the ferries, and stuff like that. He was a good legislator.

Hughes: So you had a column, and you made it clear that you felt that Walgren had taken a bum rap?

Ferguson: Oh yeah. But before all this happened, I wrote a number of columns about Walgren because he was in a position where he made news. And yet, when one of his people came to me and said, "We're trying to find something that you've written at some time that's good about Gordon so we can run it." And they couldn't because everything I'd done had been more critical than favorable. Yet I liked Gordon fine. By the way, something happened then and I never have found out who did it. Someday I hope I do. Somebody down there was trying to break me up with Gordon and with Gene Gisley—I mean make Gisley mad enough to fire me and Gordon mad enough to not talk to me anymore. And I never found out who it was…I just know that it was happening.

Hughes: And the motive there would have been?

Ferguson: So I wouldn't see that they were shadowing Gordon and Gamscam. It was part of the Gamscam. And I know Gene at one point called me into his office, and he was just irate. And he said, "I hear that you've been bad-mouthing me down in Olympia." And I said, "Gene, I've never bad-mouthed you any place." And he said, "Well then I'm told that." And I said, "Let me tell you something, Gene. Even if I wanted to, I'm too smart to do that. Do you think I'm going to go down there and do that? Everybody down there is related to everybody else. You don't dare say that a doorman there is a big jerk because the person you're talking to might be his niece or nephew. Everybody is related, and it's a big, big bear's nest. And so I wouldn't do that. I had no reason to bad mouth you." Same thing with Gordon. They were trying to break me up with Gordon because they were afraid, I'm told, that I would see what they were doing because the State Patrol was shadowing Gordon…Of course Dixy was involved in all this, and John Merkel, the U.S. Attorney. It was really a tough thing. But I stuck by Gordon all the way through. In later years, it was (still) bad at my paper because we had a new editor and he didn't like Gordon. I even wrote a column one time saying that Gordon had gone to Yellowstone Park for a trip with his wife. He was out of prison. And he had gone for a trip and when he came back, he stopped by to see me. And he was telling me what it was like. And I said, "Well, a lot of people might be thinking about going to Yellowstone and you can tell me what areas are not burned up by the forest fire and how things are." It made a good column, but it didn't come out in the paper. And I went in and I asked the new editor, "What happened to my column about Gordon and Yellowstone Park?" He said, "We don't need to have anything in our newspaper about people like *that*." All Gordon had done was tell me what was burned up and what wasn't, and what the places were like that you could stay. It was an interesting column for somebody who might want to go to Yellowstone. And this SOB has to say, "Well, we don't need anything in our paper about people like that."

Hughes: Give me your take on Dixy Lee Ray, our first female governor. She and Jimmy Carter took office in 1976. Talk about strange bedfellows.

Ferguson: She really could have been a wonderful governor, and I don't know what kept her from it so much. She was a brilliant woman. She's the one I listened to on climate change. I don't listen to all these other crappy people who think the United States is poisoning the whole world. Dixy said, "Baloney."

Hughes: When you heard her talk about nuclear power you knew she knew her stuff.

Ferguson: Oh yeah, I've got both of her books as a matter of fact. She gave them to me one day. I went to hear her speak at something in Bremerton. I went up and shook her hand. So she said, "Do you have my books?" And I said, "No." And she said, "Well here, let me give them to you." So she got the books and she wrote something in one of them, and I didn't look at it. Then I looked at it later. In one book she wrote, "To Adele, with many, many memories."

It didn't say *nice* memories, or *good* memories. But she was great. One of the last times I talked to her was after Jacques died. That was her favorite dog. I had an appointment with her in her office, and she was sitting behind her desk. I sat down and pulled a chair up in front of her desk. And I put my feet forward like this, and then I pulled them back real quick. And she said, "Oh you don't have to worry. He's not under there anymore." Tears came to my eyes; tears came to her eyes. We sat there and cried together, because we both loved dogs so much, you know.

Hughes: So where did she go wrong, Adele?

Ferguson: I used to write that she behaved like an old maid school teacher. In her college classes, I was told, if anybody sort of spoke up when they weren't supposed to or got too smart she'd say, "Out!" And they had to go. That was the kind of person she was. You know, they don't suffer fools gladly? She didn't suffer fools at all. And she was that way.

You knew Lou Guzzo, the former *Seattle P-I* managing editor who became her aide?

Hughes: Yes, I did.

Ferguson: Well Louie Guzzo wrote me a letter here a couple years after Dixy had died (in 1994). And he said, "You know one thing I always regretted, Adele, was that I never got you and Dixy together to be friends. I know that you would have been good friends because she respected you, and you respected her, but it just didn't work out." He's written me once since, when I write something about her. I still write about her once in a while. I quote her on climate change all the time. What she said was what a jackass Al Gore was and all this kind of stuff. She was a good speaker. She was just mesmerizing.

Hughes: Were you there covering that fateful State Democratic Convention at the Hoquiam High School gymnasium (in 1980)?

Ferguson: Oh yeah, Dixy's run-in with Sen. Warren Magnuson. I was there.

Hughes: Dixy had crossed Maggie and he was PO'd! That was Maggie at his Maggiest, not ready to be shuffled off to retirement and outraged that the governor was shopping around for his successor.

Ferguson: Yep. Maggie was great. I always liked Maggie better than Scoop (Jackson) because, for one thing, Maggie's people were different kind of people. Scoop's people were all hot shots. Al Rosellini's staffers were also people who wanted to be big shots. When he defeated Al in 1964, Dan Evans had staff who just wanted *Dan* to be the big shot. They were good. Dan had wonderful, wonderful staff. And they'd tell you lots of stuff. They trusted me to tell me stuff that they knew I couldn't print, but to know it helps. So they were good, and Dan Evans was a *good* governor.

Hughes: What do you think was the key factor in Dixy Lee Ray's rise to power in 1976? What was it about her?

Ferguson: She was a brilliant woman. The first time I ever met her I went to a luncheon. She was going to speak here in Bremerton. So I went up to her and said, "Hi Dixy, I'm Adele Ferguson. I'm here to hear you speak." She got her purse out and started to go over and pay for my lunch. I said, "You don't have to pay for my lunch." She said, "I don't?" "No," I said, "my newspaper will pay for my lunch." She thought she had to pay for my lunch when I was interviewing her.

Hughes: She was kind of a political naïf?

Ferguson: Oh yeah. And so when people asked her questions, she'd say, "I don't know the answer to that, but I'll find out. And if you give me your number I'll see that you get the answer." That's the way she was.

Hughes: Did she follow up?

Ferguson: Oh yeah. And later on, I used to speak a lot around the state. I don't do so much anymore, but one time I spoke to the Bellevue Republican women. When Dixy got there, she was ticked off because she wasn't being respected the way she thought she ought to be. So she kind of got a little carried away on some of the things she did…A lot of things that she did, she just sort of did out of spite. A lot of women are like that. I suppose I can be that way too, be spiteful about something. And she was a little spiteful. That's where she ran afoul of the media…At that first press conference where they made fun of her. And she was humiliated by it.

Hughes: You really think she had the room bugged?

Ferguson: Oh *yeah*. John Spellman had it bugged too. Yeah, I think they've always had it bugged so they could hear what the people were saying while they're waiting for them to come out.

Hughes: That's an interesting aside. We know the downfall of Richard Milhous Nixon was—

Ferguson: They should have burnt the tapes!

Hughes: Do you think that Washington governors and some others were surreptitiously doing some tape recording?

Ferguson: Oh yeah.

Hughes: Fascinating. Did that in any way come out in the open?

Ferguson: No, not that I know of. I wrote about Dixy's first press conference when they were running her down, insulting her, and acting like she was just a dumb old lady. She was so mad at that one, no more press conferences. We didn't have a press conference for quite a while because she was so ticked off.*

Hughes: So it all unravels for Dixy, and John Spellman, the Republican King County Executive, becomes governor, 1980.

Ferguson: I liked John Spellman OK. I thought he was a very nice guy. But he was shy; he was a very shy guy. One of the people who worked at the press house—young guy, I forget his name now—but he worked there and he cleaned it up. He used to come in and sit and talk to me in the

---

* Gordon Schultz, the former longtime UPI reporter at the Capitol, has this observation: "I don't think the conference room was bugged as such (like hidden mics etc.). What happened was the conference room was remodeled while Dan Evans was governor and they wired in a mike so the TV cameras could tap in and the press office could record what was said for the purpose of making transcripts that were distributed after each press conference. They may well have heard what was going on before the press conference started as well. But again, I don't think the microphone was hidden. It was there in plain sight." We asked Ferguson to comment on this and she declared, "I still think it was bugged!"

morning. You can learn an awful lot from the janitors. He told me that he would be out walking along in the morning and he'd run into Spellman with his bodyguard. He would say hello to the governor, and Spellman wouldn't answer back. So I always thought that was unusual for John to not answer one of the employees when they just say, "Good morning, Governor."

Hughes: And you think that that was because he was shy?

Ferguson: Well I like to say that, yeah. Now, speaking of janitors, Martin Durkan (Democratic state senator from Renton and chairman of the Ways & Means Committee) had janitors in his employ. They would check the trash sacks every evening in front of the governor's office, and from other various offices. So he got to look at an awful lot of paperwork that came out of people's offices that nobody knew he was getting.

Hughes: They didn't have shredders back then?

Ferguson: No.

Hughes: Did you ever do any Dumpster diving yourself?

Ferguson: I don't think so. I can't remember if I had any reason to.

Hughes: What was your view of Martin Durkan?

Ferguson: He was a brilliant guy and somehow he just wasn't at the right place at the right time I guess in his desire to become governor. For one thing, his brother told me, "You ought to see this guy's back. He was so badly wounded in the war you just wouldn't believe it." I'd go and talk to Martin, and the minute I'd go in his office and sit down, he'd turn the radio on. Well, that was to drown out any listening things. He was suspicious, and he was right: He was being listened to. When the phone rang—what do they call that thing that records the numbers? It doesn't record the conversation, but somebody can find out everybody who's calling in and calling out by whatever this process is. And Durkan found out that Bob Greive's right-hand man, George Martonik, was monitoring his calls.

Hughes: R.R. "Bob" Greive of King County, the Senate majority leader.

Ferguson: Yeah. He and Durkan hated each other. Durkan helped dump Greive as majority leader. I wrote about all this stuff. It's all been in the paper, so it isn't anything that new. What I haven't written about I'm not going to tell you anyway!

Hughes: What an autobiography you could write.

Ferguson: What I really ought to do is publish some of my columns.

Hughes: That would be an Olympia best seller. Given the new technology, you don't have to publish fifteen or twenty-thousand books. You can do a run of three, four, five-thousand and sell it for a decent price without having to make a big investment.

Ferguson: Another little story I wanted to tell you is about Bob Greive. We were friends. But then we had a big falling out.

Hughes: What was that over?

Ferguson: Well, because I didn't like what he was doing. When he collected money from various interests for candidates, he only used it for candidates who would vote for him for majority leader. He didn't use it to elect Democrats, or anything like that. He used it to elect people who had to swear to him that they'd vote for him for majority leader. That's how he stayed majority leader. But when we were still friends he asked me one time to be on a panel of people to ask questions of a candidate he was backing. I said, "I don't drive up to Seattle, Bob." He said, "You can go with me, it's no problem at all. I'll drive up there, we'll go up there right after session, the thing is going to be at 7:30, I'll come right back and you'll be home at a decent time." So I said, "Well, OK." So later on I was talking to, I think with Limey Flynn, a longtime lobbyist. And I said, "I'm going to go be on this panel up in Seattle for Bob Greive. I'm going to ride up with Bob." And he said, "You're going to ride with Bob Greive?" I said, "Yeah." And he said, "Bob Greive has got to be the *worst* driver in the State of Washington. I wouldn't ride down to the corner with Bob Greive." I said, "Well, geez, thanks a lot! I'm going to go up to Seattle with Bob Greive." And he said, "Isn't there anyone else going up that you can go with?" I said, "I don't know but I'll find out." So I went around and found out Martin Durkan was going to be on the panel. So I went to Durkan and said, "Limey's really worried about me driving up there with Bob Greive." And Martin said, "Forget it. You'll go with me. I've got to go up anyway.

I'll go up right after work, we'll sit through the panel and we'll come right straight back, and it won't be any problem." "Oh God," I said, "Thank you." Then I went back to Limey and I said, "Well, Limey, I took your advice. I got somebody else to ride up to Seattle with." And he said, "I am so glad to hear that, Adele. You know, the only guy down here who's a worse driver than Bob Greive is Martin Durkan!" Well, it turned out that they cancelled the thing. Later, I was invited over to Seattle to Durkan's house a number of times. Durkan would pick me up at the ferry, and he *was* a terrible driver.

Hughes: Tell me about the Pete von Reichbauer switch from Democrat to Republican in 1981, which switched control of the Senate from D to R for the first time in 26 years. Did you know von Reichbauer? She's nodding.

Ferguson: He lived kind of a strange life because it ran in his family that the men in his family died young, like in their forties or something. So this was always the story about Pete. But of course he did what he did because Spellman got elected governor and Spellman was his big buddy. He's still a King County Council member, so he's successful.

Hughes: So how would characterize John Spellman?

Ferguson: I think he was competent and honest; he was just not in-novative, I guess Evans was innovative; Rosellini was somewhat innovative. I knew one of his good friends who said one time, "You and I together, we could write a book about Al Rosellini that will sell a million copies." I said, "I want to live to be an old lady, so, no."

Hughes: By the way, I heard that you like to fish.

Ferguson: Oh yeah!

Hughes: What is it about fishing you like?

Ferguson: I just like it, I like catching them.

Hughes: What do you catch?

Ferguson: Salmon, but there's not much salmon out here anymore.

Hughes: Gov. Spellman said that he went fishing with you a couple of times.

Ferguson: He did. We were both guests of Bremerton Mayor Glenn Jarstad at Westport. Spellman and I have the same fault fishing. We start to step back from the rail. You're not supposed to do that. When you hook a fish, you're supposed to stay there and fish from there. But he does this like me, he starts a step back. He was fun on the boat. What did he say?

Hughes: I said, "Tell me about the business about Adele having this fearsome reputation and being warned to stay away from her and all that." And he said something to the effect, "Adele was always fair in what she wrote about me in her column. Mean, but always fair."

Ferguson: You know, Al Rosellini told me one time, he said, "You know Adele, you always stabbed me in the front." And when Dave Ammons wrote the story about me that was in the paper (in 1991 when she'd been at the Capitol for 30 years) he quoted it as coming from Dan Evans.

Hughes: Oh, it was Al who actually said that?

Ferguson: It was Al. So next time I saw Dan Evans I said, "Say Dan, that quote about you in there about 'you always stab me in the front,' they got that wrong because that was really Al Rosellini." You know what Dan said? "Well, I wish I'd said it."

Hughes: So what was the downfall of John Spellman? Why four years later, in 1984, did Booth Gardner—"Booth Who?" they said at first—come out of the woodwork to beat Spellman? What was it about that?

Ferguson: Well, the economy went sour and Booth was a really engaging person. He had a reputation as a shrewd businessman and an outstanding administrator. He was Pierce County executive and a new face. I know a lot about Booth Gardner.

Hughes: Have you seen him lately?

Ferguson: No, I've only seen pictures of him. How is he doing?

Hughes: He's fighting Parkinson's Disease. It's hard to see him diminished. You knew him way better than I, but I had lunch or dinner with him several times when he was governor.

Ferguson: Did you order off the bottom of the menu?

Hughes: Usually he was ordering a hamburger.

Ferguson: That's what he always had when he ate with me. First, he used to be one of my Kitsap legislators. He was a 26th District Senator. So he'd invite me out to lunch or dinner, and we'd go and he'd always order a cheeseburger. So I figured he must not have any money or anything, so I'd order something cheap too. And I said something one time to Jack Pyle from *The Tacoma News Tribune*. I said, "Jesus Christ, this guy never has any money. He always orders the cheapest thing on the menu." "Well," Jack says, "the thing about Booth is that he's got so much money that he wants to spend yours to make up for it." So from then on and the next time I got invited out, I ordered from the *top* of the menu, and I ate *big*. I thought, "To heck with that; I'm not going to eat any more of these damn cheeseburgers!"

Hughes: I saw Governor Gardner at the sayonara party when David Ammons left the AP to become communications director for Secretary of State Sam Reed. It was good to see him. It was clear that he is still very bright, but he wasn't voluble like he used to be. That's one of the debilitating things about the disease. It zaps your energy. By the way, how do you feel about the "Death with Dignity" issue that's on the ballot this year? Gov. Gardner is a key spokesman for the issue.

Ferguson: I'm not ready to vote for something like that.

Hughes: Do you see the "Death with Dignity" thing as sort of a slippery slope?*

Ferguson: Yeah. It kind of bothers me.

Hughes: You knew Booth Gardner before he became governor. Characterize what kind of an executive and a politician he was.

Ferguson: He had a *much bigger* reputation than he deserved, thanks to people like me who should have known better.

Hughes: In the spring of 1982, you wrote one of the early columns about him emerging on the statewide scene. "Booth Gardner," you wrote. "Remember the name....He may very well be the rising star of the Democratic Party in this state....He could be your next governor."

Ferguson: Yeah, and he impressed me, but he wasn't really all that he

---

* The assisted suicide issue passed handily on Nov. 4, 2008

was (cracked up to be). Greg Barlow was the guy. Barlow had worked for Booth's stepfather, Norton Clapp, in the 1970s.

Hughes: Barlow became a National Guard general, right?

Ferguson: Yep, "The General." Greg Barlow ran Pierce County for Booth as his chief of staff. The first time after Booth was elected Pierce County Executive in 1980, why Greg went in and called a meeting of all the department heads, took out the car keys to his county car, and laid them on the table. And he said, "There. We don't all need these county cars." So everybody else had to pull out their keys and lay them down. And that's how they started. Greg ran the county for Booth and Booth got all the credit. I was the only one who didn't know any better until I found out later. But I wrote one time that he had this guy working for him who was spending his money wildly. I forget who the guy was. But I wrote and said this guy is going to spend everything Booth's got before he's through. I was going through the Legislative Building when here comes this really handsome silver-haired guy in uniform, and it's Greg Barlow. So he said, "You're Adele Ferguson?" And I said, "Yeah." And he said, "I just want to thank you for the column you wrote about this guy spending all of Booth's money. I just went down yesterday and picked up his checkbook."

Hughes: What was the guy spending the money on—campaign stuff?

Ferguson: Well, not really. He was *blowing* the money, you know what I mean? He was supposed to be helping run the campaign on Booth's money, but he was blowing it. In the column I wrote about it I was saying the crap he was doing. I don't remember the specifics now. When you write five columns a week for so many years they start to blend together.

Hughes: OK. So now we're in the Gardner Administration. It's 1985. What's the hallmark of the Gardner Administration in state government?

Ferguson: Nothing. The governor spent most of his time running around visiting kids in classrooms and saying, "Do you know who I am?" Ah, he did very little. And the first thing he wanted to do when he got elected was raise the sales tax. He was not a good governor. What he should have done was take Greg Barlow with him, like when he was in

Pierce County But he couldn't do that because Norm Dicks didn't like Greg Barlow. Norm Dicks talked Booth out of bringing Greg Barlow.

Hughes: I didn't realize that Norm Dicks was so influential with Booth Gardner.

Ferguson: Oh yeah. Well after all, Pierce County is in his district....He was big buddies with Booth.

Hughes: You also had a front row seat to watch the rise of young Gary Locke as a legislator.

Ferguson: Yeah, and I always liked Gary Locke.

Hughes: He always returned reporter's calls, that's for sure.

Ferguson: He's a nice guy. And he did go together with Dino Rossi and write that budget without raising any taxes.

Hughes: What kind of marks do you give Gary Locke as a legislator and then as a governor?

Ferguson: Well, I'd give him pretty good marks except he still has that terrible Democratic disease of spending, and wanting to raise taxes instead of cutting anything. He's got that real bad. He made the most *wonderful* quote one time, though. I've probably used it five or six times, and he's never lived up to it. When he was first running for governor, I think it was, he said, "You can't always figure that your own party has all the good ideas. The other party has good ideas too. And the best way for us to handle government is for the two parties to get together and accept the other person's ideas, and make use of them. You don't have to be a Democrat." He said it better than I'm saying it. But his whole point was everybody has a voice. Listen to everybody who has something to say about it. It was very good, but he never lived up to it.

Hughes: Let's go back to females and politics and breaking barriers. Other than Dixy Lee Ray, tell me about some female legislators.

Ferguson: Well, there was Karen Schmidt. She was full of piss and vinegar.

Hughes: How about the late Ellen Craswell? Would she have made a good governor? Gary Locke defeated her in a landslide in 1996. I understand that Bruce, Ellen's husband, is still coming by your house every now and then to help you.

Ferguson: I said—and of course it just broke their heart—I said, "She'll make a good governor while she's got Bruce there to be with her, because Bruce would make a fine governor, if he could get elected."

Hughes: He was a fine politician in his own right?

Ferguson: Oh yeah, but he never got elected to anything. He told me after I wrote that, "You know when you keep saying Ellen can't win this, that's too much wishful thinking." I said, "No, it's not wishful thinking. I'm just saying she can't get elected. And she can't." All this Jesus stuff she keeps talking about. Well, that Jesus stuff doesn't work.

Hughes: She was a true believer wasn't she, an evangelical Christian?

Ferguson: Oh yeah.

Hughes: The interviewer inadvertently skipped over Mike Lowry, who was governor for four years, starting in 1993.

Ferguson: It's easy to do. I knew Mike Lowry when he worked for the Ways & Means Committee for Sen. Martin Durkan. He and his wife both worked for the Ways & Means Committee. He's a very smart guy—probably the best guy with the budget of any of those governors we've been discussing. He knew more about the budget than anybody. Bobby Williams, the Republican from Longview who was such a good budget analyst, said that when Mike was governor he'd go sit with him and they'd go over the budget. Bobby said, "This guy *really* knows the budget."

Hughes: That's high praise from Bobby Williams. They called him a "gadfly" because he seemed to be everywhere asking questions.

Ferguson: Now there was a good guy. Bobby was the guy I would call if I wanted to know something about the budget process. When he was in the Legislature he was the brains in the House for Republicans, and then even after he was out. He came here to Silverdale one time and I rushed up to him. I hadn't seen him for a long time, and gave him a big hug. He was just embarrassed as hell. He's one of those kind of guys that's not used to having people come up and hug him, women. Dan Evans used to be like that, very shy—untouchable Dan, you know what I mean? But Bobby was very impressed by Lowry's grasp of the budget. He was also impressed by Gary Locke's new budgeting method, the one about…(pauses to think)

Hughes: Priorities of government?

Ferguson: Priorities of government, yeah.

Hughes: So what went wrong for Mike Lowry?

Ferguson: Well, what went wrong is the woman. (Allegations of improprieties) But you know something, when he was in Congress I *never* heard a word about that kind of thing happening with him. Never. I never heard a word from anybody saying that Mike Lowry was easy with the hands or does anything like that. So I was surprised to hear this allegation. And I actually defended him in all the columns I wrote because I said, "These women can handle this. All they have to do is say, 'Don't do that.' " You know what I mean? "I love the job, Mike, but we can't be messing around like this."…These women all talked like they had to go through it. They didn't have to put up with that. He wouldn't have dared fire them. But they just all went along.

Hughes: That offends your sense of propriety as a strong woman doesn't it?

Ferguson: Yeah.

Hughes: The notion that a woman can't stand up for herself. So is there some complicity there a little bit?

Ferguson: What do you mean?

Hughes: Well, complicity in that your mom or your Aunt Adele ought to have given you the gumption to say, "OK buster, let's knock this off," or "This is only going to get us in trouble," like that story you told about what you used to say to guys who were hitting on you.

Ferguson: One time I was standing in the Senate, and they had called a caucus. And they all marched back in. And one of the Democratic Senators pinched me on the behind when he went by. So I said loudly enough for *everyone* to hear, in the galleries too, "If you lay one hand on me again you aren't going to have any hands left when I get through with you!" Now everybody knew what I'm talking about, see. But Mike Lowry resented some of the stuff that I wrote.

Hughes: I bet he did.

Ferguson: And I hugged him once when I saw him, and he shrank back like I was a rattlesnake.

Hughes: Who were some of the absolute best and the brightest people you covered over the years—that you thought were just exemplary public servants?

Ferguson: Well, I thought Dan Evans was an exemplary public servant. And Jimmy Andersen, who was a state senator and retired from the Supreme Court, is in that category. Andersen closed a lot of loopholes in laws concerning law enforcement, like granting immunity to private citizens who come to the aid of a police officer and creating a statewide criminal identification bureau. It was his bill that set up Medic I. Perry Woodall was exemplary. Augie Mardesich. Bill Gissberg were exemplary. I know I'm going to forget somebody. *Joel Pritchard.* There's tons of them. Just let me think.

Hughes: Do you hear from any of the old guys?

Ferguson: Once in a while. I'm going to see some of them here very shortly.

Hughes: Really, what occasion is that?

Ferguson: Well, on Election Day—and this has to be a big secret. See, this is by invitation only so you don't let it get out. But on Election Day, Gordon Walgren—it used to be Ralph Munro and Gordon Walgren—and I sort of throw a big luncheon. We don't pay for it. We just invite people. And we all meet, and it's usually old political junkies and officials, some legislators.

So we have lunch and we talk politics and we vote and see who we think is going to win in the election, and we give little talks. And this year, on our guest list we have Gov. Dan Evans, Jimmy Andersen and Dick Marquardt, the former insurance commissioner. Those are our big shots—and Ralph Munro, of course. We've invited 40 people. They just love this thing. I mean they want to invite themselves. You have to kind of fight them off because they want to bring people. Marquardt called up and said, "I don't want to drive over there by myself." So I said, "I've invited Jimmy Andersen and Dan Evans." And he said, "Dan told me, 'Well, she hasn't written anything nice about me for a while.' " I thought "What have I not written nice about him?" Well, I guess about the Indians. He authored the gambling thing.

Hughes: Is this event all off the record?

Ferguson: Well, kind of. I always tell them at the beginning of the luncheon that I may write about this but I won't identify you unless I need to identify you. It all depends. I don't do anything to embarrass anybody. Bruce Craswell, Ellen's husband, is going to come, and county officials, too.

Hughes: So, when you look back—and we'll save Gov. Chris Gregoire toward the last. But when you look back at some of the people who ran for governor or should have been governor, who would have been a great governor?

Ferguson: Norm Maleng (the Republican King County Prosecutor).

Hughes: He was one of my all-time favorite people.

Ferguson: Yeah, mine too. He was my favorite that year—1996. That was the year Ellen Craswell won the primary and ran against Gary Locke.

Hughes: What was there about Norm?

Ferguson: Well, he was brave. He spoke out on things; he wasn't a coward, and you knew exactly where he stood.

Hughes: He was kind.

Ferguson: Yeah, he was. He was a *good* man. He was a good friend. I felt *so* bad about the little girl. (Maleng's 12-year-old daughter, Karen, was killed in a sledding accident in 1989.)

Hughes: And then to lose him like that to a heart attack (in 2007) at the age of 68 was really tough. Anybody else other than Norm Maleng who really pops into your head—someone you held in high regard?

Ferguson: Well Jimmy Andersen. I knew him as a state representative, as a senator, and as a judge on the State Supreme Court. He was a chief justice.

Hughes: I'm getting ready to interview retired Justice Charles Smith.

Ferguson: Is that the black guy?

Hughes: Yes it is. Did you know him?

Ferguson: Well, not that much, but I think he was a little wishy washy on the death penalty. Be sure to ask him about that.

Hughes: I will. So in Adele Ferguson's Hall of Fame, the people that you worked with over the years in public life, who would be number one?

Ferguson: For what reason?

Hughes: Integrity, moxie, humanism, hard work....

Ferguson: Well, Dan Evans, Slade Gorton, Warren Magnuson. I had something wrong with my family once, and I needed some real help. I went to Maggie. I've never ever usually asked anybody for help, but I had a sister-in-law from Poland who was having a lot of trouble. She needed some congressional help to move from one country to another, and I got it from him.

Hughes: I thought there was a very interesting angle on Gary Locke—his sense of heritage and how far he'd come as an Asian-American. I was touched by that, it was an interesting thing. Did you get to know Mona Locke as well?

Ferguson: No, only to see her once in a while.

Hughes: Of those first ladies who do you give high marks to? Nancy Evans, for instance...

Ferguson: She didn't like me.

Hughes: She didn't? What was that about?

Ferguson: Oh, they were having a big fundraiser here for Dan at the home of Joe Mentor, a builder in Kitsap County. And they sold so many tickets that Joe had to add onto the house to make room....Joe was trying to get Nancy and I to sit together. And she said no, she didn't want to. She said, "Well she'll write down everything I say." She didn't realize I didn't really do that. So she didn't like me much. And I wrote a couple times that I wished when she came to Kitsap County that she'd quit wearing a house dress. And I thought, "You don't do that, when you come here. If you're going to come here and impress our folks at least dress up a little."

Hughes: I have a flashback to one of my all-time favorite Adele Ferguson leads.…It was the column you did at Ocean Shores where Maureen Reagan was there for a speech to Republicans. And Maureen plopped down on a sofa next to you and said, "You look lonesome!" And your response in the column was, "The hell I did." That was a great column. I thought she was an interesting lady.

Ferguson: Beautiful eyes. She had Paul Newman eyes, those beautiful blue eyes.

Hughes: How would you characterize your own politics?

Ferguson: I call myself an independent. And I always say I believe in the Republican philosophy, that government should only do for people what they can't do for themselves or it can do better. Not the Democratic philosophy, which is that government should be all things to all people. And the reason I can say I am *not* a Republican is that I'm independent (minded).…And I was pro-choice.

Hughes: Do you have strong feelings about abortion?

Ferguson: Originally I was opposed to it, and I wrote about that. Then I listened to Lorraine Wojahn, who was a senator from Pierce County. And she told about the cost of not allowing abortions and all these illegitimate kids. You had to pay for them until they were 18, and many of them are *abused.* All these little kids born that people don't want, and subsequently they'll torture, burn them with cigarettes and break their arms. Every time I hear one of those stories in the paper I just want to get a hold of some-body and kill them. And these aren't the only people seeing these kids. What about the aunts and uncles and neighbors and those people who see this and don't do anything about it?! There's nobody who could harm an animal, let alone a baby around me. I just would not put up with that. So I changed my mind. I voted against abortion when it was an initiative, but I believed what Lorraine Wojahn said. I'm pro-choice now, but I'm *definitely* against partial-birth abortion. And I often say that I'm just really embarrassed and ashamed of my women friends in the Democratic Party who condone partial birth abortion, which is murder in my view.

Hughes: Do you have strong feelings about the initiative and referendum process versus the notion of pure representative democracy?

Ferguson: I think we ought to have the initiative and referendum process. Remember the time the legislators raised their pay and the initiative came out (in opposition) and got so damn many votes? It's a balance.

Hughes: Who are some of your political heroes?

Ferguson: Well, I don't know about Ronald Reagan. I knew Ronald Reagan when he was kind of an asshole. Yeah, he was kind of a show off before he became president, when he was going to some of these meetings. And Evans didn't like him either. You could see that. My political heroes? Well, I'd say Dan Evans is a political hero of mine because he's been so damn successful.

Hughes: Best president of the United States in the 20th Century?

Ferguson: Even though he didn't impress me in the beginning, I guess I'd have to say Reagan because of the way he restored in people the love of their country. I think that Jeb Bush was the smarter brother among the Bushes and it's too bad that Jeb wasn't elected. I think things would be *so* different today if it had been Jeb instead of George.

Hughes: Tell me your view of the Chris Gregoire administration.

Ferguson: Well, she's in the pocket of the damn labor unions and Indian tribes and the defense attorneys. She made all this money, you know, on the tobacco settlement. She hired somebody to handle that for her back East. She didn't do any of that court stuff. But she went out, she got the money. I think she's a spender. Look, last time she said she wasn't going to raise taxes and that's the first thing she did. You cannot trust her....I promoted her for governor *way* back when. Before she even became in Ecology, I think. I must have done it in a news story because I can't find it among my columns. That means I did it separately. Otherwise I could look it up. I've catalogued my column. So it had to be a news story.

Hughes: What do you think has gone wrong for her?

Ferguson: What goes wrong in any of them is the lust for power. Once they're near it and can smell it and they're close to it, they want it so bad they'll do almost anything to get it. See, she said to labor, "All my decisions

I make I'll check with you first." And the Indians…That's a hundred and forty billion bucks a year we could have gotten in shared revenue from the gambling compact, and she dumped that off.

Hughes: Do you call her? Does she return her calls?

Ferguson: I haven't tried lately. I used to. I was able to get a hold of her when she was heading up Ecology. You know what she did in Ecology? She's the one who, when she was still at the Department of Ecology asked for money for increased staff. They didn't give it to her. So you know what she did? She then promptly fixed it so that it now took you a year or two to get a water right. Just to show you, "Well we haven't got time because we don't have enough *staff*." That was her.

Hughes: As a proud American and feisty female human being how do you rate Sarah Palin?

Ferguson: I like her because I think back to Jimmy Carter, who was in intelligence when he was in the Navy. And he was the *rottenest* president we've had—maybe next to George Bush. But Jimmy Carter wasn't worth a crap and he had all these credentials that should have made him wonderful.…But as for Palin, I mean what's wrong with her experience? They always act like she's only been a PTA president. She was a mayor; she was a city council member; she did everything to promote better government. She joined the PTA because she didn't like the way they were treating kids in school. She became the city councilman for things in the city she wanted changed. She became the mayor because she couldn't get it done as just a city councilman. She became governor because she wanted to do these other things. Everything she wanted was reform. She wasn't looking at being vice president or president.

Hughes: Do you have strong memories of 1992—the so-called "Year of the Woman"?

Ferguson: No. I probably didn't like most of the women that were running. I'm not the kind that hangs out with the women.

Hughes: How about Senators Patty Murray and Maria Cantwell?

Ferguson: Well, I've quit picking on Patty because she's always so nice when she sees me. She always comes up and treats me so nice. I hate to say it, but it sort of cools me off a little. And Maria, I don't care that much about Maria Cantwell.

Hughes: Speaking of female politicians, did you know Julia Butler Hansen, the former state legislator from Cathlamet who was elected to Congress in 1960?

Ferguson: I did. *I did.* I called her the "Duchess of Cathlamet." For years, she was the most powerful woman in the state as chairman of the Legislative Transportation Committee. In 1955, she and John O'Brien were the Democrats' candidates for the speakership of the House. But Julia lost narrowly in the caucus. She would have been the first woman Speaker of the House. After the vote, she went around shaking hands, saying, "No hard feelings." But then she came to the two guys who had engineered her defeat, Len Sawyer and Augie Mardesich. "No hard feelings," she told them, "but I'll get even with you sons of bitches!"

Hughes: I have to tell a Bob Bailey story about Julia. He was her district aide and he always said that Julia never wore a miniskirt because she didn't want her balls to show.

Ferguson: That's pretty good! I won't repeat the story about the time the State Patrol stopped Julia and Bob Bailey on the highway. You've heard that, I'm sure, a hundred times.

Hughes: I have not heard it! Please tell me.

Ferguson: You haven't?!

Hughes: No, I swear.

Ferguson: Julia and a couple of her friends had to get to Olympia, and they were in a hurry. Bob was driving and they were late, so she told him to speed it up. The State Patrol pulled them over. So the first thing Bailey does is try to explain they are just trying to get Julia Butler Hansen, U.S. Congresswoman, to Olympia. Then Julia gets into the act, telling the trooper, "Haven't you got anything better to do than to pull a car over and stop decent people? I mean there are people out there really breaking the law!" And she just chews this guy up and down. And the trooper gets out his ticket book, and starts to write the ticket. And Bailey quickly hands him his card that says "Senator Bob Bailey, Washington State Legislature." And the guy puts the ticket book away because that's who writes their budget—the Legislature. That's a true story. Bob told it to me.

Hughes: The day that I met Julia Butler Hansen I was a reporter for the Grays Harbor College *Timberline* in 1961. Congressman Russell Mack, a Republican from Hoquiam, had just died and she had taken office.

Ferguson: And she was PO'd because they were trying to pick a successor before he was in the ground.

Hughes: Exactly. Anyway, Julia came in, sat down at the conference table and said, "Son, do you have a cigarette?" I said, "Yes, Mrs. Hansen I do." I was smoking Parliament or some sort of highfalutin brand trying to look sophisticated. She looked at the cigarette and expertly, with the thumb of her right hand, flicked the filter off it, tapped the loose end on her watch crystal and bummed a light. It was just classic stuff. No filters for Julia!

Ferguson: She had a big fundraiser once for Sen. Magnuson. Did you hear about that, at her house?

Hughes: No.

Ferguson: So she was there and people are coming in to meet Magnuson. And Maggie was getting thirsty, so one of the guys said "We've got a bottle." I forget what he drank. "We've got some upstairs in the bedroom. You can come on up there and have a drink." And to get him up there they said, "Senator, the President is on the phone upstairs." So then he goes up the stairs. He didn't come back down. So Julia's people are now getting pissed off because they came to see Magnuson. So then Maggie tells one of the people, "Would you say that Jermaine would like to get a call from the President too?" Jermaine goes up there at the end of the fundraiser, and Julia is furious because she had lost her prime guests. Julia was really funny. I wrote a number of things about her.

Hughes: She was a great lady.

Ferguson: Yeah, she really was. She really was. She and I got along surprisingly well.

Hughes: Surprisingly?

Ferguson: Well, she's a very different kind of a woman. Julia is not your average kiss-ass. You know what I mean? Some of them are.

Hughes: I'm sitting here with another woman who doesn't exactly suffer fools gladly.

Ferguson: Well, I liked her. We especially got to be friends when she got on the State Highway Commission (1975) and later as chairman of the State Transportation Commission (1979-1981). As a matter of fact I did her a big favor. After she became head of the Transportation Committee, she used to come to these meetings, and I went to all the meetings. And she would sit up at the front table and you could see right up her skirt. You could see her underwear! So I finally went to the people there, and I said, "For God's sake would you put a board in front of that table? I don't want to be looking at Julia Butler Hansen's underwear every time I go to these meetings." They did. They put a board in front of the table.

Hughes: Did anyone over the years ever offer you any of these kinds of appointments?

Ferguson: Yes. I was offered appointments on two commissions. The Evans people offered me some kind of a labor deal. And then I was offered an appointment on one of these transportation committees.

Hughes: This would have been like a fulltime job?

Ferguson: No, but it would add to a pension if you ever did take a full time.

Hughes: Did anybody ever offer you any fulltime jobs, like on the State Liquor Control Board?

Ferguson: No, but Leroy Hittle, the former AP correspondent, gave us booze when he was on the Liquor Board.

Hughes: Tell me about the national conventions you covered over the years.

Ferguson: I went to a lot of them.

Hughes: What were memorable ones?

Ferguson: Oh, well, the ones in Florida where we had to walk home through all the tear gas.

(It was in 1972) both the Democrats and the Republicans met in Miami that year. I don't remember (a lot of details). You go to those things and all you remember is the hotel you stayed at, and that's the best you can do. One time we stayed in a gay hotel and one time we stayed in a Jewish hotel. They shut down the phones in the elevators at dusk Friday and you had to walk up all these stairs because they were Jewish and they didn't have phones and stuff on the weekend. Oh, I was in Chicago too for all the riots and protests.

Hughes: Really? You were there in '68 when the Chicago Police clubbed the Vietnam War protesters?

Ferguson: Oh yeah.

Hughes: Tell us what that was like?

Ferguson: That was wild!

Hughes: Talk about political theater. You've got rioting in the streets, and poor Hubert Humphrey getting the nomination, fighting Gene McCarthy, and the ghost of Bobby Kennedy.

Ferguson: Yeah, I was at that one.

Hughes: So how about the charge that you are anti-Indian. How do you plead to that?

Ferguson: I'm not anti-Indian. I just do not believe that anybody, even if they were Norwegians, should have the fish that belong to the people of the State of Washington. And I'm mad at the judge who gave it to them.

Hughes: George Boldt.

Ferguson: Yep. Did I ever tell you this story? I was at one of these things in John Cherberg's office one time. He had a lot of people in there. And I'm standing in there having a drink and this little old guy came up to me and said, "Aren't you Adele Ferguson?" I said, "Yes." He said, "I'd like to have you meet my wife." I said, "All right, why don't we chat a little bit?" He walks off giggling and snickering, and I said, "Who the hell was that?" And a guy said, "That's George Boldt!" He never let on that I was the one who had been chewing him up for so long. And I don't hate Indians. I really don't. As a matter of fact, I got a letter one time from Gummie

Johnson when he was representing the Indian tribes for something they wanted. And he wanted to know if I hated Indians. And I said, "No, I hate the judge who gave them the fish that belonged to the people of the State of Washington. And I don't believe they should have that."*

Hughes: Have you written about the whole mushrooming tribal casino thing, and the notion that Gov. Gregoire gave away the farm with that gambling compact? Do you think that that's OK for them to have the casinos?

Ferguson: Well, I really don't, but I don't know what you can do about it. I suppose if that's the only way they can make money, all right, but it gets bigger and bigger. And Gregoire hasn't really stopped them from getting bigger. I don't like the idea that the tribes have a monopoly on gambling and don't pay any taxes on their earnings. They shouldn't have special rights that other citizens don't have.

By the way, you know the one thing I never found out? Why did Gummie Johnson turn against the (Republican) Party? I don't know that. He did, he turned very much against the party. He was a bitter, bitter, bitter old man when he died. And I never could find out from him. When he was down there in Olympia he checked into a nursing home there. And I know that he had lunch with Supreme Court Justice Jim Dolliver every Saturday. I liked Jim Dolliver. He had been Dan Evans' chief of staff.†

Hughes: The story about Dolliver first having a chance to be appointed to the Supreme Court by Evans in 1970 and choosing not to take it is interesting.

Ferguson: Yeah, it was Dolliver who turned it down. Dan (Evans) was willing to go.

Hughes: But the State Bar Association's board was against endorsing

---

* C. Montgomery "Gummie" Johnson, who died in 2005, was state GOP chairman in the 1960s and early 1970s. He was known as a "fanatical moderate" with a strong environmental conscience. In 1965, Johnson helped purge John Birch Society members from the state Republican Party.

† Johnson married a Democratic lobbyist, and they formed a consulting firm that defended the treaty rights of Indian tribes. In 1980, he was a consultant to Gov. Dixy Lee Ray in the Democrat's unsuccessful bid for re-election against John Spellman.

Dolliver because he didn't have a lot of law practice experience. The notion also was that he might have been intellectually a lot feistier than they really liked their Supreme Court judges. In his history of the court, Charles H. Sheldon noted that "the governor could have appointed Dolliver without the bar's endorsement," but it would have been difficult for Dolliver "to win election later without its support." So Dolliver asked the governor to withdraw his name. Evans eventually appointed Dolliver to the Supreme Court in 1976 and he served for 23 years.*

Hughes: Adele, did part of your Olympia coverage extend to covering the Supreme Court?

Ferguson: Oh I was friends with all those guys.

Hughes: Who are some really impressive people there that you met?

Ferguson: *Dolliver.* Jim was the one who defended Gordon Walgren. He put out the opinion when Gordon was trying to get his bar license restored. Dolliver wrote that it's still difficult to see how Gordon Walgren ever was included in this ("Gamscam") mess because there was no reason to think that Gordon would even be involved in it. And of course Justice Jim Johnson was a good friend of mine. He was Slade Gorton's key assistant during the appeal of the Boldt Decision.

Hughes: Do you know the current Chief Justice, Gerry Alexander, really well?

Ferguson: He is the *only* member of the Supreme Court who after I wrote a column about him wrote and thanked me for it. Jimmy Andersen, who was in the Legislature for 14 years, was a great friend of mine. Bob Brachtenbach, another former legislator, was a friend of mine. As a legislator, Andersen kept plugging away at filling loopholes in laws concerning

---

* When the justice died in 2004, former secretary of state Ralph Munro recalled that during Dolliver's tour of duty as Evans' chief of staff, a throng of angry union members gathered in Olympia and angrily chanted "Evans! Evans!" Dolliver advised the governor to open his remarks by thanking them for celebrating his birthday. "It broke the crowd up," said Munro, who had also worked in the Evans Administration. "Two minutes earlier, they had been shouting obscenities; now they're all laughing."

law enforcement, like granting immunity to citizens who came to the aid of a police officer. He also helped create a statewide criminal identification bureau, and it was his bill that set up Medic I.

Hughes: Was that hard over the years to make those friendships with people you were covering?

Ferguson: No, the thing that I did was that I didn't socialize with them.

Hughes: We're talking now just about the judges?

Ferguson: *Any* of them. I don't socialize with legislators I don't make cozy friends and don't go to dinner to their houses and stuff.

Hughes: But that doesn't mean you couldn't have a drink with them?

Ferguson: Oh no, you can have a drink with them. But if you get too friendly then they can't understand it when you start cutting them up for something they need cutting up for. Somebody's got to cut them up.

Hughes: Recall for me an instance like that when somebody was really wounded, saying, "I thought you were my friend. How could you write that about me?"

Ferguson: Oh yes, it was the Speaker of the House of Representatives and he was from Vancouver—Robert Schaefer. I wrote something about him and he was so hurt that he quit speaking to me. And then I ran into him the day that we had the earthquake down there in Olympia. I happened to go down early that morning into the lunchroom in the House. I was allowed to eat in their lunchroom. He was down there, and that was the first time he had spoken to me in God knows when. And the damn earthquake hit—we're all running out to the street. (laughing)

Hughes: Talk about acts of God!

Hughes: When did you retire from *The Sun?*

Ferguson: In '93.

Hughes: 1993. Let's revisit that. What was that like down the stretch?

Ferguson: You mean why did I leave?

Hughes: Yes.

Ferguson: John P. Scripps was going to die of cancer. So they wanted to have his will drawn to avoid losing a lot of money through what happens with the papers. So they merged into Scripps Howard. But they were very honest about it; they told all the employees that. They said, "We're doing this merger and all because we want to avoid losing a lot of money to the family when Mr. Scripps dies." Well, he died, and with the new management along came a new editor out of Florida.…That was Mike Phillips and he came there with some other people and the first thing they did was try to get rid of almost everybody there that was an (opponent) type. They wanted to get rid of Gene Gisley, my editor. They got rid of him pretty fast. They kept the business manager. They didn't try to get rid of me (at first), but eventually they did want to get rid of me.

Hughes: Why? Because you had been there a long time?

Ferguson: Because I *was* the *Bremerton Sun*, you know what I mean?

Hughes: I do.

Ferguson: In Kitsap County I represent the *Bremerton Sun* more than anybody ever did except Julius Gius. Look at all the beats I was on; look at all the people I met and served and went to and did things. So he wanted to get rid of me. Julius told me that. Julius was now down in California. Julius said, "He's got to get rid of you." So one day Phillips called me in. And he called in his managing editor and his city editor and some other person. And he said, "You're going to have to make a choice: You can either continue writing politics or you can write the column. One or the other."

Ferguson: So I said, "All right, I'll take the column." I was about ready to quit—and they didn't know that—because I was so angry with them, the way that they treated me. They had a woman copy editor. I will never work for another woman. And she made changes to my column that made me look foolish. For example, if you talked about "materiel" in a war story, she'd make it "material."…So I kept writing the column, and it wasn't long before she was making more changes in the column. And I went out and I told her, "You know, if you don't understand it or if there's something really wrong with it, why don't you ask me?" She said, "I don't have to." So I went in my office, sat down, and wrote out my resignation; gave them two weeks' notice because I had piles and piles, all kinds of stuff to do.

Went in, gave it to the managing editor: "There you are." Of course that word got around real fast. So I started getting rid of stuff; did like ever good retiring person did, washed and scrubbed my desk down with soap and water, and got rid of everything. And the editor came into my room and said, "I don't suppose you're so mad at us that you won't let us keep running your column after you retire." And I said, "That's pretty slimy of you considering that you haven't spoken to me but six times in 1992." And he said, "Well, I can explain that." And I said, "Not to me you can't." So I got a call from Paul Scripps, John Scripps' son. I wrote him a letter. Well, first he called me and said, "Would you please reconsider?" My column always was number one on the list when they took a survey....The column was always right up there on top. So he said, "Would you let us run your column if I promise you that they will make no changes in your column?" And I said, "Paul you may trust them, but I don't." And I didn't trust them not to do that. All they would do was the first time I'd be gone they'd start making changes again. So I wrote him a letter and explained why I left, and what the problem was. It was too bad, we were friends.

Hughes: Did they have a retirement party for you?

Ferguson: No, no, I just walked out the door.

Hughes: You're there from 1946 to 1993 *and you just walked out the door.* Was that hard?

Ferguson: No I wasn't happy there any more. They didn't appreciate me.

Hughes: Was there a lot of fallout in the community?

Ferguson: They gave away the paper for a while (to entice subscriptions from non-subscribers). And I go by Fred Meyer's and see them giving away *The Sun*, I'd go up and I'd say, "They didn't have to give it away when I worked there." (laughs)

Hughes: Do you still take *The Sun*?

Ferguson: Oh sure. He's gone now. (The former editor).

Hughes: Has there been some bright young man or woman who came out here and said, "Adele, I wanted to meet you because you were a big part of the history of *The Sun*."

Ferguson: No, but I was a big part of the history of *The Sun*, so I've never worried about it. My pension comes from there.

Hughes: When you see now what's happening with newspapers—

Ferguson: Oh, I'm so ashamed of them.

Hughes: Tell me about that.

Ferguson: Well, I'm ashamed at what the media is doing. The media is trying to make this election (Obama vs. McCain) and I'm opposed to that. I think that's wrong. And it is the mainstream media. It isn't the small newspapers that are doing it. It's the big guys. *The New York Times*, *The Washington Post*, CNN, ABC, NBC, CBS.

Hughes: So you see strong liberal biases?

Ferguson: Oh yeah. *Oh yeah.* I think that's terrible.

Hughes: But I was also talking about the financial issues newspapers are facing, particularly with publicly-traded companies. They're making layoffs and revenue streams are eroding. I'm sure *The Sun* is not immune to that.

Ferguson: No.

Hughes: What's happening to the newspaper industry that you and I have loved for so many years?

Ferguson: I don't know. I don't know what happened to the fact that a person to be a journalist was supposed to give you the "who, what, why, where" and so forth and no opinion. And then they started (abandoning) that. The Seattle papers were doing it. When I was down there (covering the Legislature) they had their little favorites and the ones they covered up for. There's so much covering up.

Hughes: Do you see that as part and parcel of the economic problem? Newspapers are losing print subscribers but gaining readership online. But online revenues don't begin to make up for lower print advertising revenues. So the model is you can't get the same amounts of revenue from Bremerton Dodge or whatever to buy online advertising as you can in run-of-press advertising.

Ferguson: I don't have a computer. Well, I have a computer but it's one

I had made for me special. I'm not online or anything because I'm not mechanical. If anything goes wrong with that thing I've got to get Bruce Craswell up here to fix it. So I don't know how it works.

Hughes: So you're not on the Internet?

Ferguson: No.

Hughes: When you were working for *The Sun* were you on the Internet?

Ferguson: I don't think so. I forget what we did. You could get stories that were filed and stuff like that but no Internet or anything like that.

Hughes: Do you think you're missing something by not being on the Internet?

Ferguson: Oh probably. But I don't care. I'm not missing that much.

Hughes: Well, I'm still trying to make this point: What's happening now in the newspaper industry is that revenues are sharply declining because the reader base is eroding. Younger people particularly and a lot of others are accustomed to just surfing the Internet, getting all the stuff for free. And then there are these other competing interests for the advertising dollar. Do you have any reflections on all this?

Ferguson: No, I don't. I do know that you can't clip the online. Well, maybe you can clip it and mail it to your aunt. But I think newspapers should always be with us. Here's my clippings for the day. (Holds up a pile of articles clipped from papers.)

Hughes: What newspapers do you read every day?

Ferguson: I read *The Seattle Times*, the *Seattle Post Intelligencer*, *The Wall Street Journal*—good paper, too—and *The Kitsap Sun*, and I read *The Washington Times,* which comes once a week. But *The Wall Street Journal*— did you know that was the most liberal paper in the country? I didn't know that. Well, they had a list in another newspaper saying, "These are the most liberal newspapers." First one was *The Wall Street Journal*, other than the editorial pages. And then it's *The New York Times*, *The Washington Post*, *The Los Angeles Times* and all these other newspapers.

Hughes: In your opinion, are the news columns in *The Wall Street Journal* actually punctuated with liberal thought?

Ferguson: No, I don't think they are. See I go through page by page of the whole first section to see what they're doing because I like stuff I can clip. Now they've got three pages of editorial pages, and I check those out pretty carefully. They have stuff in there that no other newspaper even carries. The other day here's Joe Biden telling the world…that there's going to be a big event (if Obama is elected). Something's going to happen to test the mettle of Barack Obama. I never saw that in any other story in my papers. I didn't see it in the AP story or *The Sun;* I didn't see it in *The Seattle Times*. I didn't see it in *The P-I*. Where did he say it, and why didn't anybody else write it?

Hughes: How would you characterize your old newspaper, *The Sun,* today, versus where it was in 1975, in terms of its approach and what it's doing in news coverage?

Ferguson: Well, I think all the newspapers are crazy. For example, *The Times* and *The P-I* are inclined to give you five pages on something—on one subject. I just haven't got the time. It's got to be a really vicious murder for me to go five pages.

Hughes: It's what they call "in-depth reporting."

Ferguson: And then in my own newspaper, I don't find good sharp writing.

Hughes: What reporters working in the Northwest today do your read and admire? Did you like David Postman's stuff in *The Seattle Times*? He's jumped ship to work for Paul Allen now.

Ferguson: Oh has he? He wasn't bad. I think he was a little ahead of himself. I don't think he was as good as some of his predecessors at those newspapers.

Hughes: Do you read Peter Callaghan of *The Tacoma News-Tribune*?

Ferguson: Peter Callaghan is a good writer.

Hughes: How would you rank your old friend David Ammons, who was with the Associated Press for all those years?

Ferguson: He's a finc writer. And, he's a *good* reporter. You could *never* spot any bias, and he is a very nice guy, too.

Hughes: Who was the best reporter you ever worked with in all those years?

Ferguson: Dick Larsen (of *The Seattle Times* and later *The Eastside Journal*).

Hughes: Some of the stuff you've written in recent years has caused a firestorm, or at least a mini-firestorm. Here's this column…

Ferguson: Oh, the one about the blacks?

Hughes: Yeah. You wrote, "The pony hidden in slavery is the fact that it was the ticket to America for black people."

Ferguson: Yeah.

Hughes: You added, "I have long urged blacks to consider their presence here as the work, of God in order to bring them to this raw, new country…."

Ferguson: Why can't I think that?

Hughes: I think you certainly can, but a lot of people found it insensitive at best.

Ferguson: That column got sent all over online. It even ran in Denmark.

Hughes: And, boy, did it ever hit the fan! They accused you of being racist.

Ferguson: I wasn't being racist. I just thought, "Why are they here? How did they get here? Maybe that was the way God had of bringing them here. And would they rather be here now or there?"

Hughes: They wanted your head on a platter.

Ferguson: Oh yeah.

Hughes: Did anybody cancel you over that?

Ferguson: No. I got cancelled by two papers over something else, though.

Hughes: What was that about?

Ferguson: That was when I wrote and said that killing kids—

Hughes: The Palestinian-Israeli thing. I think I've got that here, too. You wrote it in 2002. That column had a really interesting lead: " 'Don't write that,' advised my husband when I told him my solution to bringing an end to the suicide bomber terrorism inflicted on Israel by the

Palestinian Arabs." When did you lose your husband?

Ferguson: He died in 2005. He was 87 years old. He lived five years longer than anybody in his family ever had. He had diabetes. That's what he died from.

Hughes: Did he frequently give you good advice?

Ferguson: Not that much advice. He didn't care that much about what I was writing. But *that* was good advice that time. I should have paid attention to him.

Hughes: You really sort of regret that one?

Ferguson: No, I just wish I had said it differently.

Hughes: And the upshot of that was the notion that one way to really induce peace in the Middle East is to—

Ferguson: Kill their children.

Hughes: You quoted former Israeli Prime Minister Golda Meir as saying, "This won't be settled until they love their children more than they hate Jews." And then you added, "The next time a bunch of Arab youths are throwing rocks at the Israeli tanks, mow them down. Kill them. Keep doing it until the Arabs decide whether they really hate the Jews more than they love their children." I've got all these clippings and e-mails that say this column is real evidence of your racism—that it was a racist screed and that you are fundamentally just an insensitive person. You plead innocent to those charges?

Ferguson: Oh yeah. I'm not a racist.

Hughes: So what do you regret about that? Do you think you could have just said it more deftly?

Ferguson: Yes, I could have done it a little differently.

Hughes: Someone suggested to me that for a lot of years, especially when Gene Gisley was there at *The Sun*, that you had had an editor you really trusted who might have dissuaded you from writing stuff like that. And now that you're—

Ferguson: Well, he didn't run a couple of my columns. He spiked one I wrote criticizing something the City of Bremerton was doing that he had promoted editorially. And he didn't run one about the annual Sigma Delta Chi journalism contest. I said that it wasn't always the best stuff that was chosen. It depended on who was doing the judging.

Hughes: Did Gisley give you good advice over the years?

Ferguson: Yeah, but he didn't really need to advise me. He read the columns. See, I have no editor now. The only editor I get is Bill (Will, of the Washington Newspaper Association) and he doesn't change anything.

Hughes: Bright guy, though.

Ferguson: Yeah, he's a really nice guy, too. I don't have to pay him a dime, you know. He does all this for nothing. I send him a fruitcake every Christmas.

Hughes: One of my favorite things when we were running your column in Aberdeen was that annual Yuletide fruitcake recipe. The readers loved it. Do you have the ingredients for that recipe so that we can make it part of the oral history?

Ferguson: Sure. I used to put it in the column. That is a wonderful fruitcake. And the men in particular love it.

Hughes: It's not the awful kind of fruitcake that you just pass along to someone else or use as a doorstop.

Ferguson: The one reason that many people didn't like fruitcakes and fruitcakes got a bad rep was because everybody puts citron in them. This one has dates and candied pineapples and candied cherries and nuts. That's all.

Hughes: So how did the fruitcake thing start?

Ferguson: Well, actually when I first came to Bremerton there was a guy, Cornish Southerland, standing on the street corner handing out copies of this fruitcake recipe. And I got it and I didn't do anything with it. Then after a while I thought, "Well, God, I should make it." And it was just delicious; just wonderful. So I ran the column and, God, everybody was making the fruitcake. Every year I'd get letters saying, "Oh please print the fruitcake recipe."

Hughes: So it became a perennial.

Ferguson: Oh yeah. And then I had to quit because some people complained, "You shouldn't be putting recipes in the column." I don't know why not. "Dear Abby" does it all the time.

Hughes: People complained?

Ferguson: People on the paper complained.

Hughes: Oh.

Ferguson: Editors are funny people. You know the column that I write that gets the most reaction from my readers? Any time I write about my animals. When I write about the dogs or the cat or any animals around here I just hear about it for weeks. Oh God, how they love that. I've got one written now about the chipmunk that's trying to make love to my cat. There's a chipmunk out here. The cat is sitting out here looking out the door with her nose up against the glass and this chipmunk comes running up, puts his little feet up on the glass next to hers and tries to kiss the door. And the cat goes, WHAM, like this you know.

Hughes: This is the Scarlet Pimpernel? Is that your cat's name?

Ferguson: Yes. She's named that because when we first got her she disappeared into a hole in the wall and we couldn't get her out. She was back by where the water faucets are to the washer. So when she came out eventually we boarded up the hole. She found another hole. Well, when she came out of that one, we boarded it up. There is no place that that cat can't hide. She's always hiding somewhere. Now when you leave, the minute your car goes down the driveway she'll come out. She'll say, "Well, they're gone aren't they?" She's AWOL, by God.

Hughes: You're exactly right. Animals really resonate with people.

Ferguson: Oh yeah. Thomas Friedman, *The New York Times* columnist, wrote one yesterday about his Westie pup dog. Did you read that?

Hughes: No I didn't. But he's really good.

Ferguson: Well, I read that all the way through and almost cried at the end. His dog died in his arms. But those kinds of things…People really *love* that.

Hughes: So besides the fruitcake, were there any other sort of perennial columns that you did over the years?

Ferguson: Well, I always write one about what happens at our Election Day luncheon, how it comes out, how we vote and all this kind of stuff. And I sometimes write one about my annual Christmas party. I do the annual family Christmas party, and it's fun. The kids just *adore* it.

Hughes: You mean here at your house?

Ferguson: Here. Used to have *all* my family, but it got to be too many people. I mean when you get 40, 50 people in here, I never get to sit down for the whole evening.

Hughes: Both the kids and grandchildren? They're all pretty much on the Kitsap Peninsula?

Ferguson: Everybody lives here. Except my brother who I'm close too lives over by Ravensdale in King County and one of my sisters lives over there. I just lost a brother back in Virginia. It's really funny how they go. I'm outliving everybody.

Hughes: Have you done your genealogy? Is there longevity in that Scotch-Norwegian heritage?

Ferguson: I'm not sure. See, my father died at 65, my brother died at 42. And my mother died at 79.

Hughes: What do you do for fun? I see that you're doing crossword puzzles and jigsaw puzzles.

Ferguson: Oh, well, I do everything. I go to stuff, but only in daytime. I don't go to night stuff because I don't want to come home in the dark.

Hughes: Why is that?

Ferguson: Well because I don't have any neighbors. And I get mean letters from people. People telling me I ought to be put to death. Oh yeah, I get nasty things.

Hughes: Was there ever a time in all your years in reporting and column writing where you felt that any of those threats were the real thing?

Ferguson: I don't know. I never worried a lot.

Hughes: Looking back on this fascinating life, what really just annoys the rods out of you?

Ferguson: One tiny thing that annoys me is that any time the president or another important person is going to speak they give an advance copy to the media. And the goddamn media will tell you everything that's in it before the guy even gets up in front of the microphone. That just irritates the hell out of me! I don't want the announcer to say the president is going to tell me this and this and this. Just let *him* tell me!

Hughes: Here's a veteran newspaper woman, reporter and columnist, and a lot times you've really been annoyed with your own profession.

Ferguson: Oh yeah, a lot of times. You bet.

Hughes: Because you're so easy to talk to and people enjoy being around you, did you ever sort of say to your colleagues, "Gee, guys, why do you keep doing this stuff?"

Ferguson: I've written so many columns there can't be anything I haven't written about. I was writing a column the other day about the difference between the kind of questions that these mainstreamers will ask the Republican and the ones they'll ask the Democrat. To the Democrat they'll say, "Well, Mr. Obama, which job did you enjoy the most—being a lecturer at Harvard or signing up voters?" And then they'll turn around to the Republican and say, "Mr. McCain, what's the worst thing you ever did in your life that you're the most ashamed of?" You know what I mean? See how they do it? The other day they had a "Campaign '08" special section in either *The P-I* or *The Times*. On this side they had a story about McCain, and on this side they had a story about Obama. On this side they had eight mentions of McCain and seven mentions of Obama in the same Associated Press story. On this side they had 17 mentions of Obama and two mentions of McCain. Now, you can't tell me that that isn't bias.

Hughes: Where does that spring from?

Ferguson: It springs from the fact that these people are I suppose from the '60s. I don't know But they've got an inbred hatred of conservatives. And I am a conservative. I may not be a total Republican, but I'm a conservative.

Hughes: You're certainly not a litmus test conservative.

Ferguson: No. I'm not.

Hughes: As you pointed out earlier, you're pro-choice.

Ferguson: Yeah. And I was for that little boy in Florida, Elian Gonzalez, being given back to his father in Cuba in 2000.*

Hughes: Did you write about that?

Ferguson: Oh yeah, you bet. You know what I got the most letters on of all the columns? I got over one hundred letters when I was against the rifle deal—about whether people should be allowed to buy those fancy rifles. I said I was opposed to it. And damn near all of the letters were opposed to me.

Hughes: So that was a gun-control issue, and the "fancy" rifles—you mean like high-powered rifles?

Ferguson: Well, the kind that they kill people with.

Hughes: Armor-piercing bullets and all that?

Ferguson: Yeah, I got over a hundred letters.

Hughes: That doesn't surprise me at all, having done journalism in a hunting and fishing area. So you don't want to disarm people, but you don't see why they need bazookas and armor-piercing bullets?

Ferguson: I have guns. I've killed six deer.

Hughes: When you think back on your career, what's the most memorable part? As a storyteller and observer, how would you sum it up?

Ferguson: I don't know, except that when I got ready to retire in 1993, I thought, "Boy this is going to be great to not have any deadlines to meet any more." And I'm still doing it. But I like to write.

Hughes: So you're writing every day?

Ferguson: No, not necessarily, but I'm sure writing when I have to.

Hughes: And how many columns a week?

Ferguson: Three.

---

* The custody and immigration status of the young Cuban boy was a heated controversy involving the governments of Cuba and the U.S., the boy's father, Elian's relatives in Cuba and Florida, and the Cuban-American community in Miami. A district court's ruling that the Miami relative could not petition for asylum on the boy's behalf was upheld by the courts, and Elian returned to Cuba to live with his father.

Hughes: How many columns do you figure you've written since 1965?

Ferguson: I tried to figure that out because I don't remember when I stopped writing five and started writing three.

Hughes: But if you extrapolate it and you include The Farmer's Daughter columns…

Ferguson: Not counting The Farmer's Daughter. I couldn't figure out where to start.

Hughes: So, 1965 you started out doing five, and the least you've ever done is three. From 1965 to present, 43 years.

Ferguson: Yeah. I was still writing down in Olympia, and Gene Grisley was the editor when I went to three.

Hughes: I'll figure it out. We'll come up with an estimate. What other things do you like to do when you're not researching or writing the column?

Ferguson: Well, I use to crochet. I've crocheted many beautiful, gorgeous afghans. And I drew. My husband was a fine painter. These two pictures on the wall here are by his grandmother. I'm a collector. I collect many, many things. I used to do a lot of gardening and outdoor work, and I used to like to hike, but I can't do all that so much any more. I wish I could. And I like to write. I love to read. I work jigsaw puzzles.

Hughes: What is there about jigsaw puzzles?

Ferguson: I don't know, but I'm really good at it. I can leave the room and come back and find *exactly* the piece I'm looking for.

Hughes: What does that tell us about this mind of yours?

Ferguson: I don't know. If I had to choose between booze and jigsaw puzzles I would have a *hard* time. I drink every day.

Hughes: What do you drink these days?

Ferguson: McNaughton's and water.

Hughes: Have you run into meddlesome physicians over the years who tell you not to do that?

Ferguson: Some of them, when I had my eye operation for cataracts.

Hughes: You've got the eyes of a 30-year-old, Adele.

Ferguson: Really? Oh good. When I had that operation, my directions said no drinking the night before the operation. So I said to my doctor, "How come I can't drink?" He said, "What do you mean you can't drink?" I said, "Well, you told me to ask the anesthesiologist whether I could drink and he said I couldn't." And the doctor said, "Well, I'm countermanding that right now. You can drink." So I did, and I thought, "Well he didn't think it would hurt me any." I don't drink too much. I don't get drunk. Sometimes I just drink one; sometimes two, but sometimes three, depending on how long it takes to make dinner.

Hughes: And you're cooking for yourself. John's gone now.

Ferguson: And I'm not going anywhere in my car.

Hughes: I keep saying "John," but you called your husband "Phil."

Ferguson: Yeah, I call him "Phil." Sometimes people called him "Whitey" and "Blondie." That's what they called him when he was in the Navy.

Hughes: Have you spent any time around young Tim Eyman, the initiative king?

Ferguson: He calls me constantly. And he's a guy who's on the phone for 40 minutes at a crack.

Hughes: What is that like?

Ferguson: Well, I just have to sit and listen to him. I like him. He's very smart.

Hughes: Do you think that he's just gone overboard with all these initiatives?

Ferguson: I think he is a little overboard on this latest one (opening car-pool lanes during some hours and synchronizing traffic lights). I think he's almost reached the point where he's doing it because it's a way of living for him now. I still have great suspicions of the people in power who will do anything to stay in power. I think voting by mail is kind of easy to meddle with.

Hughes: Have you ever thought about doing a book?

Ferguson: Oh, I know, but it takes time.

Hughes: I know. But history could use what you've seen. I'm sure you've read Gordon Newell's book, "Rogues, Buffoons and Statesmen." It ends in the early 1970s. Someone needs to bring that history of the Legislature and Olympia up to date. Don Brazier's books are really good, but you could make things more colorful.

Ferguson: Yeah, yeah, yeah. I've thought of printing copies of my columns.

Hughes: I think that would be a great idea. I'm surprised that you haven't done that already.

Ferguson: I've got them. I've got them all.

Hughes: It's easier than ever before because when you print a book today with modern technology you don't have to print 20,000 copies.

Ferguson: Some of those are really good columns. Not just the ones on politics but on other things. I thought one really funny one I wrote was when a guy—actually he was one of my sons-in-law at the time—he wanted a special bottle of wine. So I called the liquor store to find out if I could get this special bottle of wine. It goes like this—of course I don't remember the actual names of the wines. But they said, "Well we don't have Ansenhauersnickenbottled, but we do have Snickebookiehockeybuck." And I'd say, "No I think Ansenhauersnickenbottled is what we have." "Well, now there's Solumottlesnakinbrackin." And it just got funnier and funnier as it went with these people trying to get this *damn* bottle of wine.

Hughes: Share with us some tricks of the trade that you learned over the years as a writer. Things you fall back on invariably.

Ferguson: Always know the names of the secretaries of the people you want to talk to. So you call up. You want to talk to mayor so and so. You find out that his secretary's name is. Let's say it's Betty. You say, "Hi Betty, Adele here. How about the boss?" If you treat them like equals—treat them so that you know who they are, so they're real people and not just on the staff—they'll kill themselves to help you.

Hughes: And if you're covering education, always get to know the janitor and the school secretary. They know *everything*. Do you have any kind of interview techniques to put people at ease? You're famous for asking blunt questions. Do you think people really appreciate that?

Ferguson: Not if you ask them too blunt a question. Then they don't appreciate it.

Hughes: Know when to hold 'em and fold 'em. Know when to be blunt and when to be more soothing. Is that it?

Ferguson: Somebody told me the last time I was on a panel with the Association of Washington Business, and I asked the question afterward, "How come nobody else asked questions?" And the guy said, "Would you? If you were out here, you wouldn't ask another question if somebody like you was going to answer them." They felt I was *too* honest I guess, or too mean. I don't know what it was. But I say what I think.

Hughes: Did you ever get to interview any presidents?

Ferguson: Oh yeah. Let's see—I talked to John Kennedy. As a matter of fact I had an awful time trying to get a picture of him. Once I was doing the pictures as well as writing the story, and they were parking his car at the airport right in front of me.

Hughes: John F. Kennedy?

Ferguson: Yep. Every time I'd get my camera up one of the FBI guys would come over and stand right in front of me. Right in front of me!

Hughes: Was he president then?

Ferguson: Yeah. And I'd move, and the guy would move, and I'd move here and the guy would move. I finally said to Kennedy, "Would you make him stop that?!"

Hughes: Where was this Adele?

Ferguson: Seattle, SeaTac, I think.

Hughes: Did you get to talk to him?

Ferguson: Just briefly. When he comes through in the line you can talk to him, ask him a quick question but I don't remember anything about that. I do remember this: It was when he came through to go that baseball field in Tacoma. I was down there, and Sen. Frances Haddon Morgan from Kitsap County was there, too. Her mother, Lulu Haddon, had also served in the House and Senate. Frances was a big heavyset lady who was in the Senate for a long time. She had her granddaughter with her. So she's standing in the crowd. So just as John F. Kennedy comes by with his bodyguard, she reaches out, grabs his arm, pulls it forward, puts her granddaughter's hand in his and shakes their hands together. She said, "I wanted my granddaughter to shake hands with the president." I thought those Secret Service guys were going to kill her. Kennedy just laughed, but it wasn't long after that he was shot. You know he was shot right after he'd been here.

Hughes: So who else? Did you talk to President Clinton?

Ferguson: No. But I talked to Gerald Ford. I also talked to Jack Kemp and Nelson Rockefeller.

Hughes: Best interview you ever did?

Ferguson: I don't know. I just don't think about it in those terms

Hughes: You said something earlier to the effect when you're a reporter that usually once it's done, it's over.

Ferguson: It really is.

Hughes: Do I summarize correctly that you believe Dan Evans is by far and away the best governor we've had on your watch?

Ferguson: I hate to say that while Al Rosellini is still alive. I can say that Dan Evans and Al Rosellini were the best.

Hughes: Have you been around those two when they've been together?

Ferguson: No, not that much, on a rare occasion. But I've been on the panels that ask them questions—one time when they had this panel over in Eastern Washington. I was invited to come over and they were going to do Evans and Rosellini. I was told that I was the only reporter picked by both sides to be on the panel. I was told the Evans people said, "Well, geez, you know she's going to jump all over you about such and such." And they said, "Yeah, but she'll get all over him (Rosellini), too."

Hughes: So you always tried to be—what did John Spellman say—that she was "mean sometimes, but fair"?

Ferguson: I always tried to be fair.

Hughes: Well, we're winding down today. Tell me about how this place where you live came to be called Hansville?

Ferguson: I got tired of living near Seabeck because most of the people who lived there were old timers and did not welcome anybody who hadn't been there a hundred years like they had. So I thought, "Let's get out of this place." I began reading the papers. Looked at *The Seattle Times* houses-for-sale section.

Hughes: What year was that?

Ferguson: 1965. So I kept reading the ads for houses and I saw this one up here: "150 feet of waterfront home," the ad said. And I thought, "Gee, that really sounds good." I wanted to get away from my folks, and they lived right next door practically. So I drove up on my lunch hour at noon the very next day. I worked until my deadline, which was 11 o'clock.

Hughes: So how long does it take to get here from *The Sun* (newspaper offices in Bremerton)?

Ferguson: Forty-five minutes. So I came up here and these people were living here. It turned out they had leased the place with an option to buy at the end of one year. The year had gone by and they had decided to try and get it cheaper than 27,000 bucks, so they dallied. And the owner got tired of it. He advertised. I answered. All my life I'd wanted an emerald ring. I went down on the beach and found a green plastic ring out of some kind of a toy box or something, and I picked it up and I thought, "That's some kind of a sign." That ring tells me that I want this. And it was beautiful here! So I went back and I told my husband, "We have to have that place!" We didn't have any money, but we did have another place over near Poulsbo that was kind of on the water, so we put that up and went to the bank. Of course, we always paid our bills. My folks never paid anybody. I was the kid who had to go out and tell the bill collector they weren't home…

Hughes: In 1966, I was earning $78.50 a week for a five-and-a-half-day week as a cub reporter with *The Aberdeen Daily World*. Were you doing a lot better than that on *The Sun*?

Ferguson: *Oh no*, I wasn't doing a lot better than that. *The Bremerton*

Sun didn't pay that highly, and I had even been there for quite a while. So anyway, we told them we'd take the place. And we scratched up the down payment, which was twenty-five hundred bucks or something. And about this time the people who were in here decided they didn't want to leave. They told the owner, "Now we're ready to sign. We want to exercise our option to buy the place." The owner says, "You're too late. You should have done it when the year was up." Well, they wouldn't get out of the house. So they set a date for the house to be vacated and for us to get in. Phil and I drove up every night from out by Seabeck just to look at our house. We did this for I bet a month and a half, two months, waiting to get these people out of here. Well, finally the day came. We loaded our furniture onto a U-Haul truck and came up, and they're still in our house! But the owner of the house and the real estate agent told them it was time to go. We passed each other in the doorway. I mean they're bringing stuff out, and we're bringing stuff in.

Hughes: It wasn't "God bless you and have a wonderful life"?

Ferguson: Oh, they were just furious. But not too much later, their daughter got in some trouble at school. She was accused of something that she didn't do. Falsely accused. And somebody told them to come talk to me because I would write about it. They came and talked to me, and I wrote about it and the daughter got off. Then we were friends. (laughter)

In any case, we moved into the house and were madly in love with the house and have been ever since. All the people up and down where I live here are former University of Washington faculty members. At one time somebody put on a big sales pitch at the UW and a whole bunch of these people bought all these houses up and down here. And they just came over on holidays or for the summer or something. So we were all alone up here.

Hughes: Is that Point No Point down there where the lighthouse is?

Ferguson: Yeah, that's Point No Point. This is Foulweather Bluff up here at the other end.

Hughes: Do you know the derivation of "Hansville"?

Ferguson: Nah, I did once but I don't really care. I suppose Hans must have settled it....*

Hughes: So how many people live here?

Ferguson: I don't know. There's a gang of them now.

Hughes: Here you are in this wonderful place overlooking Puget Sound.

Ferguson: Admiralty Inlet.

Hughes: We're at the northern tip of the Kitsap Peninsula?

Ferguson: Yeah. Skunk Bay.

Hughes: Has anybody over the years made any funny metaphors on that—"Adele Ferguson is still writing columns at Skunk Bay"?

Ferguson: No. (smiling) And across the road here I own 20 acres. Mount Baker is straight across from me. So is Whidbey Island.

Hughes: So do you get to Olympia much these days?

Ferguson: Not much anymore.

Hughes: There's all these clippings here, and you listen to the radio and you watch TV. What are you writing columns about today?

Ferguson: Well, let's see, what did I write about last week? I can't recall.

Hughes: Sometimes I couldn't remember, either. Isn't that awful?

Ferguson: Yeah, people say to me, "Gee I really liked your column this week." I say, "What was it about?"

Hughes: That is the most horrible feeling. I'm so glad you said that. There were times I'd think, "My God, am I losing it? But you write so many and you can't remember what they are. And you're moving on to something else all the time.

Ferguson: And once you put it behind you, it's behind you. The last one I wrote was about an old newspaper friend of mine who once told me that in the year of the Great Depression in 1929, her devout Catholic, widowed mother got a phone call from her priest saying, "Go down to the bank immediately and take out all your money." But she couldn't find her girdle so she didn't go and put it off until the next day. And the next day the bank didn't open!

---

* Hansville is named for Hans Zachariasen, one of the first settlers, in the 1880s.

Hughes: Well, here's a column you wrote just the other day— "Candidates Long on Talk, Short on Substance." So there you go. Some things never change?

Ferguson: Yeah. That's from this year.

Hughes: Was there a question that you really want to answer that you wish I'd had the wit to ask?

Ferguson: No. Are you coming back, or are you done? You're going to sit down and wonder where the holes are?

Hughes: Yeah, exactly. I haven't had so much fun in a long time.

Ferguson: I'll probably think of some more funny stories!

ADELE FERGUSON INTERVIEWS
November 13, 2008

Hughes: We're back with Adele Ferguson at her Hansville home. Wiccy and Daisy, her dogs, are under foot, and The Scarlett Pimpernel, a tabby, is around here someplace.

Ferguson: Under the bed.

Hughes: Under the bed again. Well, we're almost done transcribing the first part and you were talking about someone we couldn't identify from the tape—*The Seattle P-I* reporter who resented you when you arrived at the Capitol in 1961.

Ferguson: It was Stub Nelson. He was the guy I told you about who got the nose bleeds. Whenever he got very stressed and was just up to here not knowing what to do to next, he got nosebleeds.

Hughes: So it was Stub Nelson who got snotty with you when you inadvertently sat in his chair?

Ferguson: Yes, yes.

Hughes: Do you know Stub's real name?

Ferguson: I never heard he ever had one. Everybody called him Stub.

Hughes: That's a great name for a reporter. Later on did you and Stub make amends?

Ferguson: Oh yeah. But for a long time none of them, except Leroy

Hittle, would even speak to me. They thought I was just playing around. You know what I mean? Leroy was the AP guy. Everybody loved Leroy. And he helped me so much; he just took me under his wing. We used to have these little cubicles all down the wall, and Leroy's office was here. He gave me one on the end so I'd be closest to him. Stub was in there too because there wasn't that much room. But eventually, even though I didn't get along with these guys very well, eventually I was one of the ones who wrote the rules for how the press had to behave. Well, they named me and I forget who else—Bill Mertena of the AP maybe—to write rules. Did you know Mertena?

Hughes: I did. Good guy.

Ferguson: Bill Mertena, incidentally, hated "GOP." He just had fits when anybody used "GOP" for Republicans in a story. Didn't bother me none. I thought one of the reasons they use GOP, because in the headline it's shorter.

Hughes: Sure, "Dems" and" GOP."

Ferguson: I use Rs and Ds sometimes. After I've used the other, of course.

Hughes: So how long did it take for the ice to melt with the guys at the Capitol in Olympia?

Ferguson: A couple of months—two, three months.

Hughes: But that wasn't true with any of your sources?

Ferguson: Oh no, no, no. Most of my sources to begin with were lobbyists.

Hughes: How did your annual Election Day luncheon go on Nov. 4?

Ferguson: Well, we did have some stellar guests at the Silverdale Yacht Club Broiler. We used to have it other places, wherever we could hold enough people. But Gordon Walgren and I are the hosts. For some years it's just been the two of us, and Ralph Munro. Many times both he and Gordon have picked up the tab for the whole thing. One of them paid for the booze and one of them paid for the food. Everybody's hopeful that they'll do it again. (laughs) But anyway, Gordon and I meet and then we decide who to invite. It's by invitation. Although enough people hear about it and want to come that if they ask us, and they aren't too rotten, we'll say, "Just drop by." But there are some people we leave out of it because *other* people there don't like them. We don't embarrass people by having somebody they hate come to the luncheon. But this last time we had 40 names. I said to Gordon, "I've got so many here, and I want to be sure we have some Republicans." See I generally look at the Republicans, and Gordon looks at the Democrats. He says, "I think that you're getting ahead of me. I've got to get more Democrats in here." I said, "Well, I don't care." Dick Marquardt, the former insurance commissioner and ex-legislator, calls me every once in a while. And last year when he called me, it was after our luncheon, I said, "Why don't you come next year to our luncheon on Election Day?" "I will," he said. I said, "OK." So this year he said, "You remind me." So this year I told him, "Now remember the luncheon is noonish at the Silverdale Yacht Club Broiler, and it lasts a couple hours. And you have to pay for your own lunch." So he said, "OK." And then he calls back, he said, "You know, I don't want to drive over there all by myself. I'm going to ask Jimmy Andersen to come with me." Jimmy is a for-mer Supreme Court Justice, old friend of mine. I love the guy. Wonderful guy. Then he called me back and he said, "I decided we'd ask Dan Evans to come." And Dan came. Andersen was a great friend of Gordon's too. Andersen and Gordon put together a package of crime bills in the Senate. I think Andersen defended Gordon. I can't remember whether or not he testified, but he defended Gordon in his "Gamscam" thing. I also invited an old friend of mine who was a federal judge. That's Bob Bryan. He was here in Kitsap. He was Dan Evans' chair for his campaign one time. This year, after most everybody was gone, Bob and Gordon and a few other people stayed behind. And Bob said something about, "I was glad to see Dan. After all, Dan named me to the Superior Court. He came over and asked me how would I like to be a judge?" And I said, "Well, you know, Bob, my recollection of that was that the second time, or whatever, they asked you to be the chairman of his campaign for governor, you turned him down. And you didn't get that appointment to the court when it was open. Later on you got one." Bob says, "Oh no, that's not the way it was. He came over and offered me the appointment, and I took the appointment. (Bryan was a Superior Court Judge before he became a U.S. District Judge.) And so I said, "I remember very clearly that you didn't get it when you were supposed to get it." Well, he denied that, you know. But everybody at the table said, "I like your version of it best, Adele!"

Hughes: The luncheon was on Election Day. What was the consensus on the outcome of the election?

Ferguson: There were only four of us who went for McCain. And I said, "Who are the other three people here?" And I knew Marquardt was one of them, but he didn't put his hand up. Earlier, he told me on the phone, "McCain is going to win this because of the 'Bradley Factor.'" And I said, "Well, I keep hearing that there never was a Bradley Factor." I mean they just say that people tell people they're going to vote for the black guy, but they're not going to do it.

Hughes: Ralph Munro was a strong McCain backer, wasn't he?

Ferguson: Oh yeah. McCain came to Bremerton and drew one of the biggest crowds you ever saw in Bremerton.

Hughes: Did you really think that McCain could still pull it out?

Ferguson: Well, I hoped so. And I thought, by golly, this guy (Obama) has got no more experience than a freshman in high school to come in here and want to be president. But let me say, too, that while I liked Sarah Palin, she doesn't have any more experience to be president either, and I think she's making a big mistake now to keep shooting her mouth off about maybe running for president in '12. I think that's a big mistake. I think what she ought to say is, "Well, we'll see how things look then." I thought, "Don't do that." Now you're laying it out there, and now Bobby Jindal and these other guys are going to look upon her as being too pushy.

Hughes: Bobby Jindal, the governor of Louisiana, is a very impressive young man.

Ferguson: Isn't he? I really like him.

Hughes: So this is quite a luncheon you had. There's Dan Evans, and Gordon Walgren, and Jimmy Andersen, and Dick Marquardt—

Ferguson: And Ralph Munro, and bunch of county officials and ex-county officials, and ex-mayors, and ex-legislators. Betti Sheldon was there. She was at the center of one of our biggest mistakes. When she was running for the Legislature against Ellen Craswell, we all voted on who we thought would win. We voted almost unanimously that Ellen Craswell was just going to whip the crap out of Betti Sheldon. And Betti burst into tears and left the luncheon. So we never did that again.

Hughes: What was the outcome? Did Ellen win?

Ferguson: No, Betti won! (laughs uproariously) We tell that story frequently at the lunch.

Hughes: You said one of the things you really wanted to talk about today was your old friend Clyde Ballard, the Republican from East Wenatchee who became speaker of the House in 1995. (Ballard was Speaker for two terms before sharing the speakership with Democrat Frank Chopp in the wake of a 49-49 tie.)

Ferguson: Clyde was one of the most decent guys who ever served in the Legislature He and his wife operated an ambulance service.

Hughes: Tell me more about Clyde.

Ferguson: Well, Clyde and his wife did not drink. I forget who started this, but the tradition was that the Speaker of the House would have the press in once a week and pour the drinks and have peanuts and stuff.

Hughes: Is this the so-called "Committee Room X"?

Ferguson: No, you'd get your hair cut in Committee Room X and you'd get a drink while you're in there. Room X was on the third floor of the House up in the corner. And they had a guy—Rep. Ralph C. "Brigham" Young—who was a barber. They had cases of beer up there and stuff. I could always tell when my legislators had been there because they always fell asleep after they came back down.

Hughes: So you could get a haircut and a Budweiser from "Brigham" Young!

Ferguson: Let's see, who's the chairman of the Transportation Committee in the Senate?

Hughes: Mary Margaret Haugen.

Ferguson: Is she a hairdresser?

Hughes: I don't know.

Ferguson: Well, she cut my hair a few times.…You couldn't get out to go downtown. She cut in the women's lounge.

Hughes: I got you off the topic of Clyde Ballard.

Ferguson: He didn't drink; his wife didn't drink. But I told him the social hour was a good idea. "This really works out well," I said. "It gets the press together for about an hour with the speaker and we can talk just off the record unless you want it to be on the record." And it sort of breaks the ice between these two groups of people. This was weekly. And so then the question was how was Clyde going to do that when he didn't drink? Well, then he concluded that he certainly didn't have to drink. They got all their booze from lobbyists, you know. They didn't have to pay for it. So Clyde and Ruth would go ahead, and they started having the weekly meetings. He and Ruth were absolutely terrific. Ruth never was paid for what she did. She just ran his office and took care of everything. She was great, absolutely great, and Clyde was too. I called them quite a bit after they left the Legislature.

Hughes: Here is a series of really good columns you wrote starting in February of 1967 talking about Tom Copeland and Speaker Don Eldridge, and "What power really means in Legislative Circles." I don't know much about Tom Copeland, one of the Republican leaders of that era.

Ferguson: Tom Copeland was a very wealthy farmer. He raised peas, and he did a *lot* of behind-the-scenes manipulating.

Hughes: And he lost to Don Eldridge for Speaker, then ended up running the House, the business end of it.

Ferguson: Yeah, and he was good at it.

Hughes: Eldridge won the speakership in 1967, with the help of the Evans' Republican Coalition. And you did a really good column here headlined, "Some have misjudged Speaker Don Eldridge." "Don Eldridge has fooled a lot of people this session," you wrote. "He's a lot tougher than they thought he was going to be. And he's going to fool a lot more people before it's over." Tell me more about him.

Ferguson: He was a good friend. I admired him. He was a very smart guy. He and I used to meet and have lunch together after he left the Legislature (and was appointed to the Liquor Control Board by Dan Evans). He'd call me up and I'd go down to Olympia and we'd sit and shoot the breeze. He and I were friends, and I got along with most of the House speakers pretty good, although I got irked at Joe King. I shouldn't even say this, but I will anyway—what the hell. When Joe King was speaker, he had the booze receptions. And here we are in this room full of people—reporters and all, and everybody was eating the peanuts and drinking the booze. So Joe says, "We are going to pass the state income tax in this session."

And I said, "No, you're not."

He said, "What do you want to bet?"

I said, "Well, what do you want to bet?"

He said, "I'll bet you a bottle of good booze that we will pass the state income tax in this session." Put it on the ballot, you know.

I said, "OK, I'll take the bet." Well of course we didn't. I never got the booze.

Hughes: I don't think in our lifetimes we're going to see Washingtonians approve an income tax, do you?

Ferguson: Not when it has to go through them. They just aren't going to do it.

Hughes: Gov. Evans made the best run I've ever seen. He made logical presentations on why it would be fairer, but the electorate wasn't buying it. (Sorting through copies of her columns) You say you've got all of these columns indexed, Adele?

Ferguson: Yeah.

Hughes: Are they in scrapbooks?

Ferguson: They're up there in books, page by page. See, this is my columns indexed.

Hughes: How far back does that go?

Ferguson: Back to the beginning—1965.

Hughes: And so you painstakingly kept a copy of each column, put it in a scrapbook?

Ferguson: Some of them are missing because I took them out to use and then didn't put them back, but not very many.

Hughes: So what's your technique here in terms of indexing?

Ferguson: It's alphabetical. And then I have other books that list each category, and then the numbers and the dates for the columns.

Hughes: You've got good handwriting. Did you develop shorthand, your own kind of shorthand?

Ferguson: No. But I used to love to watch Richard Larsen, *The Seattle Times* reporter. He took all his notes about half and half. He'd do half real shorthand and the other half just notes. He was a great guy, and a true gentleman, Mr. Larsen was.

Hughes: At The Legacy Project, We did some research on two interesting Kitsap legislators, Lulu Haddon, and her daughter Frances Haddon Morgan, who was in the House and Senate for 10 years from 1959-69. Apparently Lulu Haddon, the mom, who was in the House and Senate from 1933-42, was something of a trailblazer in her own right.

Ferguson: Oh sure. Lulu was Finance Commissioner of Bremerton once. Lulu was very political, and so was Frances. Frances was something else. She cried her bills into existence. If she had a bill that she wanted, and they didn't want to help her get it out of committee she just let tears go by the bucket. And when they made her chairman of one of the committees, anybody who got a bill put in there that required the parents or caretakers of retarded kids to contribute to their care, by money, you never saw that bill again. She put it in her purse and it *never came out.*

Hughes: Did she have a developmentally disabled child?

Ferguson: Grandchild. One time she hid out. For two or three days they couldn't find her, and they needed her to help get a bill out. But she told me later, "You know, I was in the grocery store one of those days, and

Jim Dolliver (Evans' chief of staff) walked in and saw me in there. And he just looked at me and acted like he didn't see me." (laughs) You know what the Evans' people did? They liked her because they knew that what she did wasn't for *her*. It was for those who can't speak for themselves. And so they put her on the Canal Commission in order to give her enough years to get a pension. But in the end she didn't get a pension. When Dixy was governor, Frances went into the governor's office one day to rest. They've got these couches out in the waiting area, and she sat down to rest her feet. And the girls who worked in there, one of them came over and asked her what she was doing there. And she said, "Well, I'm just here to see people. And I was tired so I thought I'd come here and rest my feet." And she said they made it very plain to her that the couches were not for people to rest their feet. So after that, Ralph Munro, the secretary of state, got a great big armchair and put a metal tag on it that said, "This chair belongs to Frances Haddon Morgan." He put it in his outer office. And Frances, when she was tired, would go sit in Ralph's office and rest her feet.

Hughes: What a remarkable guy.

Ferguson: Yeah, really, and you know he wasn't popular with Republicans. Isn't that odd?

Hughes: It is odd.

Ferguson: Democrats loved him. He worked hard for the older people, for the retarded kids, for *anybody*! Ralph gave me that clock up there; that red clock. It came from Russia. And when he came to the luncheon the other day, he brought me a bouquet of flowers. He's that kind of a guy.

Hughes: Any other really memorable characters from over the years?

Ferguson: Oh there were lots of them. Rep. Bud Kalich, of course, was a wonderful guy.

Hughes: A rare popular Democrat from Lewis County—ex-fighter pilot.

Ferguson: I went down there and went elk hunting with him. He had an old ranch or farm down there, with old apple trees. And he wanted to preserve these old types of apples that they don't sell anymore.

Hughes: Heirloom apples.

Ferguson: Yeah, that was one of his things.

Hughes: You know, Adele, you really need to do something about these dogs of yours. They're so savage. (Dogs are nuzzling interviewer's crotch.) What kind of dog is Wiccy?

Ferguson: Labrador.

Hughes: I've never been around a Labrador that is this sweet—the face, the eyes, her beautiful whiskers. How did Wiccy come to be called "Wiccy"? Are you fond of the Wiccans?

Ferguson: No, I did it because she was such a problem to me. See, when I first got her my daughter had picked her up by the side of the road someplace. And she had her for a week or so. My daughter picks up all those dogs and finds homes for them. So she brought her out here and gave her to me. And she would run off. She was always down at the road looking for whoever dumped her off. And when a car would go by, sometimes she'd chase it. I knew she was going to get killed. So I paid a thousand to have this fence put in all the way around to keep her in. I never saw a stray I didn't pick up if I could catch it.

Hughes: What's the most difficult column you've had to write—just really a gut-wrencher?

Ferguson: I don't know. I'm pretty good at writing when people die. The one I wrote about Paul Conner, everybody just loved that one. Paul was in the Legislature from the 24th District for more than 30 years. *Nobody* ever wrote some of the stuff I wrote. Bob Schaefer, you know, he was Speaker of the House, he was a foundling. Did you know that?

Hughes: I didn't.

Ferguson: He was left in a basket on the doorstep someplace. I don't know if it was a home or an orphanage or something like that, down in Vancouver. And I wrote a whole column saying, "Isn't it too bad that somewhere there are a couple of people who don't know that the baby they left on that doorstep became the Speaker of the House of Representatives.

Hughes: You were here when the legendary Tyee Motel at Tumwater burned in 1970?

Ferguson: Yeah, but I didn't stay at the Tyee.

Hughes: Quite a watering hole for the legislative crowd wasn't it?

Ferguson: Yeah, there were a lot of trysts, you might say, out there. Incidentally, I wanted to mention now that we've got President-Elect Barack Obama, that State Rep. Sam Smith, a black man from Seattle, stayed at the Olympian Hotel, as I did, in the 1960s. And at least once during every session, he'd have a party for all the black people from around the state—you know 40, 50 people. And I was the only press person who was invited. You never saw people so dressed up in your life. I mean they'd wear the most *gorgeous* dresses and jewels and furs. Just looked *great*. And they were nice people. We all had a good time. Sam would go down in the House restaurant and get a paper plate or two and then he'd heap lunch meat on it, so he'd have that for hors d'oeuvres to take it to the party.

Hughes: I'm curious about your opinion on term limits. Helen Sommers who has been there for 36 years is now retiring. She is currently the state's longest serving legislator.

Ferguson: She was a *good* legislator, but I think that we will never be able to do anything about Congress without term limits. Because you've got people like Barney Frank and Chris Dodd, who screwed up Fannie Mae and so forth, who are now writing the legislation and conducting the hearings to do something about that mess. That's crazy! I always felt that in Congress, the senators should be allowed two terms and the House members six terms or 12 years. And you couldn't go from one to the other. And then when it comes to the state Legislature, I think often about the people who have been there that you really miss. Lt. Gov. John Cherberg, who served for 32 years, was a hell of a guy. He was one of my best friends down there.

Hughes: Have you been down to Olympia lately?

Ferguson: Not lately.

Hughes: So you're doing the classic thing of the 21st Century, working from home. You're clipping articles and reading and writing but you're not doing it with computers or using the Internet?

Ferguson: Well, I had a computer made for me, but I only wanted it to take my column and let me get the column out and run it though a printer. And I had a fax machine. And the reason I do that is because if anything goes wrong with my machine, which it does once in a while, I've got nobody to fix it. I am the most un-mechanical person that ever lived. You know who fixes my machine? Bruce Craswell, Ellen's husband. He and Ellen once invited me to lunch at their house, and the other guests were their pastor and his wife. And so we just sat and shot the breeze. I'm telling you, we sat there all afternoon. They were just enthralled hearing my stories.

Hughes: I'll bet they were! And Ellen was a true believer, a naïf. She must have just been stunned to hear some of this colorful insider stuff you talk about.

Ferguson: Yeah. And I should say, too, that I admired Ellen. Ellen was great. But Sen. Phil Talmadge, a Democrat from the 34th District (1979-1991) couldn't stand Ellen—not as a person, but for the way she was—the fact that she wouldn't vote for the tax increases and all this kind of stuff.

Hughes: Tell me about Phil Talmadge.

Ferguson: Well, I liked Phil. One day we were in Cherberg's office. Phil never had drinks in there, but he'd come in. I don't know if he was a drinker or not, but he didn't drink in there. He came in one day when I'd had two or three. So I said, "You know, Phil, do you realize that every time you stand up to speak most of the people at the press table put down their pens?" He said, "Why?" I said, "You're the world's greatest expert on everything. You speak on every topic, on every issue, and while you do know something about them, you're too widespread. Why don't you stick to things you *really* know well, and then everybody will look *forward* to hearing you speak." He thanked me. And for I guess two or three days he did keep his mouth shut but he broke loose after that.

Hughes: He's a really bright guy, isn't he?

Ferguson: He is. He really is.

Hughes: He had a very interesting career on the Supreme Court too, didn't he?

Ferguson: Yeah, and left voluntarily. He didn't get beaten. I'm not sure what he's up to now.

Hughes: In your wildest imagination, after all that you saw there, having a front row seat, did it enter your mind that it would be interesting to be in the Legislature yourself?

Ferguson: No, I never wanted to be in the Legislature. I never wanted to be on-call to people. I never wanted to be where people would call you and you had to be nice to them. My husband and I both made several trips with Lt. Gov. Cherberg on his trade missions; pay your own way and everything. But we went on these trips and I had to be nice. Most of the other people on the trips were legislators, and some lobbyists, and some business people they took along. The whole point of the trip was we were going to get business for the State of Washington, so we had some rich business people on the trip too. But anyway, I had to be nice, even though I would really get irked over something. Some of the legislators, for example, wouldn't help carry luggage. They would just drop out of sight and leave it for the rest of us to do. But I couldn't make a big fuss about anything because I had to be friends with these guys when we got home. So that's the part—that you have to be nice when you get back home again. I don't like having to be nice all the time.

Hughes: Did I ask you about Jeannette Hayner, who became Senate majority leader in 1981 when von Reichbauer switched parties.

Ferguson: You didn't. Jeannette Hayner eventually decided that she was going to do the drinks once a week like the others, even though she didn't drink.

Hughes: She was the first female Majority Leader, right?

Ferguson: Right. And she was persuaded by her caucus, or somebody that these press people are going in and having drinks with the Speaker of the House, and they're having drinks with Clyde Ballard and whoever, so why don't you do it? Well, she didn't drink and she didn't want to be accused of spreading beer and rum to these people. But she did it, and sometimes they'd have little sandwiches and cookies. But she answered questions and socialized, and I think she kind of liked it after a while.

Hughes: And was she a good majority leader?

Ferguson: Yeah. I think she took the office from Jim Matson from Yakima, a really nice guy who everybody liked. He was one of Walgren's best friends. Anyway, he was the one before and she got it; they pulled that coup and got it.

Hughes: What kind of relations do you have with Speaker Frank Chopp?

Ferguson: Not very good, even though he's from Bremerton. See, he sort of came at the end of when I was there representing *The Sun*. I left in '93, so he was not there long enough for me to get too cozy with. But I got along fine with Wayne Ehlers, who became speaker in 1983. I liked Wayne, except I never forgave him. He's the guy who got the initiative passed that set up the salary commission (for statewide elected officials). And I *always* say, If you want to know the guy who fixed it so that they get a raise damn near every time they meet, thank Wayne Ehlers because he did it. At one time, when Wayne was Speaker and Denny Heck and Dan Grimm—a future state treasurer—were in the Legislature, those three guys were running the House and none of them had a job. They were all living off their overtime that they got. They could call meetings any time they wanted to, so they just lived off the Legislature, the three of them. I wrote about it!

Hughes: Denny Heck, who became Booth Gardner's chief of staff, seems like someone who would be your kind of guy.

Ferguson: Eh, not exactly. Neither was Dan Grimm, but Wayne was. He was a jolly guy.

Hughes: Let's go back to 1970. I see here in one of your columns that there's an episode that somehow escaped my radar. This concerns Slade Gorton's friend Mary Ellen McCaffree and the possibility that she could be Speaker of the House.

Ferguson: I remember writing that. She was my neighbor up here for a while. She lived up here in Hansville.

Hughes: You wrote this: "Mary Ellen McCaffree of Seattle, just the ticket. Smart, experienced, unflappable, with the added advantage of being one of a tiny handful of legislators who are in so with the governor that they could have just about anything they wanted from him. Whether she wants this is something else again, but she'd be tough to beat."

Ferguson: She didn't go for it. When she was up here she lived just up from the store here in Hansville. Her husband was the president of the Senate of the University of Washington. All this property up here, all the way down, much of it belongs to former faculty members of the UW. They were one of them.

Hughes: It's *fabulous* here.

Ferguson: But you wonder why we've got so many problems today, people can't pay their mortgages and stuff. Look at the houses they're building. Everybody builds a house that's way too big for them because they think they're going to make a mint when they sell it. This house is valued at a half a million, but we paid $27,900 for it.

Hughes: What did your husband Phil do for a living?

Ferguson: He was in the Navy for eight years, and then he became an electrician in the Navy Yard. And then he went to work as a consultant. Then he wrote manuals on how to store your atomic weapons and stuff like that. He didn't go to college. But I didn't go to college either.

Hughes: So you had these trade mission opportunities. Did these devolve from covering the Legislature?

Ferguson: Cherberg just liked to travel, and he never had to pay. The guy who organizes the trip doesn't have to pay. Everybody else paid. Actually, it wasn't that much, and it was great because when you went you were treated the same as the lieutenant governor. You got to meet the second-in-command in all the countries. You don't get first-in-command when you're *Lieutenant* Governor. So we went on all these trips. I persuaded him to go to Egypt. He had not thought of that before. We also went to China for three weeks.

Hughes: When was that?

Ferguson: 1980 I think it was. Every time we went out on the streets we were surrounded by crowds of people, all wanting to practice their

English on us.

Hughes: We're winding down. If you were doing this interview, what would you ask yourself, Adele?

Ferguson: I made list notes to myself of people I didn't want to *not* mention.

Hughes: Tell me about them.

Ferguson: Perry Woodall, a Republican from Eastern Washington, was a wonderful guy, tremendous lawyer and always looked out for the Mexicans. He took care of his people. He had a seat in front of Marshall Neill, who later went on the Supreme Court. Perry would get up and make all these speeches. In the middle of talking, he'd come back to Marshall and have him look it up in the law. Then Marshall would turn the book around so Perry could read the law, and Perry would carry on. Perry was one guy who wouldn't tell you what went on in caucus. It was sort of a thing with him that the members of the caucus are not supposed to tell what goes on when they shut the caucus door, so he wouldn't tell you anything about that, but he'd tell you *everything* else. Some of the others were *dying* to tell you what went on in the caucus. I always found out about the Democratic Caucus. Bob Bailey tried to explain to his caucus one time why so much stuff was getting out of the caucus. "Everybody thinks Red Beck is doing it," he said, "because Red talks to Adele all the time." But he says, "I have a feeling sometimes that it's me." Red did tell me everything. Red said, "Now, they made me chairman of the Constitutional Convention Committee. And I just have one thing to do all session: Make sure that no bill gets out of committee that calls for a Constitutional Convention!"

Frances Haddon Morgan got up one time on the floor of the House —and they had a bill on the floor that had to do with using nicknames. They wanted to stop people from using nicknames like "Red" Beck. So she got up there and declared, "Now, people won't all use their real names. For example, Frances Haddon Morgan is not my real name. My real name is Frances Rose Morgan; my mother's name is Haddon." Then she says, "And there's Adele." Everybody looks at *me*. Now they're talking about *me*. "Adele

Ferguson. That's not her real name either. She's got another name." And pretty soon she sits down. I went out in the court and ran around to her side of the chamber; she's out there now in the wings. And I said, "Frances, if you ever mention my name again on the floor of the Senate, I'm *never* going to mention yours in *The Bremerton Sun*." She decided that I was really OK when she found out I had a sister who was retarded. I was in the same boat with her. She had the (retarded) grandson and I had the sister.

What else I was going to tell you about was that I wrote an amendment once. I never got involved in writing legislation. Some of the other reporters did. They had a bill that had to do with riding horses on public lands. So I wrote an amendment while I'm sitting at the press desk. It said, "Horses being ridden on public highways must be plainly labeled 'horse' in a sign affixed to their tails so drivers coming up behind them won't mistake them for legislators." They passed it, and then they tabled it. They were having a little fun!

Hughes: That's great.

Ferguson: I did actually help write a bill with a guy from over in Eastern Washington who became head of a big federal office in Seattle and now he's back in Washington, D.C.—Rollie Schmitten. Our bill had to do with protecting white deer. There used to be white deer up here. I don't know if there are anymore, because I haven't seen any white deer for years. But you could see them when we were out in our boat; you'd see them on the beach. We wanted to make it so that people didn't just kill them for their hides. So we drew up a bill. Our bill took care of albino animals. I heard that the Game Department later got it rescinded.

Hughes: Who speaks for albino animals? Adele Ferguson does!

Ferguson: Now Karen Schmidt was a fine legislator; she was one of my legislators. She wrote the death penalty bill and really went through hell for it because she got calls in the middle of the night. You know, people screaming and carrying on. There are more of these damn do-gooders who believe the death penalty is a terrible thing. I think it's fine. I think we ought to do more of it. But Karen was a fine legislator.

John O'Brien knew how to get things done. He was great. One of his constituents told him she was tired of going in grocery stores and if her kid had to go to the bathroom they wouldn't let the kid go to the bathroom. They only had a toilet for employees. So he wrote a bill that said henceforth after Jan. 1 or whatever, that any store as big as thus and such square feet must a have a separate toilet for the public. And of course you know what happened? All the grocery stores immediately put signs up that said their toilets were available to anybody who wanted to use them. So then his bill just never got anywhere. They didn't need it. But that's how you legislate. That's how smart guys legislate. And all new grocery stories, regardless of size, had toilets for customers anyway from then on.

Hughes: Can you make any generalizations about what you've observed in the Legislature over the years? What's different today than in 1961 when you started covering Olympia?

Ferguson: Of course I haven't been down there since '93, so I've been out of it a while. But before I left, it used to be that all during the session there were always parties and receptions, and fundraisers. And then when they passed new laws that said you can't have the fundraisers and all, and it got to be too expensive to have these things. The nightlife disappeared. Before that, it was fun and everybody went. The staffers all went, and the reporters would go to get some good hors d'oeuvres or you'd hope that before it was over somebody would ask you if you wanted to go out to dinner. Once I went to a reception and waited and waited and nobody asked me to dinner, so I went ahead and started eating the hors d'oeuvres. Then Gordon Walgren comes up and asks if I want to go out to dinner with them. "Why the hell didn't you ask me an hour ago?" I said. "I wasted all this time eating this crap."

Hughes: So some of the so-called reforming really zapped some of the energy out of the Capitol?

Ferguson: It zapped the fun out of it. And it used to be that lobbyists were pretty powerful people, and pretty important people. But somehow the anti-lobbyist group got them painted as the bad ones. I always thought they were handy as hell. If you want to know something they're not going to lie to you, even if it's not to their benefit. Some of the most honest people down there were the lobbyists because their reputations rose and fell on whether they could be trusted with what they said. I know reporters who don't want to hear anything "off the record" because they can't write it. When I first went down there (in 1961) I talked to the insurance lobbyist and he said, "I'd like to invite you to dinner with some legislators. But it will have to be a dinner where you can't write anything about it." And I thought, Well then I can't come along. That's when I didn't know any better. I learned that's not the way you do it.

Hughes: Were there any stories that you sure *wished* you could write about.

Ferguson: Well yeah, and I'm not going to talk about them either. I've got some real good *dirt* on some of those people down there, but I'm never going to write about it, and I don't talk about it.

Hughes: But is it safe to say that in terms of your conscience that if you would have felt some of that dirt absolutely had to come out that it would have?

Ferguson: Oh yeah. I wouldn't conceal something that was lawbreaking or hurtful. It's just stuff. I'll give you an example of a very mild case: Red Beck was the senator down in the 26th District. And he was just a great advocate for the gas tax. I knew that Red bought all his gas from the Navy Yard where he didn't have to pay the tax. He was ex-Navy. But I never wrote about it. See what I mean? I never wrote that because I figured you could figure it out real easy for yourself. If they'd have asked him, I suppose he would have had to admit it, but I never, ever wrote the truth, which was that he never paid the gas tax because he bought his gas in the Navy Yard. I knew about people's romances, too, but those are really no-nos. Some of the top people down there were romancing quite handily with some of the people. But that's just gossip. I didn't write about that stuff.

Hughes: I wonder if as much of that goes on today as it used to.

Ferguson: I would imagine. People are the same.

Hughes: I was always really impressed at how you were able to be both a columnist and a reporter at the same time. How did you manage that?

Ferguson: It wasn't hard.

Hughes: Why wasn't it hard?

Ferguson: I guess you just wear a different hat. I know the rules.

Hughes: You're still a newspaper junkie like I am. Do you worry about the profession—the loss of readers and revenues?

Ferguson: I don't like what some of the people *in it* are doing. Their English is poor. I almost clipped out something I saw in this morning's paper. They wrote that somebody "got a hold of" something. And I thought, "Come on, you don't say 'got a hold of,' for God's sake, in a news story." And then I read a story where they said that in the final results of the governor's election last time, Gregoire had a 129-vote margin over Rossi. But that's not the final result. It was 133 votes when the court got through. And I wrote a letter to the publisher and said, "For God's sake, doesn't anybody keep up with what's going on? If you call the Secretary of State's Office and ask them what the final vote was, it would be 133."…And I don't like the fact that they choose sides in the news columns. That's what a journalist is supposed to *not* do. A journalist is supposed to be just the facts, ma'am, and not embroider it with what you think or anything. That's not true journalism.

Hughes: So you're seeing a lot more of that, blurring the distinction between news and opinion?

Ferguson: *Oh yeah.* And I've been places on panels where there are other people, maybe a columnist or two, and they'll say something like "Today we have a group of journalists." And I'd correct them and say, "No, I'm not a journalist. Peter here from the Tacoma paper, he's not a journalist; he's a columnist. He's an opinion writer, and a good one, too. *I'm* an opinion writer. We can tell you what we think about it but you're not supposed to do that in news stories."

INTERVIEW III

January 23, 2009

Hughes: There's a real possibility that the *Seattle Post-Intelligencer* may go out of business as a printed newspaper. Now, the *P-I* hasn't always been my favorite newspaper, but—

Ferguson: Mine either, but I don't want to see it go under. I think it must be mainly the online competition. That's what's doing it.

Hughes: That and this recession. So what's your message to Mr. and Mrs. Greater Seattle about what it's going to be like without that voice in a town that needs more voices in the media?

Ferguson: Well, I believe in newspapers. *I believe in newspapers.* I don't care what they do on television or online or all this other computer stuff. You can't clip them and mail them to your aunt in Dubuque. Once in a while I would do a column and just ask people, "What don't you like about your newspaper?" And usually the answer I would get was, "They never follow anything up. They'll have a story in about something that's really interesting, and never say another word about it. You never know what happened."

Hughes: That more so than any perception of a political bias?

Ferguson: Yes. And my own newspaper here in Kitsap County, I used to write notes to the editor and say, "Any time you run a story about somebody hired for a public job why don't you put the damn *salary* in there?!" Everybody wants to know what we are paying this person. And they never do it. They'll put ages in sometimes, and I think all politicians' ages should be in their stories. And they don't do it all the time.

Hughes: Who's your favorite reporter lately—someone you think just does a terrific job?

Ferguson: Well to me, no one reporter so much, but for favorite columnist, Charles Krauthammer. He's very good.

Hughes: Do you watch TV much?

Ferguson: I watch CSI!

Hughes: Do you watch any of the hot new news shows, like Anderson

Cooper?

Ferguson: I watch Sean Hannity. I don't watch Olbermann. I watch Hannity, and sometimes Bill O'Reilly. But O'Reilly's ego is almost more than I can stand....In the morning I get up at 5. I watch the news from about 5 to 5:30 on Channel 5, and the next half hour on Channel 4, and the next half hour on Channel 7 and then I give it up for the day.

Hughes: And then you start thinking about what to write in your column. Have you written anything about our new president?

Ferguson: Yeah I have.

Hughes: What have you said about Barack Obama?

Ferguson: I started out by noting that in the final days of the Bush Administration there was a Fox News interview asking the two Bushes—father and son—questions like, "What memorable events went on in this office?" And I thought, *"That isn't what I'd ask."* I want to ask the senior Bush, "Why, why, why every time they jump all over you about 'Read my lips, no new taxes,' don't you tell them the truth? Which was, that the Democrats came to you and offered to make a deal. You signed a tax increase, and they pledged to put all the money saved from downsizing of the military into reducing the federal deficit. Nobody ever says that! It was in the papers and I had clippings. I talked to Slade Gorton about it and did a story with him. But nobody remembered it!

And I would have asked the younger Bush, "Why, with the reputation of the Republicans for fiscal responsibility, did you let the first budget come through loaded with all the goodies for Republicans, and Democrats as well, instead of vetoing it? And you didn't veto anything until stem-cell research came along." No wonder the Republicans were mad at him over that.

Then I would ask Jimmy Carter, "Why can't you obey the historical tradition that ex-presidents do not cast aspersions or criticize their successors' actions?" He's an asshole! Carter goes overseas and does it all the time.

And I would ask Bill Clinton, "Why do you take these occasional jabs at George W. Bush when he restored you to respectability by asking you serve with his father on the fundraising drive for the tsunami victims and the victims of Hurricane Katrina?"

And I said I would like to ask Barack Obama, as I've asked before and got no answers, "Where were you, and who was there—the who, what, where—when you decided to run for president? Or are the people who were involved persona non grata?" You know that may be why he can't talk about it. It may be Jeremiah Wright and those people.

Hughes: It certainly is an amazing historical moment—our first black president. Did you think there was a real chance that he would be elected?

Ferguson: I *so* disliked the Clintons, and I was so hopeful that they wouldn't get back in again. Remembering that they left with the furniture...I didn't really think so, no. But I was wrong once before.

Hughes: Really?

Ferguson: Somebody called me and asked, "Well, what do you think about Clinton now that he's been caught with Monica and the cigar and all that kind of sleazy stuff?" And I said, "He's toast!" (whispering) *I was wrong.*

Hughes: What's the most memorable column you ever wrote from the standpoint of the impact it made?

Ferguson: Well, I don't know about impact, but I think my most memorable column was about a dog named "Dice." (It was published in October of 1974). People love pet stories, and this one was really something. Dice was a dark brown German shorthair who belonged to Bill and Laura Breuer of Olympia. I wrote that "He was no ordinary dog—he was one of the greatest hunters around and they treated him like one of the family. He rode in the front seat of the car right up there between his owners. Bill and Laura and Dice were practically inseparable."

Then, as he got older, Dice started to get sick. The Breuers took him to the vet, who said Dice had colon cancer. They sent a specimen of tissue to WSU for verification and the sad word came back that nothing could be done. The best thing to do, the vets said, was to put Dice to sleep rather than subject him to more pain and suffering. So the Breuers put Dice in the car between them and took him on his last ride to the vet. They left him there and drove around for the rest of the day, crying.

About two months later, Bill and Laura's son, Chet, who was chief of detectives with the Olympia Police Department, got a call from the dog hospital. They wanted him to come and get Dice. But Dice was supposed to be dead. Here's what happened: After Bill and Laura left the dog, the veterinarians didn't have the heart to give him the fatal needle. They'd known Dice since he was a pup and he was like family to them, too. So they decided to wait a day or two until their newest partner came on board and get him to put the dog out of its misery. While they were waiting, the phone rang. It was WSU. Did they still have the dog with colon cancer? They did. "Well," they said, "We've got a new drug we want to try out. How about giving it to Dice? It won't cost anybody anything and it might help." The upshot, of course, was that the drug worked! And Dice was ready to go home. They called Chet because they knew that his folks thought Dice was dead. Chet called John Sullivan, a family friend, for advice. "How do I tell them he's not dead without giving one of them a heart attack?" Sullivan said, "Do it just like you told me." The next day, Sullivan was at home when Bill and Laura drove up with Dice sitting in his usual spot between them. He pretended not to notice the dog as Bill and Laura got out of the car, all smiles. "Come on over here," said Bill. "I want to show you something." Sullivan tried to look at the tires and the hood and everything else on the car until he was ready to be surprised by an equally happy Dice.

Well, Dice lived for a couple more years and finally died of old age. The Breuers vowed that they would never have another dog. Sullivan tried to give them one out of a litter of shorthair puppies, but they refused. Dice was the love of their lives, and they couldn't go through all that all over again.

Sullivan told them he had to be gone for a week or so, and he didn't have anyone to watch the last pup in the litter. Wouldn't they please just puppysit for him? They were reluctant, but they loaded the pup into the car and drove off.

"Funny thing," I concluded. "It's been a long time since, and Sullivan has just never gotten around to retrieving that pup." I guess I'm not the only one who gets sentimental about animals. People just loved that column, and so do I!

Hughes: What a great story! Adele, if you left this mortal coil tomorrow, how would you like to be remembered?

Ferguson: "She tried to be honest." (laughs)

Hughes: I think you succeeded.

Ferguson: Well, I don't know, but I've never really lied about anybody.... I think what they used to say about me, which was a compliment, was that I had an "institutional memory."

Hughes: You certainly do. I thank you for letting us spend this time with you, Adele. It's been great.

Ferguson: Well, thank you for asking me. I know I'll think of more things I wanted to say!

— 30 —

Some memorable columns

 adele ferguson reports:

The header for Adele's column in the 1960s

Nov. 15, 1965

A Very Pretty Baby Is Now 18 Years Old

Frances was the prettiest baby I ever saw.

She was fair and blue eyed and no one noticed at first that her eyes were slanted a little more than those of her brothers and sisters.

She immediately became the pet of all those older brothers and sisters and she thrived on it.

She didn't start to walk or talk when she should have but then lots of babies are slow, they said. The slanted eyes became more obvious and the little hands became almost square with blunt fingers. When her teeth came in, they were not even but irregular. Everybody loved her just the same, and it was some time before the truth began to dawn on some of them.

It was a truth her horrified parents refused for a long time to believe—that their fair-haired baby girl was mentally retarded.

She learned to walk and she didn't walk—she fairly flew. She was like a wild bird, ever seeking escape, and at night she would slip out a window and like a tiny ghost in her nightgown, race up the road. More than once, startled motorists who had jammed on their brakes to avoid hitting her

174

when she darted from the roadside in the dark, returned her to her home where firmer effort was made to keep windows and doors locked beyond her ability to get them open.

She could disappear in an instant, sometimes to slip into a neighbor's home and dump everything she could find into a sticky mess.

Matches had to be kept from her reach and she had to be watched constantly that she didn't turn on the kitchen stove burners. Because she had a remote sense of pain, she could lay her hand on a hot burner and suffer a severe burn before the hurt of it reached her brain.

The truth had to be believed now, despite tearful protestations from some of those brothers and sisters who did not want to believe it. And for her own protection the little wild bird had to be caged.

After a long wait, speeded up somewhat because too many narrow escapes made it an emergency, her parents made the heartbreaking but necessary journey to Rainier State School at Buckley and left her there. They visited her regularly, and after awhile they were allowed to bring her home for visits. She always recognized them when they came, and spoke to them in her hoarse gibberish.

She grew up into a big, hulking girl who still rushed around, who was dangerously destructive but who could hold a visitor's baby in her arms and gently and lovingly croon to it. But for any length of time away from the school beyond a few hours, her loneliness for the others like herself who were part of her world was unbearable to watch.

She would go off by herself and sit in silence, tears streaming down her face. So after a few times they didn't bring her home anymore, but visited her instead.

My sister, Frances, is 18 now. She is a big, husky girl with odd, square hands and feet. Her teeth are a jumble in her mouth and she wears a square Dutch-boy haircut which accentuates the slanted eyes.

But I never saw a prettier baby.

They know Julia inside the Pearly Gates

It's been a while since I talked with the Duchess of Cathlamet, and now the opportunity to chat with one of the truly great characters in politics is gone forever.

I knew Julia Butler Hansen was dying, and she knew she was dying—in fact, only a couple of weeks before her death at 80, she summoned former aide (and ex-state senator) Bob Bailey to her bedside to work out the details of the eulogy at her funeral.

Don't worry about it, he assured her, Alan Thompson (another former aide, now House chief clerk) and I will take care of it. But Julia liked to manage everything, something the guardian of the Pearly Gates surely has found out by now.

For years, she was the most powerful woman in the state as chairman of the Legislative Transportation Committee. It was Julia who fixed it so that the House had one more member than the Senate on the committee so that a House member would always be chairman.

If you wanted roads in your district, you got along with Julia—that was before the adoption of the six-year plan by the highway department. It was pork barrel all the way.

Once Rep. Art Avey of Kettle Falls, an inveterate prankster, tried to bollix things up for Julia by demanding to know why the highway budget didn't go through Ways & Means the way every other appropriation bill did.

Julia was furious but Speaker John O'Brien ruled that highway bills had always been handled separately and that was that.

Julia stormed off the floor, snarling, "Somebody ought to tell that son-of-a-bitch Avey to buy lots of road graders because he's not going to have any paved roads in his district."

She challenged O'Brien once for the speakership and lost, 27-23, and after the vote was over, went around shaking hands. "No hard feelings,"

Congresswoman Julia Butler Hansen, whom Adele dubbed
"The Duchess of Cathlamet." *Photo by John Hughes*

she murmured graciously, until she came to the two men who engineered her defeat, Rep. Len Sawyer (who later became speaker and was forced to resign) and Rep. August P. Mardesich (who later became Senate majority leader and was forced to resign.)

"No hard feelings," said Julia to them, "but I'll get even with you, you sons-of-bitches."

She went to Congress in 1961, serving until 1975, and Bailey was her district aide and a state senator at the same time. Once while driving her and a couple of her friends to Olympia for some meeting, they were late and she told him to speed it up.

He did and was pulled over by a state trooper. Bailey was trying to explain why they were in a hurry, when Julia got into the act. What was he doing stopping decent citizens when he ought to be out catching crooks or something? demanded Julia of the officer. Couldn't he find something better to do with his time?

That did it. The trooper pulled out his ticket book and started scribbling. Bailey tried to explain who his passenger was, you know, CONGRESSWOMAN Hansen, but the trooper was not impressed.

When Bailey pulled out his driver's license, however, and the trooper saw "state senator" on it, he tore up the ticket. Congress doesn't have a handle on the State Patrol budget but state senators do.

My favorite story about Julia, though, was the time someone wrote her up in *Reader's Digest* as The Most Colorful Character I Ever Met, and quoted her on her salty language. Julia was horrified and furious. She even cried. Then she collared her then administrative assistant, Don Brown, demanding, "How could he do this to me? How could anyone say such things about me? How dare they print such a thing? Don, do I talk like that? Do I use words like that? What a nasty, untrue thing to say about me. GET THAT SON-OF-A-BITCH ON THE PHONE!"

Why can't they all just get along?

Why anybody would put any reliance in the political judgment of Sen. Don Benton, R-Vancouver, is beyond my comprehension.

Isn't this the guy who, as state Republican chair, squirreled away over $1 million in campaign donations in 2000 to pay cash for an office building in Olympia so he could move party headquarters there from Tukwila after the election? Money that might have made the difference in U.S. Sen. Slade Gorton's effort to keep his seat against the challenge of millionairess Maria Cantwell, which he lost by a couple thousand votes? The GOP might even control the Legislature today if some of that money had been spent on tight legislative races.

When Benton came around seeking signatures on his letter to Senate leadership protesting the plan to have all lawmakers put on the feed bag together during the two years they won't have use of their private dining rooms while the Legislative Building is being refurbished, his fellow senators should have reached for the Raid and hung a bag of garlic around their necks.

Instead, 36 of the 49, about half and half Democrats and Republicans, signed it. Actually, only 34 names appear. Two came to their senses and had their names blacked out.

I believe those who said they didn't read before signing because they'd have to be as politically out of sync as Benton otherwise, whose hyperbole included "THIS IS UNACCEPTABLE," yes, in capital letters, unacceptable being the very thought of breaking bread with representatives instead of enjoying with their upper chamber peers the gourmet services of two French cooks.

Senators have always looked upon themselves as the House of Lords and their cohorts across the rotunda as the House of Commons. Or, perhaps, as college seniors compared to high school freshmen. I don't know why they should be so uppity. I never saw a House member take off his shoes and socks and trim his toenails at his desk as a senator from Spokane once did.

Let me say, first, that I approve of the lawmakers' private dining rooms, not so much to get away from lobbyists, but for convenience and time saved. If they had to go out to lunch, it would take hours for them all to come back, and some might be a little the worse for wear. Not that there wasn't temptation in the Senate dining room when they had wine there. One of my fellow reporters who ate there used to show up for the afternoon session with rosy cheeks and rosy nose and doze at the press desk. We poked him awake when he snored.

I ate in the House restaurant for the 30 plus years I covered the Legislature in Olympia, paying just as they did. I chose the House over the Senate because the House was more of a fun place. I never broke the rule that what was said down there was off limits. The problem usually was the reverse. Members would want to tell me something and I'd have to say no, not here. Tell me afterward in the hallway or upstairs.

I also sat on the minority side, which most of the time was with the Republicans. I wanted to be out of earshot of the majority who liked to strategize over lunch and I didn't want them to think I was eavesdropping. My informants in the majority usually clued me in on what was being said anyway, which I considered to be legit as long as I hadn't overheard it in the lunchroom myself.

Anyway, Senate leadership apparently is unmoved by the distress of 36 of the members, giving no consideration to suggestions that they be bused to the French restaurant their chefs operate in Olympia, or that meals be catered.

They're going to have to eat with the House members even if it does make them feel like remote cousins at Thanksgiving who have to sit with the kids at card tables far below the salt.

House members aren't so bad. I ate with them, didn't I? So what if they spill their milk once in awhile? Can't we all just get along? Well, can't we?

Will Gregoire stand up to Indians over fishing?

In the fall of 1999, when the Association of Washington Business met at Semi-Ah-Moo, then-Attorney General Christine Gregoire was a guest speaker on the salmon crisis, and I got to ask her a question that was a major point of controversy.

When the U.S. Supreme Court OK'd the 1974 Boldt decision, giving treaty Indian tribes up to half the salmon, it authorized the state to use whatever measures were necessary for conservation of the resource. Is it the position of the state that that includes shutting down tribal as well as non-tribal harvest?

"Yes," she said, "but it would be very tough to do."

How tough we don't know, because we've never tried it. Sports and commercial fishing seasons were frequently shut down as a succession of fisheries directors and governors catering to the tribes failed to use their authority, shifting their attention to habitat improvement instead.

There is a reason for reopening this old wound, which I have decried from its inception. I maintain that salmon are a resource that belongs to all the people, not a handful of fellow citizens awarded super rights by judges attempting to atone for past wrongs to long dead ancestors.

Gov. Gregoire has asked state officials to look into the Makah Tribe's winter harvest of 20,000 Chinook salmon, which is either 12 or 40 times as many as they had been allotted under state guidelines, depending on who's doing the talking.

Phil Anderson, state Fish and Wildlife salmon policy coordinator, said the catch was supposed to be about 500 in the areas of Neah Bay, Sekiu and Port Angeles. Other state fishery representatives not quoted by name in the media, said the allotment was 1,600 or 1,800. Tribal chair Ben Johnson said they always planned to quit when they reached 20,000, which indicates they had no intention of abiding by the allotment they had worked out under state guidelines. U.S. Sen. Slade Gorton got a provision in the law that the Endangered Species Act, with its regulations for conservation, applied equally to all Americans, but the tribes negotiated a deal with the Clinton Administration allowing them to decide for themselves on a case-by-case basis whether or not to comply. Tribes nationwide poured cash into the state in 2000 to replace Gorton with their good friend Maria Cantwell.

All the news items on the Makah case said that state officials could not legally dictate the number of fish tribes can take, but I think that's an assumption based on those Clinton executive and secretarial orders. My copy of United States v. State of Washington on the salmon case reads, in Article 107: "For the state to show that a specific fishing regulation is necessary for conservation, it must utilize run size predictions, valid escapement goals, the least restrictive regulation of tribal fishermen and it must view the entire run as a divisible resource."

Fisheries officials at first said over fishing of the Chinooks in the Strait by the Makah means the 2005 Chinook catch will have to be reduced for other commercial, tribal and sports fishers to make up for it. But they were already chickening out at their annual meeting on harvest negotiations March 1 in Olympia. If such a level of over fishing happens again, Anderson said, they risk losing their management agreement with the feds that runs until 2009. Cluck cluck cluck!

It is long past time the state settled whether the authority of a state to protect and preserve its resources outranks some federal bureaucrat's dictates, a la Clinton, the Makahs and the ESAct.

If we the state deal them out of the Chinook harvest until they've made up the loss, I have no doubt they'll fish anyway, in their belief they have that right. Then let's take them to court. In the meantime, we'll find out whose side our new governor is on. All of us together, including the tribes, as one body of citizens to whom the laws on conservation apply equally? Or a handful of super citizens, who decide for themselves which laws they choose to obey.

Stopping free speech—Olympia-style

As if they didn't have enough to keep them at each other's throats in Olympia in the final days, House Democrats decided it was no longer allowable for one member to refer to another in government-funded writings as "lacking in honesty with taxpayers," or be called "tax-and-spend liberals," or "disingenuous."

That's in e-mails or newsletters to their constituents. Since the Democrats are in charge, it's the Republicans they are aiming at, of course. The example cited is that of Rep. Gary Alexander, who wrote that Democrats were displaying a lack of honesty with taxpayers.

That's mudslinging, said House Clerk Rich Nafziger, and is an extension of the rule that forbids lawmakers from insulting each other during floor speeches. They can continue to say what they please at news conferences, etc., but so long as they are communicating with the use of taxpayer money, from now on they have to keep it clean.

Republicans, of course, are furious. I mean, how can a Republican give a political speech without calling Democrats tax-and-spend liberals? Isn't truth a defense? And I don't see why saying someone is "lacking in honesty" is so offensive. Saying your opponent is as crooked as a dog's hind leg may be carrying it too far but how else can you call someone a liar without coming right out and saying it?

As for disingenuous, I suspect they figure too many people don't have any idea what it means so why take the chance on the inference it's an insult?

So far, they've confined their actions to censorship and writing a new rule and no one has proposed passing a bill to enforce it.

In Jerusalem a few years ago, behavior turned so brutish in its Parliament with members leaping out of their seats to shout insults, that the Ethics Committee chair circulated a list of 68 insults, including "swamp fly," "king of the swamp," and "poodle," that she wanted banned under threat of reprimand and suspension. Others among the 68 were "blood drinker, boor, fascist, filth, eye-gouger, Jew-hater, Nazi, Philistine, terrorist, traitor, government of murderers, gut-ripper, degenerate, defacer of property, humbug, nincompoop, poisoner of wells, spiller of blood, thug, total nonentity, threat to the state, thug, monster and brain defective."

Members admitted they misbehaved on occasion but said calling in the language cops was too much. They argued, sure, but afterward they went out and had a drink together.

In the early days of the Knesset, Israel's first prime minister, David Ben-Gurion, had such contempt for his political nemesis, opposition leader Menachem Begin,

Lieutenant Governor John Cherberg opens the session. *Seattle Argus*

that he never spoke his name. He'd refer to him as "the gentleman sitting next to Dr. Bader." Over the years, it got wilder, hence the list, which I don't know the fate of, so I think it was just a kind of shot across the bow of the offenders.

It was the reverse in our state Senate when Lt. Gov. John Cherberg ruled the roost. He'd introduce members as "the great and renowned senator from…..," the esteemed and honorable senator from…," "the respected and excellent senator from…." When members razzed him for his excessive use of adjectives, he warned them what he'd use in place. How, asked Cherberg, would they like, "The chicken-livered and chauvinistic…," "The pussyfooting and pusillanimous…," "The vacillating and vacuous…..," "The wishy-washy and waffling senator from…"

They decided they liked the super saccharine approach better.

July 8, 2008

The Rosetta Stone was easier to decipher

An open letter to Bill Gates, president of Microsoft:

Dear Bill,

First off, let me explain that just because I used the familiar salutation of Dear Bill doesn't mean that I harbor any affection for you. To the contrary, after using your Microsoft Works program in my new computer, I understand perfectly why it took you this long to get engaged.

Your bride would want to know what you do for a living, and after you had spent two, maybe three months explaining to her how Microsoft Works works in a computer, she would go out in the kitchen and get a butcher knife and come back and kill you.

I've had the same feeling. In fact, for anyone contemplating the purchase of a personal computer and accompanying software, let me advise that your first step should be to remove any deadly weapons from your home, to prevent the temptation to do harm to yourself or the machine.

When I was forced to buy a computer, after years of using those in the offices where I worked, I told my husband to get one that was simple. All I want it to do, I said, is allow me to write my column, store it so I can make changes in it if necessary before it has to be sent out, and get it out of the computer and onto paper for the mailing.

What I wound up with is what is known as "state of the art." That means that I can play games, figure my income tax, do color graphics, communicate with any astronauts in space stations and monitor the progress of the North Korean nuclear weapon capability.

The man at Costco who sold it said it would be an "easy walk" to do what I wanted it to do, my husband said. This is the same man who told George Bush the voters would never elect an Arkansas hillbilly president and Ross Perot got that way by being thrown too many times from his horse.

An instruction manual came with the program and, at first reading, I thought this was the last undiscovered work of Agatha Christie. I mean, there is no way you can get from A to B to C in this book. Clues are scattered along the way like air drops over Bosnia, only occasionally landing where they do some good.

I should have been suspicious when I saw the title: "Concise Guide to Microsoft Works for Windows."

Bill, 198 pages ain't concise, not where I come from. And the fact you call this book a "remarkably friendly application that can help you process any type of data—words, numbers or sets of records"—cuts no ice with me.

The Rosetta Stone was easier to decipher.

Do you know what it's like, Bill, to be caught in the machine, desperate to get out and can't, to be unable to stop underlining, which you never meant to do in the first place but hit the wrong button and don't know which one?

To have program after program rush by you as you frantically push-buttons in hopes of finding the right one, stacking up like pancakes until you're afraid they are going to burst off the screen and fall in your lap.

What I wanted to know was supposed to be on Pages 18 to 20, but I read Pages 18 to 20 more times than I have recited the Pledge of Allegiance, and I've been going to political dinners for over 30 years, remember, and I still couldn't figure it out.

Anyway, the only reason I am able to even write you at all, instead of being hopelessly lost in the maze of Microsoft is that a child stopped by the house. A simple child who asked to see the computer said it looked like it was compatible to what they used at school, sat down in front of it, and did in 40 seconds what I had been trying to do for two weeks. I didn't even know she could pronounce compatible. And when she was through, instead of asking for a cookie, she said: "Get a cover for your keyboard so you don't get cat hairs in there. These things are murder to clean."

So, I guess there is hope for our public school system, and the younger generation. I just wish, Bill, that you had a Dick meets Jane kind of manual for those of us who date back to the days when newspaper stories were written on typewriters, then cut and pasted.

And if I don't figure out pretty soon how to make this thing disgorge stuff I've written and it has hiding somewhere in its digestive tract, I'm coming to see you. Hide the butcher knives.

Yours truly, Adele Ferguson

Oct 1, 2008

Sometimes the justice system is neither

Cassie Holden would probably be a mother today with three or four kids in school, or maybe she'd be a teacher or a doctor.

At 12, her whole life lay ahead of her when she came over from Pocatello, Idaho, in June 1988, to visit her mother in Bremerton and went for a walk before dinner from which she never returned.

It was two days before they found her, raped and beaten to death with a rock. The man who did it was arrested in the rape of another young woman in Kitsap County and Cassie's DNA was found on his shoes.

Jonathan Lee Gentry was as old then, at 32, as Cassie would be today if she had lived. He had a long criminal record and his jury had no trouble voting for the death penalty.

So where is he today, 20 years later? Thanks to defense attorneys who have spent 18 years on our nickel digging up excuses for him to evade the death he deserves, he's the longest serving resident of Death Row. The state Supreme Court has upheld the sentence twice, in 1995 and 1999.

Just the other day his latest appeal was turned down by a federal judge who said allegations of misconduct by his prosecutors wasn't enough to get him off the hook. But Assistant Atty. Gen. Paul Weisser said it will take at least two more years to deal with appeals still pending.

What in God's name is wrong with this country when a proven murderer can play the justice system like a fiddle? Well, not the murderer but his lawyers who get paid by us. The longer it takes, the more they make.

Remember Charles Rodman Campbell, who slaughtered two women and a child? His lawyers dragged it out for $226,000. That was when public defenders got $50 an hour.

The Supreme Court got the attention of the Washington Assoc. of Criminal Defense Lawyers back in 1994 when it gave them a tongue lashing in an opinion of upholding the death penalty for Brian Keith Lord, for the kidnapping, rape and bludgeoning to death of a Poulsbo girl. The court blasted not only Lord's two court-appointed attorneys but all other members of the bar who handle such cases.

The message was stop throwing in everything but the kitchen sink in such matters. Don't leave it to us to sort out the meritorious claims from the frivolous and repetitive. A brief submitted by Lord's lawyers that was 1,200 pages long and raised 67 issues for further appeals "borders on abuse of process. We hereby provide notice that such behavior WILL NOT be tolerated in the future."

The stunned WACDL asked the court to strike the tongue lashing language so it wouldn't go into the legal record. The court said what you see is what you get. The WACDL came up with a proposal for changing the ways attorneys are picked for death penalty cases. Let us, instead of the superior court judges, pick them, they said, and pay those attorneys per case between $60,000 to $200,000 rather than $50 per hour.

Eventually an Office of Public Defense was established which supplies names of available public defenders for death penalty cases to the high court. And about 10 years ago, their $50 per hour pay was raised to $125 per hour.

So, life goes on for a rapist and killer as his lawyers pull every string possible to fulfill their obligation to get him off regardless of the viciousness of his crime and the fact of his guilt, while the parents of Cassie Holden have only memories of a happy little girl visiting her mom who skipped off for a walk and ran into Jonathan Lee Gentry.

Adele's famous fruitcake recipe

Adele learned it from her friend Cornish Southerland, who learned it from his mother:

Two cups of pecans	1 cup flour
16 ounces pitted dates	1 cup sugar
8 ounces candied cherries	1 teaspoon baking powder
8 ounces candied pineapple	1 teaspoon vanilla
4 eggs	Pinch of salt

Bowl 1: Put half the flour in a large bowl, together with the dates cut into small pieces, so they don't all stick together. Add halved cherries and pineapple cut into small pieces. Add nuts.

Bowl 2: Mix remaining flour, sugar, baking powder, salt and vanilla. Beat the eggs and put them into the flour mixture. Pour over floured fruit in Bowl 1 and mix well.

Line one standard loaf pan or two small ones with waxed locker paper. Spray pan first, then paper. Press the bake mixture into place. What you see is what you get—it doesn't grow any—so pick your pan accordingly.

You do not have to use waxed locker paper if you are good at getting a cake out of a plan without breaking it up. I find it easier to lift the paper-wrapped cake out, then peel off the paper. The original recipe called for using regular waxed paper, but I could never get the stuff off the cake so I switched to locker paper.

Bake for 2-and-a-half to 3 hours at 300 degrees, with a pan of water under the cake on the shelf of the oven. If you use a glass loaf pan, one reader advises that you should lower the temperature to 250 degrees. Otherwise the cake may be too crusty.

When cake is done, cool it in the pan. Next, dip an old piece of sheet fabric or some cheesecloth in rum, brandy or sherry and wrap the cake in it. Wrap that in aluminum foil and put the cake in some cool spot to season. Check it weekly and re-soak the cloth if it has dried out. The cake will ripen in a couple of weeks, but the longer the better. By the way, don't worry about how hard the cake is when it comes out of the oven. The seasoning time will mellow it marvelously.

Also, it doesn't matter what size the eggs are. There's no butter or shortening in this recipe, so don't let the absence of that worry you. Under no circumstances add citron!

The cake can be decorated while it's still hot by glazing it with a mixture of white Karo syrup, a little brown sugar, some hot water and a little plain gelatin. I don't know the quantities. Cornish Southerland says she does it by feel. I don't decorate mine at all.

If you want to turn Cornish Southerland's Mother's Fruitcake into Bill's Fruitcake, use a quart of whole Brazil nuts, almonds and pecans instead of just pecans. Otherwise, the recipe is the same.

The cake keeps beautifully. You can put it in the freezer and save it until next Christmas. It can be cut straight from the freezer.

ACKNOWLEDGMENTS

I've known Adele for 45 years. In fact, *The Daily World* at Aberdeen, from which I retired as editor and publisher in 2008, was the first newspaper in the state to publish her syndicated column. Invaluable to this project was Don Brazier's fastidious two-volume *History of the Washington Legislature* (1854-1963 and 1965-1982). It was a labor of love for Don, a former legislator and avid Washington historian. He spent countless hours reviewing microfilm and poring over documents. For anyone interested in the history of the Legislature it stands as the definitive reference work. Ralph Munro and his successor as secretary of state, Sam Reed, offered a trove of stories about Adele—all of them true—while Dan Evans, Slade Gorton, Gordon Walgren, David Ammons, Bob Partlow, Gordon Schultz, Walter Hatch, Peter Callaghan, Dick Larsen, Sid and Bette Snyder, Bob Bailey, Robert L. Charette, George W. Scott, Steve Excell and Lillian Walker gave us many more. The wonderful cover portrait of Adele is by Terry Poe of the Kitsap Newspaper Group. We thank them for letting us use it. We also thank the amazing staff at the Washington State Library and State Archives, as well as our friends at the Kitsap County Historical Society Museum, the Puget Sound Navy Museum and, of course, *The Kitsap Sun*, which sponsored the printing of this book. My teammates at The Legacy Project, Trova Heffernan and Lori Larson, are the glue for these projects, together with Carleen Jackson and Laura Mott of the Heritage Center and Kathy Campbell and Kurt Gorham at Gorham Printing.

JOHN C. HUGHES
for The Legacy Project, January 2011

kitsapsun.com

INDEX

Wow!

Presented to:

_____

By:

_____

On:

_____

Published in the UK in 2005 by Candle Books
(a publishing imprint of Lion Hudson plc).

Reprinted 2006

Distributed by Marston Book Services Ltd,
PO Box 269, Abingdon, Oxon OX14 4YN

Worldwide co-edition produced by Lion Hudson plc,
Mayfield House, 256 Banbury Road, Oxford, OX2 7DH, England.
Tel: +44 (0) 1865 302750   Fax: +44 (0) 1865 302757
Email: coed@lionhudson.com
www.lionhudson.com

ISBN-13: 978-1-85985-557-7
ISBN-10: 1-85985-557-1

Printed in China

Guess What?
Story Bible

Written by Tracy Harrast

Illustrated by Paul & Alice Sharp

CANDLE
BOOKS

Table of Contents

How the World Began

Genesis 1:1—2:3

In the beginning, ⬤ created heaven and the earth. The earth was dark and was covered with ⬤.

Then God said, "Let there be ⬤." And there was light. God saw that the light was very good. He called the light "⬤" and the darkness "⬤". That was day one. Then God made the ⬤ on day two.

The next day he made dry ⬤ appear, and he created plants and trees. Then on the fourth day, God made the ⬤, moon, and stars.

God made birds and  on the fifth day.

When the sixth day came, God made land

. Then he made a and a woman in

his own likeness. He told them to have children.

God saw everything he had made, and it was very ██████. He blessed the ██████ day because that was the day when he rested.

 **Seek & Find**

How does resting help us?

What could happen if we worked all the time?

When you've been outdoors, which of God's creations have made you think about his greatness?

The First People

Genesis 2:7–25

After God made the world, he made the first man from . The man's name was Adam. God put Adam in a garden called and told him to take of it.

God didn't want Adam to be 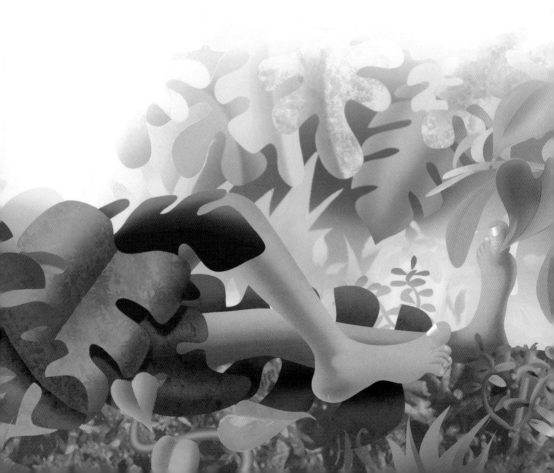, so he decided to make a friend who was just right for him. While Adam was asleep, God took out one of his 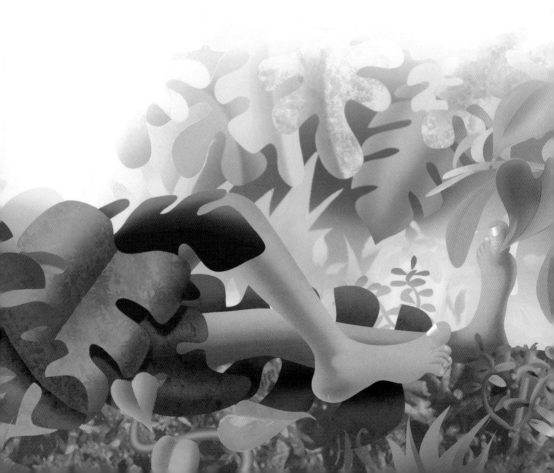 and made a 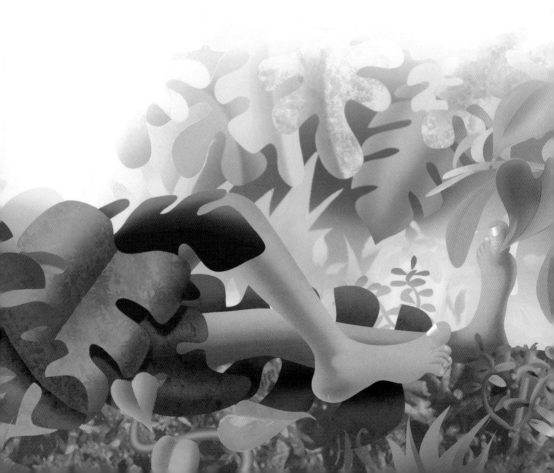 from it.

When Adam woke up and saw her, he was happy. He said, "Her bones have come from my . Her body has come from my body. She will be named 'woman', because she was taken out of a _____."

That's why a man will leave his [image] and mother and be joined to his [image]. The two of them will become [image].

Adam and Eve were both [image], but they didn't worry about it. They were happy in the Garden of [image] . . . for a while.

Seek & Find

God made us, too. How can we show him we're thankful for our bodies?

Do you want to get married one day?

A Snake Lies in the Garden

Genesis 2:16–17, 3:1–23; Romans 5:13–18

God told Adam, "You can eat any ⬭ in the ⬭ except one kind. Don't eat fruit from the tree of the knowledge of good and evil. If you do, you will ⬭."

The devil was a sly and tricky serpent. He ⬭ to Eve: "You won't die. God knows if you eat it, you will be wise like him."

Eve saw that the fruit looked good. She wanted to be ⬭ so she ate some. She gave some to Adam, and he ate it too.

Now Adam and Eve worried about being ⬭. They made clothes from ⬭ and hid from God. God asked, "Have you eaten the

fruit I told you not to?" Adam blamed Eve.
Then Eve blamed the ▓▓▓. God ▓▓▓▓▓▓▓ all
three.

Adam and Eve had to leave the garden.
God gave them animal skins to wear.

Because Adam sinned, all people would now die one day, just as God had said. But Jesus changed all that. Turn to page 86 to read more about Jesus.

 **Seek & Find**

Like Adam, we all sin. Have you trusted Jesus to take away your sins?

Animals on the Ark

Genesis 6:5—9:17

People became so bad that every thought they had was ⬭. God was very sad.

God told a good man named ⬭, "Make an ⬭ from wood. A ⬭ will destroy all life in the world. But your family and the ⬭ you bring on the ark will stay alive."

Noah did everything as God commanded. He built the ark. Then he brought his family and at least ⬭ of every animal, male and female, onto the ark. He brought ⬭ for them, too.

Then rain fell for ⬭ days and nights. Water covered the ⬭. Everything that had been ⬭ on dry land died.

The ark came to rest on the mountains of . When the land was dry enough, Noah brought his family and the animals out of the . Then he built an  and worshipped God.

God promised, "Never again will a  destroy the earth." As a reminder, he created a  in the clouds. We still see the reminder today!

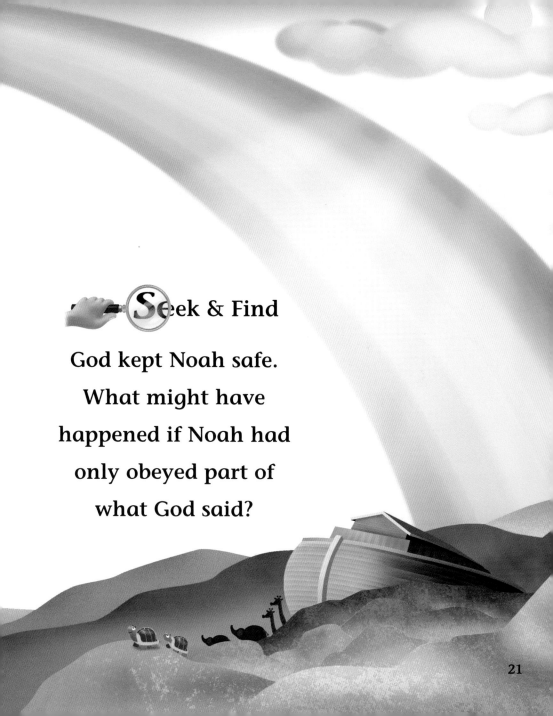

Seek & Find

God kept Noah safe. What might have happened if Noah had only obeyed part of what God said?

Count the Stars

Genesis 12:1—21:5

God told Abram to move to a new ⬚. But he didn't tell Abram exactly where. Abram ⬚ God to show him. When Abram reached Canaan, God said, "I will give this land to your ⬚."

But Abram and his wife, Sarai, could not have a ⬚. Abram asked God for help. God told Abram, "Look up at the sky. Count the ⬚ if you can." Then he said, "This is how many ⬚ will be in your family one day." Abram believed God. God changed Abram's name to ⬚ and Sarai's name to Sarah.

23

One day, three  came to visit. Abraham invited them for dinner. One angel said, "When I return about this time next ⬭, Sarah will have a ⬭."

Sarah was in a ▒▒ nearby. She overheard and ▒▒▒▒. She thought she was too ▒▒ to have a baby. But she had a son exactly when the angel had promised; Sarah was 90, and Abraham was 100! They named their baby ▒▒▒.

Seek & Find

God didn't tell Abraham his whole plan about where to move. Why not?

From Pit to Palace

Genesis 37:2—50:20

Joseph's dad made a ⬤ for him. His 11 brothers were ⬤. When Joseph said they bowed to him in his ⬤, they got so mad they threw him into a ⬤! Later, they sold Joseph as a slave.

Joseph ended up in ⬤ in Egypt, though he had not done anything wrong. The king's wine taster was in prison with him. He told Joseph a ⬤. Joseph said it meant he would be set ⬤. The man promised to help Joseph, but he ⬤! Two years later, the king was having ⬤ and wanted to know what they meant. Finally the wine ⬤ remembered Joseph!

27

Joseph told the king his dreams warned of a seven-year [image] when food wouldn't grow. The king gave Joseph a powerful job helping Egypt store [image].

Then the famine hit. Joseph's ████████ came to ██████ for food. They were afraid when they found out that the man in charge was Joseph. They ██████ to him as they had in Joseph's ████████. He ████████ them and said, "You planned to harm me. But God wanted to ████ many lives."

 **Seek & Find**

What event in your life seemed bad at first, but later God turned it into good for you or others?

A Baby in a Basket

Exodus 2:1–10

A  in Egypt wanted to keep her baby safe from an evil ●. She placed him in a basket and floated the basket in the ●. The baby's sister, Miriam, watched nearby.

A ⬚ was bathing in the river. She spotted the basket and opened it. When she saw the crying baby, she felt ⬚ for him. Miriam asked, "Do you want me to get someone who could ⬚ him for you?" The princess paid the baby's own ⬚ to feed him!

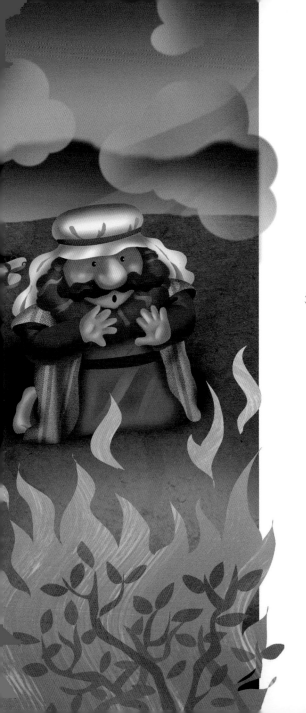

When the baby grew older, he went to live with the ░░░░░░ and became her son. She named him ░░░░░.

When Moses grew up, he left Egypt and became a ░░░░░░░. One day God spoke to him from a ░░░ that was on fire! The Lord said, "I have seen my people

suffer in Egypt as slaves. I have heard them cry
out to me. I want you to bring them out of
Egypt. I will be with you." Moses was in for a
big adventure!

 **Seek & Find**

**When the slaves cried out to God,
he heard them and sent help.
What help do you need from God?**

An Escape Through the Sea

Exodus 7:14—15:21

The people in  were mean to God's people, the Israelites. The ___ were ___. They worked for free. The Israelites were sad. They prayed to God to help.

God sent Moses to tell ___, the king of Egypt, to let the slaves leave. Pharaoh said, "No!" So God sent ___ to change his mind. Before each plague, Moses gave Pharaoh another chance to let the Israelites go. But Pharaoh was very stubborn. Even after ░░░░░, gnats, flies, locusts, dead animals, sores called ░░░░░, hailstorms, and three days of ░░░░░░░, Pharaoh still said, "No!" When his son ░░░░ during the tenth plague, finally Pharaoh let the Israelites go. As they left, Pharaoh changed his mind again. He and his army chased them on ░░░░░░!

35

God made a way for the Israelites to escape. He  the waters of the ⬭ Sea. The Israelites went through on dry ground. Then they ⬭ praises to God.

Seek & Find

If you were there, how would you have felt as you walked through the sea? How has God helped you through a problem that didn't seem to have an escape?

Miracles for Moses

Exodus 4:1–9, 16:31, 35; 17:3–6; Numbers 21:4–9;

John 3:14–15

God performed many amazing ⬛ for Moses. He caused Moses' staff to turn into a ⬛. Then God changed it back into a staff. Moses' hand turned ⬛ when he put it in and out of his coat. When he put his hand back inside his ⬛ God turned it back to normal.

As the Israelites followed Moses through the desert, they got ⬛. Moses hit a ⬛, as God told him to do, and ⬛ poured out of it.

38

God fed the Israelites while they were in the desert for 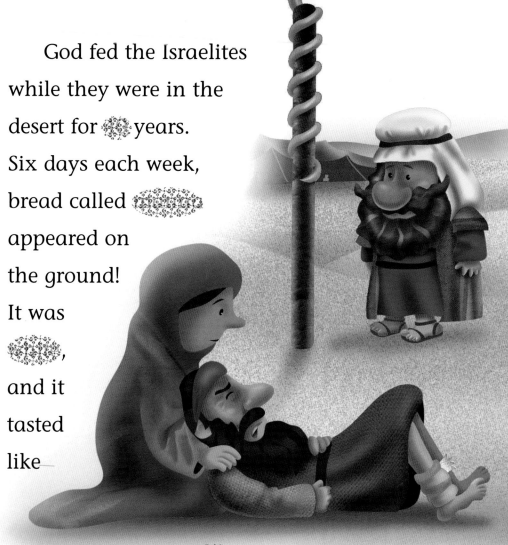 years. Six days each week, bread called ⬚⬚⬚⬚ appeared on the ground! It was ⬚⬚⬚, and it tasted like— wafers made with ⬚⬚⬚.

When Israelites were dying from snakebites, God told Moses to make a ⬚⬚⬚

snake on a pole. Whoever looked at it would live. Whoever would not look at it would die. Later, Jesus explained that he is like that. Whoever looks to  to save them will forever. Whoever doesn't look to him will not.

Seek & Find

Would you like to see miracles happen?

Why or why not?

Ten Commandments

Exodus 20:3–17, 34:1–8, 28–29

The Lord came down to Moses on Mount _____. He said, "I am a God who is tender and kind. I am gracious. I am slow to get _____. I am faithful and full of love.

"I _____ those who do evil. I forgive those who refuse to obey. And I forgive those who sin. But I do not let guilty people go without punishing them." Moses bowed down and _____ God.

Then God wrote the Ten Commandments on two _____ tablets:

1. Do not put any other _____ in place of me.
2. Do not make statues of gods.

3. Do not misuse the of the Lord your God.

4. Remember to keep the Sabbath day .

5. Honour your father and mother.

6. Do not commit .

7. Do not commit adultery.

8. Do not steal.

9. Do not .

10. Do not desire anything that belongs to .

Moses carried the tablets down the .
His face was _____ because he had spoken
with God.

Seek & Find

Jesus said God's laws are about loving

God and people *(see Matthew 22:36–40).*

How does keeping each of the

Ten Commandments show love?

Big Battles of the Bible

Exodus 17:8–16; Joshua 6:1–20, 10:1–15;

Judges 4:1—5:1

God helped the Israelites win [picture] when they trusted him. When they fought the Amalekites, the Israelites kept winning if [picture] held up his staff to God in heaven. This showed that the Israelites depended on God. But Moses got tired. So two [picture] held up [picture] arms until his people won the battle!

One of the most famous battles happened in [picture]. God told Joshua how to win. Joshua and his men [picture] around the city while [picture] blew ram's horn [picture]. When Joshua and the men shouted, the [picture] around the city fell!

46

Joshua's men marched in and took over Jericho. In another battle, God sent a ▓▓▓▓▓ that killed more Amorites than were killed by

. Then God answered Joshua's prayer that the  would stay in the sky until they won!

God used a woman named  in a battle, too. She had a message for Barak from God. She told him God wanted him to lead the Israelites to . Barak refused to go without her, so Deborah went along. When they won the battle, they praised God together with a .

Seek & Find

What are three ways you praise God when he helps you?

God Guides Gideon

Judges 6:11—7:25

The Lord told Gideon he would lead Israel's ⬚ against another army. Gideon asked, "How? My family is ⬚, and I'm the least ⬚ member of my family." The Lord answered, "I will be with you."

Gideon wanted to be sure. He put a piece of ⬚ outside and said to God, "If only the wool is ⬚ tomorrow morning and the ground is ⬚, I will know that you will use me to save Israel." The next day, the wool was wet and the ground was dry.

Then Gideon said, "Let me use the wool for one more ⬚. This time keep the wool ⬚

and make the  wet." That's what God did. So Gideon gathered a big army.

God said, "You have too many . I do not want Israel to brag that their own has saved them."

God told Gideon to let most

of his army go home. He only kept 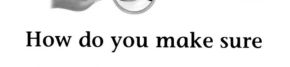 men.

When it was time to fight, Gideon's small army held 🔵, broke 🔵, and blew 🔵.

They shouted, "A 🔵 for the Lord and for Gideon!"

Then the other army 🔵 away!

🔍 Seek & Find

How do you make sure you're doing what God wants?

Samuel Listens to God

1 Samuel 3:1–19

A boy named Samuel lived in the ▨▨ with the prophet Eli. Eli taught him how to ▨▨ the Lord. In those days God didn't give many messages to his people. But one night after Samuel went to ▨▨, God called out to him.

Samuel ran to Eli and said, "▨▨ I am. You called out to me." Eli said, "I didn't call you. Go back and lie down."

It happened again and Samuel went to Eli a second time. Eli sent him back to ▨▨ this time, too.

The third time, Eli figured out that the Lord was calling Samuel. So Eli said, "Go and lie

down. If someone calls out to you again, say,
', Lord. I'm listening.'" So Samuel did.

The Lord came and stood there. He called out again, "Samuel! Samuel!" Then Samuel replied, "Speak. I'm listening."

God  Samuel some of his plans. In the

morning, Samuel gave Eli
the message God had given
him. As Samuel grew up, the
Lord was with him. Everything
he said to Samuel came true.

Seek & Find

**God finished his message when Samuel
said he was listening. When you pray,
do you listen for the Holy Spirit to
speak to your heart?**

David Fights a Giant

1 Samuel 16:4—17:50

King Saul wanted someone to play the ⬭ to calm him. His servant said, "David plays the harp. He's a brave ⬭. He's very hand-some. And the ⬭ is with him." When David played the harp, Saul felt better.

One day a ⬭ named Goliath dared Saul's army: "Choose someone to fight me. If he wins, we will be your ⬭. If I win, you will be our slaves." Saul and his whole army were ⬭.

David said, "I'll fight him." Saul replied, "You're too ⬭." But David said, "The Lord saved me from a ⬭ and a ⬭. He'll save me from this giant, too."

David took his sling and five . Goliath

threatened, "You'll regret this!" But David said,

"You come to fight me with a . But I'm

coming against you in the name of the !"

David swung his sling. A stone hit Goliath on the ⬚⬚⬚ and killed him. Goliath fell flat on his ⬚⬚⬚.

S̶eek & Find

What has God done for you in the past that helps you trust that he will help you again?

Are you facing a giant problem?
If so, what help do you need from God?

61

God and Elijah

1 Kings 19:1–18; James 5:17

The Bible says Elijah was an ordinary person, just like us. But Elijah had great faith, and God performed many amazing ⬤ for him.

To help Elijah prove to others that God was real, God made ⬤ come down from heaven onto an ⬤. During a famine, God sent ⬤ to bring food to Elijah each day.

One day while Elijah was in a ⬤, the Lord gave him a message: "Stand on the ⬤. I am going to pass by."

As the Lord came, a powerful ⬤ tore apart the mountains. But that wasn't the Lord.

Then there was an earthquake. But that wasn't the Lord. Then a  came. But that wasn't the Lord either.

After the fire, there was only a gentle whisper. It was God's voice.

Elijah told God he was █████ and that he was the only believer left. God told him there were actually ████████ of people who still believed.

God showed Elijah he was with him in both big and █████ ways.

Seek & Find

Sometimes you might feel like you're the only one who believes in God, but actually there are millions of believers. Who do you know who loves God?

A Queen Risks Her Life

Esther 1:1—9:32

King Xerxes chose a very beautiful ⬤ woman named Esther as his queen.

Esther's cousin Mordecai had ⬤ her after her parents died. Mordecai would not ⬤ down to an evil noble named ⬤. Prideful Haman was angry. Haman knew Mordecai was Jewish. To get revenge, Haman asked the king to pass a law that all of the Jews would be ⬤. The king didn't know Queen Esther was Jewish.

Esther needed to beg the king for mercy. But the ⬤ said no one could approach the king uninvited. If they tried, they would be put

to ⬚⬚⬚ unless the king held out his ⬚⬚⬚⬚⬚ .
Mordecai told Esther, "It's possible that you
became queen for a ⬚⬚⬚ just like this."

Esther asked the Jewish people to [fast]—not eat or drink anything—for three days. She fasted, too. Then she went to see the king. He held out his gold rod. Esther was [safe]!

The king had evil Haman killed the same way Haman had planned to kill [the Jews]. Then the king gave the Jews permission to [fight] for their lives. No one could stand against them!

 **S**eek & Find

How can you help the

people in your life?

Psalms

(NIV)

Psalms are poems, prayers, and praise for God. Many are songs. Some favourites are...

The Lord is my ⬤⬤⬤, I shall not be in want. He makes me lie down in green ⬤⬤⬤, he leads me beside quiet waters...

Psalm 23:1–2

God is our refuge and strength, an ever-present help in ⬤⬤⬤.

Psalm 46:1

This is the ⬭ the
Lord has made;
Let us rejoice and
be ⬭ in it.

Psalm 118:24

I have hidden your word in my
⬭ that I might not sin against you.

Psalm 119:11

Your word is a ⬭ to my feet
and a light for my ⬭.

Psalm 119:105

Seek & Find

How would memorising your
favourite psalms help you?

Proverbs

(NIV)

The book of Proverbs is filled with advice about how to live a 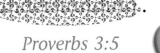 life. King ⬭⬭⬭ wrote most of it for his son. Some favourites are…

Trust in the Lord with all your ⬭⬭⬭ and lean not on your own ⬭⬭⬭.

Proverbs 3:5

The way of a fool seems ⬭⬭ to him, but a ⬭⬭ man listens to advice. *Proverbs 12:15*

He who walks with the wise grows ⬭, but a ⬭ of fools suffers harm.

Proverbs 13:20

A gentle answer turns away ⬭, but a harsh word ⬭ up anger. *Proverbs 15:1*

He who is kind to the poor ⬭ to the Lord, and he will ⬭ him for what he has done.

Proverbs 19:17

Seek & Find

How would you say these proverbs in your own words to give advice to a friend?

73

Walking in Fire

Daniel 3:1–30

King Nebuchadnezzar made a huge gold
⬤ . He commanded everyone, "When you
hear the ⬤ , fall down and ⬤ the
statue. If you don't, you will be thrown into a
flaming ⬤ ."

Shadrach, Meshach, and Abednego
refused to worship the statue. They told the
king, "The God we ⬤ is able to bring us out
of the flaming furnace ⬤ . But even if we
knew our God wouldn't ⬤ us, we still
wouldn't serve your gods."

The king was very angry. He ordered his strongest  to tie up Shadrach, ⬭⬭⬭, and ⬭⬭⬭ and throw them into the flaming furnace. But the three men in the fire didn't ⬭⬭.

The king jumped to his feet. He was amazed when he saw they were ⬚ and that there was someone with them in the fire. He said, "The ⬚ man looks like a ⬚ of the gods."

The king let them come out of the ⬚. Not one ⬚ on their heads was burned. Their ⬚ weren't burned either. And they didn't even smell of ⬚!

Seek & Find

When someone tries to get you to do something wrong, what might happen if you say no?

How could God help?

Lions Miss a Meal

Daniel 6:1–28

Daniel was a ⬚⬚⬚ under King Darius. Daniel did a better job than anyone else. So the king planned to put him in charge.

The other leaders were ⬚⬚⬚. They looked for a way to get Daniel in trouble. But they could never catch him doing anything ⬚⬚⬚.

So they talked King Darius into passing a ⬚⬚ that for ⬚ days people could only ⬚⬚ to the king. If they prayed to any other man or god, they would be thrown into the ⬚⬚ den.

Daniel still prayed *to God* ⬚⬚ times a day with his ⬚⬚⬚ open. The other leaders told

the king that Daniel disobeyed the law about .

Guards threw  into the lions' den. The king said to him, "You always serve your  faithfully. So may he save you!"

As soon as the sun began to rise, the king hurried to the lions' den. He called, "Daniel! Has your God saved you from the lions?"

Daniel answered, "My God sent an ▨ that shut the lions' ▨! " Daniel did not get hurt. He had trusted God.

 **S**eek & Find

Would you pray even if your school made a rule against it?

When have you trusted God to protect you from danger?

Three Days in a Fish

Jonah 1:1—3:10

God told Jonah, "Go and preach in ⬭." But Jonah tried to run away from God. He took a boat to ⬭ instead.

A wild ⬭ tossed the ship. All of the sailors were afraid. The captain woke Jonah and said, "Get up and call out to your ⬭ for help! Maybe he'll see what's happening to us. Then we won't die."

Jonah said, "This terrible storm is my ⬭." He told the ⬭ to throw him over-board. When they did, the stormy sea became ⬭. God sent a huge fish to ⬭ Jonah so he wouldn't ⬭. Jonah was inside the

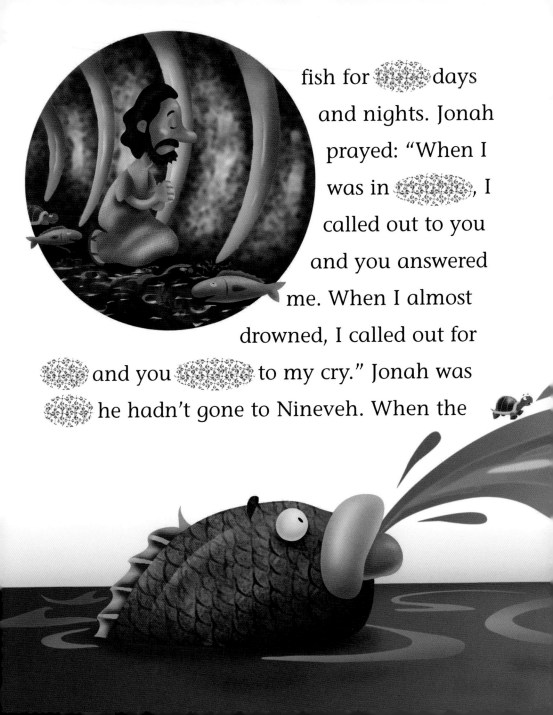

fish for ▓▓▓ days and nights. Jonah prayed: "When I was in ▓▓▓, I called out to you and you answered me. When I almost drowned, I called out for ▓▓▓ and you ▓▓▓ to my cry." Jonah was ▓▓▓ he hadn't gone to Nineveh. When the fish ⬚ Jonah onto the shore, Jonah headed to Nineveh.

Jonah ⬚ the people that they needed to stop doing bad things. They believed him and ⬚. God saw this and decided not to ⬚ them.

Seek & Find

Why is it a bad idea to try to run from God?

God's Son is Born

Matthew 2:1–11; Luke 2:1–20

Mary was expecting a baby. But
she and her husband, Joseph,
had to go to ▨▨▨▨▨ to
put their names on a
▨▨ list. There was
no room in the
▨▨, so they
stayed in a
stable.

While they were there,
Mary gave birth to the Son of
God. She wrapped him in
 and placed him in a
_____, a box for animal
_____.

In fields nearby, shepherds
watched their flocks at night. An
_____ appeared to them and
said, "Do not be
afraid. I bring

you good news of great joy. Today a Saviour has been born; he is Christ the Lord.

"You will find the baby wrapped in cloths and lying in a manger." Suddenly the sky was

full of ⬚ praising God. They said, "Glory to God in the highest, and on earth ⬚ to all."

The shepherds hurried to Bethlehem and found Jesus. Then they spread the word. Everyone who heard was ⬚.

Mary kept all these things like a secret treasure in her heart. Later, wise men followed a ⬚ to find Jesus. They gave him ⬚ and worshipped him.

 **Seek & Find**

Which Christmas traditions remind you most about Jesus?

John Baptises Jesus

Matthew 3:13–17, 4:1–11

Jesus came to the ⬤ River to be baptised
by John. Jesus had never sinned, but he said,
"It is ⬤ for us to do this. It carries out God's
holy plan."

As soon as Jesus was baptised, the Spirit of
God came down on him like a ⬤. A voice
from heaven said, "This is my Son, and I ⬤
him. I am very ⬤ with him."

Then Jesus went into the ⬤ He did
not eat for ⬤ days. The devil tempted him in
⬤ different ways, but Jesus didn't ⬤.

First, Satan tried to tempt Jesus to turn
stones into ⬤ because he was hungry.

Next, he tried to get Jesus to jump off the ⬭ and force ⬭ to catch him. After that, the devil offered the world's ⬭ to Jesus if he would ⬭ to him. Jesus said, "Get away from me, ⬭!"

Jesus never gave in to any of the devil's temptations. He fought back each time by quoting the ⬭. Finally, the devil left.

Seek & Find

Can you find a Bible verse
to memorise that would
help you fight temptation?

Everlasting Life

John 3:1–21

A Jewish leader named Nicodemus came to visit Jesus at ⬤. Jesus told him, "No one can see God's kingdom without being ⬤ again."

That puzzled Nicodemus. He wondered how he could be born ⬤ .

The first time you are born, your ⬤ will one day die. If you are "born again", the Holy Spirit will be with you always. You get new life that will last ⬤ God gives us new life by his Spirit when we put our ⬤ in Jesus. When we trust him to take away our ⬤ because he died on the ⬤, we are born again. We have

life. Jesus told Nicodemus that everyone who believes in him can live with God forever.

Jesus said, "God loved the so much that he gave his one and only . Anyone

who believes in him will not die but will have
eternal . God sent his Son to  the world
through him."

S eek & Find

Have you trusted Jesus as your Saviour?

Miracles at Sea

Matthew 8:23–27, 14:22–33, 17:24–27;
Luke 5:1–11; John 21:1–14

Jesus performed amazing miracles on the Sea of  and its shore. One day, Jesus told Peter to take his into deep water. "Let the down and catch fish," he said. Peter hadn't caught any the night before, but he obeyed Jesus anyway. He caught enough fish to fill  boats! Jesus said, "From now on you will catch ."

On another day while Jesus was on a boat, a big came up. Jesus' helpers him up and said, "Lord! Save us! We're going to drown!" Jesus ordered the winds and waves to . Everything became ! His helpers were .

Very early one morning Jesus walked on  to his helpers who were on a . Then Jesus let  walk on water.

But Peter took his eyes off Jesus. He got  and began to . He cried, "Lord! Save me!"

Right away Jesus caught him. "Your ⬚⬚⬚ is so small! Why did you doubt me?" Jesus asked.

On another day Peter asked Jesus for ⬚⬚⬚ to pay a ⬚⬚⬚. Jesus said, "Throw out your ⬚⬚⬚ line. Open the mouth of the first fish you catch. You will find the exact ⬚⬚⬚ you need inside."

Seek & Find

**How could remembering
that Jesus calmed the storm
help you when you are afraid?**

A Boy's Lunch Feeds 5,000

John 6:3–14

As Jesus sat on the side of a ⬭, he saw a large crowd coming. So he said to Philip, "Where can we buy ⬭ for these people?" He asked this to test Philip. Jesus already knew what to do.

Philip answered, "Eight months' pay would not buy enough for each one to have a ⬭!"

Andrew said, "Here is a boy with ⬭ small loaves of bread. He also has two small ⬭. But how far will that go in such a large ⬭?"

Jesus said, "Have the people sit down on the grass." There were more than 5,000 people there. Jesus took the loaves and gave . His disciples handed out the  to those

who were seated. Jesus gave them as much as they wanted. And they did the same with the ⬚.

All of the people had enough to eat. Then Jesus said to his helpers, "⬚ the leftover pieces. Don't ⬚ anything." The leftovers from the five loaves of bread and two fish filled ⬚ baskets!

Seek & Find

What has God given to you
that is more than you need?

Your Faith Has Healed You

Matthew 11:4–5, 8:5–13, 15; 12:22; Mark 5:25–29;
Luke 7:12–16; 8:49–55; John 11:43–44; Acts 3:2–8

Many ⬤ people asked Jesus to heal their eyes, and he did. ⬤ men could walk after meeting Jesus. He helped deaf and mute people to hear and ⬤, too.

As Jesus touched a sick woman's hand, her ⬤ left. When another woman touched his ⬤, her bleeding problem stopped right away. Jesus made sores disappear from many people's ⬤. When Jesus made a sick person well, he often said, "Your ⬤ has healed you!"

Jesus even healed people who seemed past ⬤. He brought Jairus' 12-year-old ⬤ back to life after she had died.

Jesus felt sorry for a  whose dead son's body was being carried out of the 🏛️. He made the dead man return to life and 🪑 up!

After Jesus' friend Lazarus had been dead in a tomb for 🔢 days, Jesus said, "Lazarus,

come out!" Everyone was very ▨▨▨ to see Lazarus walk out of the ▨▨ alive!

Sometimes Jesus healed from far away, too. He healed a ▨▨ army leader's servant who was in a different city.

Jesus let his followers heal using his ▨▨, too.

 **Seek & Find**

When you get well after being sick, do you usually thank God for healing you?

Do you know someone who needs you to pray for healing?

The Lord's Prayer

Matthew 6:9–15 (NIV)

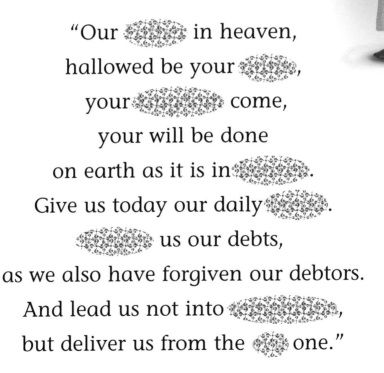

Jesus taught us this prayer:

"Our ⬤ in heaven,
hallowed be your ⬤,
your ⬤ come,
your will be done
on earth as it is in ⬤.
Give us today our daily ⬤.
⬤ us our debts,
as we also have forgiven our debtors.
And lead us not into ⬤,
but deliver us from the ⬤ one."

Then Jesus reminded everyone, "██████ people. If you do, your ██████ in heaven will forgive you. But if you do not, your Father will not forgive your sins."

Seek & Find

How are your prayers like the Lord's Prayer, and how are they different?

What do you say in your prayers?
What do you thank God for?

More Than a Teacher

John 6:48, 8:12, 10:3, 4, 9–14; 14:6

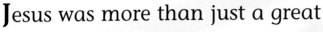

Jesus was more than just a great
████. He asked Peter, "Who do you say I
am?" Peter answered, "You are the ████. You
are the ███ of the living God."

    Jesus told people how he was like familiar
everyday things. He said, "I am the ████ of
life." Bread keeps us alive, and so does ████.

    He said, "I am the ████ of the world. Those
who follow me will never walk in ████."
Light helps us not to trip in the dark. Jesus
helps us see how to live without falling
into sin.

Jesus also said, "I am the ▨. Anyone who enters through me will be ▨." He said, "No one comes to the ▨ except through me." There is no way to get to God without Jesus.

Jesus told them, "I am the good ▨." He said, "I know my sheep, and my sheep ▨ me." We follow Jesus like sheep follow a shepherd. Jesus doesn't want us to just learn *about* him, he wants us to ▨ him and ▨ him.

 **Seek & Find**

Is Jesus like a storybook character to you, or do you know him like you know your family?

What Matters Most

Matthew 19:19, 22:37–40; Luke 6:31–35;

John 15:12

Jesus said, "▩ the Lord your God with all your heart and with all your ▩. Love him with all your ▩. This is the first and most ▩ commandment."

He continued, "The second is like it. 'Love your neighbour as you love ▩.'"

How can we show love to other people? Jesus' ▩ Rule is "Do to others as you want them to do to ▨." He said to love one another as he has loved us.

Jesus even wants us to love our ▨. He said, "Suppose you love those who love you. Should anyone ▨ you for that? Even 'sinners' love those who love them. And suppose you do good to those who are ▨ to you. Should anyone praise you for that?"

Jesus said people would know we are his ▨ if we love one another.

Seek & Find

**Sometimes people we love may
not even know that we love them.
How can we show them?**

The Good Neighbour

Luke 10:25–37

A man talked with Jesus about the command to love his neighbour. He asked Jesus, "Who is my ⬤?" Jesus answered with a story.

A man went from ⬤ to Jericho. ⬤ attacked him. They stripped off his ⬤ and beat him. Then they went away, leaving him almost dead.

A Jewish priest went down that same road. When he saw the man, he ⬤ by on the other side. Another priest did the same thing!

But a man from ⬤ came along. When the Samaritan saw the man who had been attacked, he felt ⬤ for him. He washed his wounds and put  on them. Then he put the man on his own . He took him to an and cared for him.

The next day the Samaritan gave two  coins to the ▒▒▒▒▒. "Take care of him," he said. "When I return, I will ▒▒ you back for any extra ▒▒ you may have."

Jesus asked, "Which of the three was a ⬬ to the man who was attacked?" The man talking with Jesus answered, "The one who felt ⬬ for him."

Jesus told him, "Go and do as he did."

Seek & Find

Jews usually wouldn't speak to Samaritans, but Jesus said to love them. Are there people you avoid that you shouldn't?

God's Kingdom

Matthew 13:24–33, 44–50; Mark 4:26–32

Jesus told stories called ⬚⬚⬚. Many were about the ⬚⬚⬚ of God. He said God's kingdom is like a fishing ⬚ that a fisherman lowered into the lake. The net caught good and bad fish. The fisherman kept the good fish and threw away the bad. Like the fish in the net, good and bad ⬚⬚⬚ are together right now, but one day ⬚⬚⬚ will separate them.

Jesus said the kingdom of heaven is like a ⬚⬚⬚ seed. It was tiny, but then it grew into a huge tree. Jesus' church started very small, but now there are ⬚⬚⬚ of Christians.

Jesus said his kingdom is also like yeast.

Yeast is what spreads quickly through  dough to make it rise. God's kingdom has spread quickly like yeast throughout the

Jesus said the kingdom of heaven is like a man found in a field. The man sold all he had so he could buy the . Jesus said it is also like a valuable that a salesman sold everything to buy. Someone who understands the value of God's will give up anything for it.

 **Seek & Find**

Are you part of God's kingdom?

Is Jesus your King?

You Are Loved

Matthew 19:13–15; Mark 10:13–16; Luke 18:15–17;

John 3:16; 1 John 3:1

Some people brought little ⬭ to Jesus. They wanted him to place his ⬭ on the children and ⬭ for them. But his helpers told the people to ⬭.

Jesus wasn't too busy for the children. They were important to him. He said, "Let the little children ⬭ to me. Don't keep them away. The kingdom of ⬭ belongs to people like them. Anyone who will not receive God's kingdom like a little child will never ⬭ it." Then he took the children in his ⬭. He put his hands on them and ⬭ them.

Jesus loves children, including . He thinks of you as his friends. He said, "No one has greater  than the one who gives his  for his friends." He loved you enough to die so that your sins would be forgiven.

God the Father loved you so much that he gave his one and only ▨ so you could live with him forever. He even ▨ you into his family when you ▨ in Jesus. First John 3:1 says, "How great is the love the Father has given us so freely! Now we can be called ▨ of God."

 **S**eek & Find

Do you feel God's love for you?

The Upset Sister

Luke 10:38–42

Two of Jesus' friends were  named Mary and Martha. One day Martha opened her home to Jesus and his helpers.

Mary sat at Jesus' _____ and _____ to what he said. But Martha was thinking about how to get food and the house _____ for her guests. She was so worried about cooking and _____ that she was missing a chance to hear what the Son of God was _____! Martha came to Jesus and asked, "Lord, don't you _____ that my sister has left me to do the work by myself? Tell her to  me!"

Jesus answered, "Martha, Martha, what could prevent you from spending  with me in prayer and Bible study?" It is easy to think

too much about everyday cares and forget
what matters most. Spending time with ████ is
more ████████ than other things. He can help
us not to be ███████ and upset.

 **S**eek & Find

What sometimes keeps you
from spending time with Jesus
in prayer and reading the Bible?

When you're worried and upset,
how does praying help you?

The Shepherd and Sheep

Luke 15:4–10; John 10:11, 14, 27

Jesus called himself the Good _____ and he called believers "_____". A shepherd risks his _____ to protect his sheep from wolves; later Jesus would give his life to save us.

Jesus said, "I _____ my sheep, and my sheep know me." He also told people, "My sheep listen to my _____ and _____ me."

But even when his sheep _____ away, Jesus still loves them. He wants them back and he will go after them. He said, "Suppose one of you has _____ sheep and loses one of them. Won't he leave the 99 in the open

country? Won't he go and look for the one  sheep until he finds it?

"When he finds it, he will joyfully put it up on his shoulders and go home. Then he will call his friends and neighbours together. He will say, 'Be happy with me. I have found my lost sheep.' "

Jesus continued, "I tell you, it will be the same in heaven. There will be great joy when one sinner turns away from sin. Yes, there will be more joy than for 99 godly people who do not need to turn away from their sins."

Seek & Find

What are some temptations that cause people to wander away from Jesus?

Coming Home

Luke 15:11–32

Jesus told a story about a man with ⬤ sons. The younger son asked for his ⬤ of the family's wealth. Then he went far away and ⬤ it all on wild living.

When he had spent everything, he got a job feeding ⬤. He was so ⬤ that he longed to eat the pigs' ⬤! But he decided to go home instead. He said to himself, "I don't deserve to be my father's ⬤, but I could be one of his ⬤."

While the son was still far away, his father saw him. He was filled with tender ⬤ for his son. He ⬤ to him. He threw his arms

around him and  him.

The son said to him, "Father, I have against heaven and against ." But the father gave him a robe, a ring, sandals, and a big party!

The older _____ said that was not fair. The father replied, "My son, you are always with me. Everything I have is _____. But we had to celebrate and be _____. Your brother was _____, and now he is _____!"

Seek & Find

How is sinning like being lost?

When you repent, how does God feel?

Don't Worry

Matthew 6:25–34

Jesus said, "Do not worry about your  and what you will  or . Don't worry about your body and what you will . Isn't there more to

life than eating? Aren't there more important
things than ?

"Look at the . They don't plant or
gather crops. But your Father in heaven

them. Aren't you  much more than them?

"Why do you _____ about clothes? See how the _____ grow. They don't _____ or make clothing. But not even King _____ in all of his glory was dressed like them. Won't God dress you even better?

"But put God's kingdom _____." If you put God first and try to follow him, he will take care of the rest.

We don't need to worry about tomorrow. Jesus said, "░░░░░░░ will worry about itself. Each day has enough ░░░░░ of its own."

Seek & Find

In 1 Peter 5:7 it says, "Turn all your worries over to him. He cares about you." What worries do you need to turn over to God?

Jesus' Last Meal

Matthew 26:26–30; John 13:1–5; 14:18–19, 27; 16:22

Jesus knew when he was about to ⬚, so he met with his disciples to eat his last ⬚. First he washed their ⬚ to show that it is important to be humble and to serve others. He said, "I have given you an ⬚. You should do as I have done for you."

Then Jesus gave thanks and broke some ⬚. He handed it to his disciples and said, "Take this and eat it. This is my ⬚."

After that, he gave thanks and handed a ⬚ to them. He said, "Drink from it. This is my ⬚. It is poured out to forgive sins."

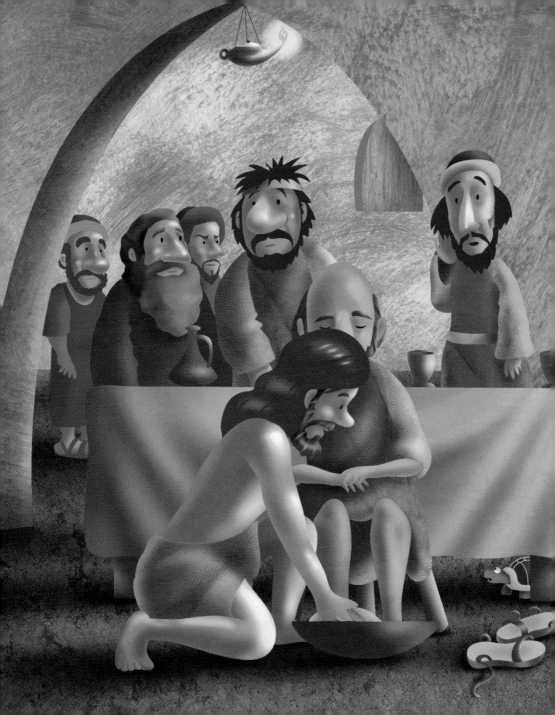

Jesus comforted his disciples. "I will not leave you like ⬛⬛⬛. I will come to you. Because I ⬛⬛⬛, you will live also."

He told them, "I leave my peace with you. I give my

to you. I do not give it to you as the world does. Do not let your hearts be 〰️. And do not be 〰️."

Then they sang and 〰️ about what was ahead.

Seek & Find

What does Jesus want believers to remember when we eat the bread and drink from the cup of Communion?

Why Jesus Died

Matthew 26:47–54; 27:45–54

Evil leaders were so jealous of Jesus that they wanted to ⬚ him! Jesus' disciple Judas led them to the Garden of ⬚. He showed them which man Jesus was by giving him a ⬚ on the cheek. Then the bad men started to take Jesus away.

Peter wanted to rescue Jesus. He cut off one of the men's ⬚, but Jesus healed it. Jesus said he could have called down thousands of ⬚ for help if he had wanted. But he planned to die for our sins as the ⬚ tells us he would. So Jesus let the men take him.

Even though Jesus had never done anything , people said he was guilty and had to die. Soldiers nailed him to a . Jesus was willing to die as the punishment for our ⬚. It was the only way that we would be able to be with him in ⬚.

There was ⬚ for three hours in the middle of the day while Jesus was on the cross. When he died, the temple ⬚ that kept men apart from God was torn. The ground ⬚, and rocks split. The guards said, "He was surely the ⬚ of God!"

Seek & Find

Why did Jesus choose to die on the cross for you?

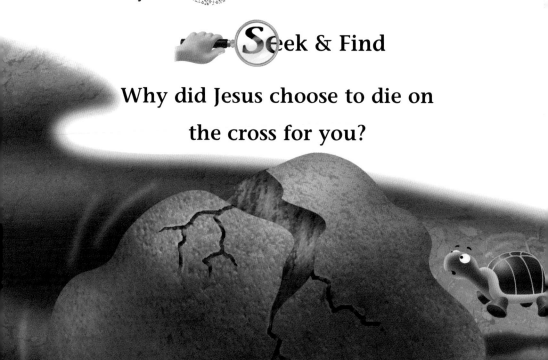

Jesus is Alive Again!

Matthew 28:1–20; Luke 24:15, 42;

John 20:10–20, 26–29; 21:1–14; Acts 1:9–11;

1 Corinthians 15:3–6

Jesus' body was in the tomb for _____ days. At dawn on _____ morning, Mary Magdalene and Jesus' mother Mary went to the tomb.

There was a big _____. An angel rolled back the _____ that had sealed the tomb. He told the women, "I know that you are looking for Jesus who was _____. He is not here! He has _____, just as he said he would!" As the women ran to tell the disciples, Jesus met them, and they _____ him.

Other people saw Jesus, too. He walked with two men on the road to ▨▨▨▨▨. He appeared to his disciples in a ▨▨▨▨ room. He let them feel the ▨▨▨▨ holes in his

hands and feet. He told Thomas, "Because you have seen me, you have ░░░░░. Blessed are those who have not ░░░ me but still have believed."

On one morning, Jesus made breakfast on the ░░░░ for his disciples. Another day he even appeared to 500 people at once.

Jesus went back to heaven by rising up in a ░░░░. Angels said he would come back one day the same way.

Seek & Find

What part of your Easter celebration reminds you that Jesus returned to life?

God Sends Power

Acts 2:1–41; Galatians 5:22–23

Jesus promised to send the Holy ⬭. While the
believers were together, a sound like strong ⬭
came from heaven. It filled the whole ⬭.

Small ⬭ came upon each believer.
All of them were filled with the Holy Spirit.
They began to ⬭ in languages they had
not learned.

Jews from every country in the world were
visiting Jerusalem. They heard the sound. They
were puzzled because they each heard the
believers ⬭ their own language!

Peter said to the crowd, "⬭ who
calls on the name of the Lord will be ⬭."

He told them, "You  Jesus to the cross.
But God raised him up and made him both
Lord and Christ." The people felt  and
asked what they should do. Peter replied, "Turn

away from your sins and be ▨▨▨▨ in the name of Jesus Christ. Then your sins will be ▨▨▨▨. You will receive the ▨▨▨ of the Holy Spirit." About ▨▨▨ people believed and were baptised that day!

Seek & Find

What did Peter say people needed to do to be saved?

Have you done that?

Paul's Adventures

Acts 27:42—28:5; Romans 5:8; 8:38–39;

2 Corinthians 1:9, 6:5, 11:33; Galatians 6:9

Saul was mean to Christians and tried to put them in ⬚. One day Jesus appeared to him in a ⬚. Then Saul believed in Jesus. He was very ⬚ after that. Even his name changed, to ⬚.

Paul visited many countries and taught about Jesus. Sometimes he was put in ⬚ for it. He wrote ⬚ from prison that became ⬚ of the Bible. The Holy Spirit gave him great truths to write: "I am absolutely sure that not even death or life can ⬚ us from God's ⬚." He wrote, "While we were still

sinners, ⬡⬡⬡ died for us."

Instead of being sad in jail, Paul ⬡⬡⬡ praises to God. He said hard times happened so he would rely on ⬡⬡⬡ instead of himself.

Sometimes people beat Paul and threw ⬡⬡⬡ at him. Once when people wanted to kill Paul, he hid in a ⬡⬡⬡ and friends lowered it over the city wall. Another day when he swam to shore after a shipwreck, a  bit him!

No matter what he faced, Paul kept serving God because he loved ⁘ and people. He said, "Let us not become tired of doing ⁘."

Seek & Find

What is the biggest change you've seen in someone who started believing in Jesus?

The Roman Road

Romans 3:23; 6:23; 5:8; 10:9 (NIV)

Romans were famous for the many ▨▨ they built. In the book of the Bible called Romans, there are ▨▨ verses that explain that the road to heaven is through ▨▨. These verses are sometimes called the "Roman Road". They say:

1 *"For all have ▨▨ and fall short of the ▨▨ of God."* That means everyone has done wrong things against God and is not good enough to deserve to go to heaven.

2 *"For the wages of sin is ▨▨ but the ▨▨ of God is eternal ▨▨ in Christ Jesus our Lord."* Sin deserves death, but instead, God offers us a gift: we can live ▨▨ because Jesus died for our sins.

3 "But God demon-strates his own ████ for us in this: While we were

still ████, Christ died for us."

God loved us enough to let his Son die for us even while we were still bad.

4 "If you ████ with your mouth, 'Jesus is ████,' and believe in your ████ that God raised him from the dead, you will be ████." If you believe in Jesus, you can go to ████. Tell others!

 **Seek & Find**

Can you memorise the verses of the Roman Road so you can tell others about Jesus?

Grace is Amazing

John 3:16; Romans 3:20, 11:6; 1 Corinthians 1:30;

Galatians 2:21, 5:6; Ephesians 2:8; James 2:18; 1 John 4:19

Grace is God's kindness. We didn't do anything to it. God is so loving that he wants us with him in heaven even though we don't deserve it. Jesus said, "I am the ⬭." He is like a bridge that connects us to ⬭ the Father. This is how much God loved the ⬭: He gave his one and only ⬭. Anyone who believes in him will not die but will live ⬭.

Keeping rules and doing good things isn't what makes us [image]. God's rules show us how much we do that is wrong.

Our righteousness comes from what Jesus did for us on the [image]. Being saved doesn't come from anything we do. It is God's [image].

If we have faith in Jesus, we show it by what we [image]. The Bible says, "The only thing that really counts is [image] that shows itself through [image]."

 **eek & Find**

Are you amazed that God loves you so much?

The Body of Christ

1 Corinthians 12:12–31

Now that Jesus has gone to ●●●●●, he uses
believers to help people. He does his work
through ●● as if we were his own hands and
feet. The ●●●● calls believers the Body of Christ.

Just as every part of the body matters,
every ●●●● is important, too. Different parts
of the body have different ●●●●. Believers do,
too, so it's good that we aren't all exactly the
●●●● .

Just as each part of a body ●●●●● with
the rest of the body, believers belong together,
too. Parts of a ●●●● need each other, and so do
believers.

Seek & Find

Describe some ways that Jesus
uses you to help people.

Love Like God Does

John 13:35; 1 Corinthians 13:1–13; 1 John 4:16

Of all the abilities God could give us, the most important is ⬭. The Bible says that even if we have enough faith to move ⬭, if we don't have love, we're nothing. Suppose we serve God by giving everything to ⬭ people. It won't mean anything if we don't ⬭.

People mean different things by "I love you." The ⬭ tells us what real love is. It's when we treat people like ⬭ does. God is love. If we love one another as Jesus loved, everyone will know we ⬭ him.

If we truly love, we are  and kind.
We don't want others' belongings. We don't
or act proudly. If we really love someone,
we won't be . We won't easily get or
keep track of what people do .

172

If we have real love, we will ⬮ those we love. We'll never give up on them. We will look out for what is best for other people. We will always trust and ⬮.

The most important things are ⬮, hope, and love. But the greatest is ⬮.

Seek & Find

Think of someone you love.

Do you treat that person with love?

Fruit of the Spirit

Galatians 5:16–26

The Holy Spirit gives believers the  to say no to ▒▒. Even though we don't have to sin, sometimes we still do. That's because we have what is called a "sinful nature". It ▒▒▒ against the Holy Spirit. So sometimes we do ▒▒▒▒ things we don't want to do.

If we let the Holy Spirit help us become like Jesus, he produces good qualities in us called "████ of the spirit". These are love, joy, peace, patience, ████████, goodness, ████████████, gentleness, and ████████.

 **S**eek & Find

Which fruit of the spirit do you want most? Why?

God's Armour

1 Corinthians 10:13; Ephesians 6:10–17; James 4:7

Because we can't see the _____, some people don't know he's there. But he's real, and he wants to harm us. The Bible promises that if we say _____ to him, he will run from us. God will not let the devil _____ us more than we can stand. God will always give us a way to _____.

Let the Lord make you _____. Depend on his mighty power. Wearing God's _____ you can stand firm against the devil's evil plans. Our _____ is not against human beings. It is against evil forces in the unseen world.

So put on all of God's _____ . You will be able to stand up to anything. Buckle the _____ of truth around your waist. Put the breastplate of ▨▨▨ on your chest. Wear shoes fitted with ▨▨▨ that comes from the good news of ▨▨▨.

Pick up the shield of ▨▨▨. You can use it to put out ▨▨▨ that come at you like flaming ▨▨▨ from the evil one.

Put on the ▨▨▨ of salvation. Hold the ▨▨▨ of the Holy Spirit. The sword is God's Word.

Seek & Find

How are temptations you face like flaming arrows?

Jesus is Coming Back

Matthew 24:31–51, 25:14–46; 2 Peter 3:4–19

Jesus promised to ⬛⬛⬛, and he told us to be ready. He has waited because he is ⬛⬛⬛. He is giving people a chance to turn away from ⬛⬛.

The Bible says, "Try your best to be found ⬛⬛ and without ⬛⬛" and to "be at ⬛⬛ with God." It also says to "grow in the ⬛⬛ and knowledge of ⬛⬛."

Jesus said when he comes he will separate people into two groups. The group he will welcome into ⬛⬛⬛ are those who help others that are ⬛⬛, hungry, thirsty, in prison, or need a place to stay. He said, "What you

179

have done for people who seemed least impor-tant, you have done for 🔳."

He said to be like a servant who kept working while his 🔳 was away on a trip. When his master returned, he said, "You have done well, good and 🔳 servant!"

Jesus said he will return when we don't 🔳 him. He will come in the 🔳 with great power and glory.

Seek & Find

**What will you say to Jesus
when you see him?**

Your Home in Heaven

John 14:2–6; Acts 2:34; 5:31;

Revelation 3:21; 4:3–11; 5:8–14; 21:4, 12–27

When Jesus was leaving the earth, he said, "There are many ⬚ in my Father's ⬚. I am going there to prepare a place for ⬚. I will come back and take you to be with me."

He said, "I am the ⬚ and the truth and the ⬚. No one comes to the ⬚ except through me."

Jesus and God the Father live in a ⬚ place. Their glory gives the city its ⬚. The Father is seated on a ⬚, which has a ⬚ around it that looks like an emerald. Jesus is at his ⬚ side. People and ⬚

worship them. There is music, singing, and joy. Everyone is full of 🔷. No one feels 🔷 or dies. No one cries anymore.

In front of God's throne is what looks like a sea of 🔷 as clear as crystal. The city and its main street are made of clear, pure 🔷. The city has a wall with 12 open 🔷. Each gate is made from one 🔷. Sparkly gems decorate its 12 foundations.

Only those whose names are in the Lamb's Book of 🔷 will go inside.

Seek & Find

Have you trusted in Jesus to save you? If so, what do you look forward to most about heaven?

A

altar—A table or raised place on which a gift, or sacrifice, was offered to God.

amen—A word that means "it is true" or "let it be true".

angel—A spirit who is God's helper. A spirit who tells people God's words. See also cherubim.

anointed—To be set apart as God's special servant.

apostle—One of the twelve men who spent about three years with Jesus. They taught others about Jesus, too. See also disciple.

ark of the covenant—A large gold box that held the stone tablets of the Ten Commandments. The ark was God's throne on earth.

armour—A special outer covering like clothes made of metal. People wore it to help keep them safe in battle.

B

Babel—A city where people tried to build a tower up to the sky.

Babylon—1. The capital city of the empire of Babylonia. 2. Any powerful, sinful city.

baptise—To sprinkle, pour on or cover a person with water. It is a sign that the person belongs to Jesus.

believe—To accept as true. To trust. See also faith.

blessed—1. Made joyful. 2. Helped by God.

C

chariot—A cart with two wheels pulled by horses. People, especially soldiers, rode in them.

cherubim—1. Spirits like angels who have large wings. They were and are a sign that God is sitting on his throne. 2. Spirits who serve God.

chief priest—See high priest.

Christ—A Greek word that means "The Anointed One". It is one of the names given to Jesus. It means the same thing as the Hebrew word Messiah. See also Jesus.

clean— 1. Something that God accepts. 2. Something that doesn't have sin.

clean animals—Animals that God said were acceptable to eat or to give as offerings.

commandment—A law or rule that God gives. See also law.

covenant—1. A treaty, or promise, between two persons or groups. In the Bible it is a promise made between God and the people. 2. Promises from God for salvation.

cross—A wooden post with a bar near the top that extends to the right and left. A cross looks like the letter "T". The Romans killed people by nailing them to crosses.

crucify—To kill people by nailing them to crosses.

cud—Food that is chewed again. An animal such as a cow brings its food back from its stomach to its mouth. This food, or cud, can be chewed again. God told the people of Israel they could eat any animal that chews the cud and has hooves that are separated.

D

dedicate—To set apart for a special purpose, often for God's use.

demon—An evil spirit.

devil—The one who tempts people to sin. See also Satan.

disciple—A person who follows a teacher. This person does what their teacher says to do. See also apostle. See also Twelve, the.

doubt—A lack of faith or trust in something or someone. To not be sure.

E

Eden—The place where God made a garden for Adam and Eve.

eternal—Forever. Without beginning or end.

evangelist—A person who tells others the Good News of Jesus.

evil—Bad. Wicked. Doing things that do not please God.

evil spirit—A demon. One of the devil's helpers.

F

faith—Trust and belief in God. Knowing that God is real, even though we can't see him. See also believe.

faithful—Able to be trusted or counted on.

famine—A time when there is not enough food to eat.

fast—Going without food and/or drink for a special reason.

fig—A sweet fruit that grows on trees in warm countries like Israel.

G

glory—1. God's greatness. 2. Praise and honour.

God—The maker and ruler of the world and all people.

grace—The kindness and forgiveness God gives to people. This is a gift. It cannot be earned.

H

hallelujah—A Hebrew word that means "praise the LORD".

harvest—Picking a crop when it is ripe.

heaven—1. God's home. 2. The sky. 3. Where Christians go after they die.

Hebrew—1. Another name for an Israelite. 2. The language spoken by the Israelites. The Old Testament is written in this language.

hell—A place of punishment for people who don't follow Jesus. They go there after they die.

Herod—The first name of five rulers from the same family. They ruled over Israel during the time of the New Testament.

high priest—A person from the family line of Aaron. He was in charge of everything in the holy tent or in the temple. He was in charge of everyone who came there to work and worship, too.

holy—Set apart for God. Belonging to God. Pure.

Holy Spirit—God's Spirit who creates life. He helps people do God's work. He helps people to believe in Jesus, to love him and to live like him.

honour—To show respect to. To give credit to.

hosanna—A Hebrew word used to praise God.

hymn—A song of praise to God.

I

Immanuel—A name for Jesus that means "God with us".

Israel—1. The new name God gave to Abraham's grandson Jacob. 2. The nation that came from the family line of Jacob. 3. The northern tribes that broke away from Judah to serve their own king.

Israelites—People from the nation of Israel. God's chosen people.

J

jealous—1. How God feels when people worship other things. 2. How we feel when someone else has something we want.

Jesus—The Greek form of the Hebrew name Joshua. It means "the Lord saves". See also Christ. See also Immanuel. See also Saviour.

Jews—Another name for the people of Israel. This name was used after 600 B.C.

judge—1. To decide if something is right or wrong. 2. A person who decides what is right or wrong in legal matters.

K

kingdom—An area or group of people ruled by a king.

L

law—Rules about what is right and wrong that God gave the people of Israel. See also Law, the.

Law, the—The first five books of the Bible.

locust—A type of insect similar to a grasshopper. A huge number of them sometimes eat and destroy crops.

Lord—A personal name for God or Christ. It shows respect for him as our master and ruler.

M

manger—A food box for animals.

manna—Special food sent from heaven. It tasted like wafers, or crackers, sweetened with honey. God gave it to the Israelites in the desert, after they left Egypt.

mercy—More kindness and forgiveness than people deserve to get.

Messiah—A Hebrew word that means, "The Anointed One". It means the same thing as the Greek word Christ. See also Jesus.

miracle—An amazing thing that happens that only God can do. This includes such things as calming a storm or bringing someone back to life.

miraculous signs—Amazing things that God does to point us to him. These things cannot be explained by the laws of nature.

myrrh—A spice with a sweet smell. It came from plants and was made into perfume, incense and medicine.

N

Nazarene—A person who came from the town of Nazareth. Jesus was called a Nazarene.

O

oath—A promise made before God.
obey—To do what you are told to do. To carry out God's commands.
offering—Something people give to God. It was and is a part of their worship. See also sacrifice.
oxen—Large cattle that are very strong. They were used to pull carts or ploughs.

P

Passover—A feast that happened every year. It reminded the people of the time when God "passed over" their homes in Egypt. Because the people put blood on the doorways, God did not hurt them.
paradise—A perfect place. Another name used for heaven.
pasture—A field of grassy land where cows or sheep may eat.
Pharaoh—The title of the ruler of Egypt in Bible times.
Philistines—Strong enemies of Israel, especially during Saul and David's time.
pierce—To poke through with a sharp instrument.
pillar—1. A tall, upright post that helped to hold up a building. 2. A pillar could also mark a special place.
pillar of cloud—A cloud God used to lead the people of Israel. They could see it all day long when they were in the desert.
pillar of fire—A column of fire God used to lead the people of Israel. They could see it all night long when they were in the desert.
plague—1. A sickness that kills many people. 2. Anything that brings a lot of suffering or loss.
praise—To give glory or honour to someone. To say good things about someone or something.
priest—A person who worked in the holy tent or the temple. He was responsible to give his own as well as other people's gifts and prayers to God.
prophet—A person who hears messages from God and tells them to others.
proverb—A wise saying.
psalm—A poem of praise, prayer or teaching. The book of Psalms is full of these poems.

R

Rabbi—The title of a teacher of Jewish law.

resurrection—Coming back to life in a whole new way and never dying again.

right hand—A place of honour and power. Jesus is at the right hand of God.

Rome—1. The empire that controlled a lot of the world when Jesus lived here on the earth. 2. The capital city of that empire. It is in Italy.

S

Sabbath—The seventh day of the week. On that day the Israelites rested from their work and turned their thoughts towards God.

sacred—Set apart for God. Holy.

sacrifice—1. To give something to God as a gift. 2. Something that is given to God as a gift of worship. See also offering.

salvation—Free from the guilt of sin. Jesus died for our sins and rose up from the dead. With this sacrifice, he paid for our sin. He has saved us if we believe in him.

Satan—God's most powerful enemy in the spirit world. Also called the devil.

saved—Set free from danger or sin.

Saviour—The One who sets us free from our sins. A name belonging to Jesus Christ. See also Jesus.

Scripture—God's written Word to us. We also call this the Bible.

scroll—A long strip of paper or animal skin to write on. It was rolled up on two sticks to make it easy to use and store.

shepherd—A person who takes care of sheep or goats.

sin—To disobey or displease God.

Son of Man—A name Jesus gave to himself. It shows he is the Messiah. See also Messiah.

soul—A person's true inner self.

spiritual—Having to do with the things of God or the Bible.

staff—A stick a shepherd uses to take care of sheep or goats.

synagogue—A Jewish place of worship and teaching.

T

temple—1. Any place of worship. 2. The building where the people of Israel worshipped God and brought their sacrifices. God was present there in a special way.

tempt—To try to get someone to do bad things.

threshing floor—A place where heads, or tops, of grain are beaten or stepped on. This is done to knock the seeds of grain from the stems.
tomb—A place to put dead bodies. It was often a cave with a big, stone door.
treaty—An agreement between two people or groups or nations.
Twelve, the—The men who Jesus chose to be his special followers. See also disciples.

U

unclean—Something that God does not accept. Not pure. Not pleasing to God.

V

vineyard—A place where grapes grow and are picked.
vision—A dream from God. The person who saw it was usually awake. God gave these kinds of dreams to people to show them what he was going to do.

W

wafer—A thin, crisp cracker. Wafers were one kind of offering the Israelites brought to the Lord.
widow—A woman whose husband has died.
wisdom—Understanding that comes from God. Wise thinking.
worship—To give praise, honour and glory to God.

Y

yeast—Something added to bread dough to make the bread rise.
yoke—1. A strong piece of wood. It fitted on the necks of two oxen so that they could pull carts or ploughs. 2. A piece of wood put on the neck of a slave or a prisoner.

Z

Zion—1. The city of Jerusalem. 2. The hill on which King David's house and the temple once stood. 3. Another name sometimes used for heaven.